THE SEMANTICS OF TIME

The languages of the Athabascan family are noted for their rich
aspectual systems—inventories of grammatical forms that denote
the nature of the action of a verb in relation to its beginning,
duration, completion, or repetition, but without reference to its
position in time. Koyukon is an Athabaskan language spoken
along the Yukon and Koyukuk rivers in Alaska. Among
Athabaskan languages, Koyukon has the most elaborate and
profusely varied possibilities of morphologically marked
derivational aspect.

This work comprises three parts. The first describes the
aspectual system, which sorts out a complex network of four
modes, fifteen aspects, four superaspects, and some three hundred
aspect-dependent derivation prefix strings. The second analyzes
the organization of verb theme categories, which are directly
linked to aspectual categories. The last assesses the function of the
aspectual system as a whole.

MELISSA AXELROD received a Ph.D. in linguistics from the
University of Colorado in 1990. She has worked for the Alaska
Native Language Center, University of Alaska, Fairbanks, and
currently teaches in the English Department at California State
University, San Bernardino.

STUDIES
IN THE ANTHROPOLOGY OF
NORTH AMERICAN INDIANS

Editors
Raymond J. DeMallie
Douglas R. Parks

THE SEMANTICS OF TIME
Aspectual Categorization in
Koyukon Athabaskan

MELISSA AXELROD

Published by the University of Nebraska Press,
Lincoln and London

In cooperation with
the American Indian Studies Research Institute,
Indiana University,
Bloomington

© 1993 by the University
of Nebraska Press. All rights
reserved. Manufactured in
the United States
of America.The paper in this
book meets the mini-mum
requirements of American
National Standard
for Information Sciences —
Permanence of Paper for
Printed Library Materials,
ANSI Z39.48–1984.
Library of Congress
Cataloging-in-Publication
Data. Axelrod, Melissa.
The semantics of time:
aspectual categorization
in Koyukon Athabaskan /
Melissa Axelrod. p. cm.—
(Studies in the anthropology
of North American Indians)
"In cooperation with the
American Indian Studies
Research Institute, Indiana
University, Bloomington."
Revision of the author's
thesis (doctoral)—University
of Colorado, 1990. Includes
index. ISBN 0-8032-1032-9
1. Koyukon language—
Aspect. 2. Koyukon lan-
guage—Verb.
3. Koyukon language—
Discourse analysis.
I. Title. II. Series.
PM1594.A94 1993
497'.2—dc20
92-42719 CIP

For Julie Jones

Contents

Figures

Tables

Acknowledgments

I am grateful to a number of people for assistance in this research. My deepest debt of gratitude goes to Eliza Jones, my teacher, partner, and friend. Eliza's intelligence and insight into her language provided the foundation for this study; her patience and humor sustained me to its completion. *Enaa baasee'*, Eliza.

This book is a revised version of my doctoral dissertation (University of Colorado, 1990). To my committee members—Michael Krauss, Allan Taylor, Laurel Watkins, and Dorothea Kaschube—I owe a great deal of thanks. I am especially grateful to David Rood, my dissertation director, for his assistance and support. My second reader, Barbara Fox, provided suggestions, encouragement, and wit that were invaluable. James Kari gave me the benefit of his knowledge and experience in a very useful reading. Manuel Arce also read the manuscript and offered many helpful comments.

I thank the faculty and staff of the Department of Linguistics, University of Colorado, Boulder, and of the Alaska Native Language Center (ANLC), University of Alaska, Fairbanks. I owe special thanks to Michael Krauss, who taught me Athabaskan linguistics and allowed me to participate in ANLC's work to maintain and preserve the rich heritage of Alaska's native languages. Support for the *Koyukon Athabaskan Dictionary* has come from the National Science Foundation, the National Endowment for the Humanities, the State of Alaska, the Alaska Humanities Forum, and ANLC.

I revised the manuscript for publication while I was a visiting professor at the University of Costa Rica, and I am grateful to that institution for providing me with the time to complete the work. Most of the revisions were suggested by Paul Hopper and Chad Thompson, who read the manuscript for the University of Nebraska Press. I thank them for their thoughtful and stimulating reports. Douglas Parks, coeditor of the series in which this book appears, deserves abundant thanks for his patience, advice, and support.

I owe more to my family and friends than I can possibly express. Their constant support, encouragement, sympathy, and good humor were the most important elements in my ability to complete the project. Thanks and love to my family: to my parents and to David, Steven, Rise, and Jeremiah. Thanks also to my dear friends Manuel, Emmanuel, and José Arce; Rebecca Burns-Hoffman; Jule Gómez de García; Linda Oliver Bruemmer; and Meryl Siegal.

Abbreviations

Modes

FUT	future
IMPF	imperfective
OPT	optative
PERF	perfective

Aspects

BIS	bisective
CNCL	conclusive
CONS	consecutive
CONT	continuative
DIR-REP	directive-repetitive
DUR	durative
MOM	momentaneous
n MOM	momentaneous derivative with *ne-* imperfective or *ne-* perfective mode prefixes
gh MOM	momentaneous derivative with ∅ imperfective or *ghe-* perfective mode prefixes
l MOM	momentaneous derivative with ∅ imperfective and *le-* perfective mode prefixes
ll MOM	momentaneous derivative with *le-* imperfective and *le-* perfective mode prefixes
∅ MOM	momentaneous derivative with ∅ imperfective and ∅ perfective mode prefixes
NEU	neuter
n NEU	neuter derivative with *ne-* imperfective or *ghe-* perfective mode prefixes
gh NEU	neuter derivative with *ghe-* imperfective or *ghe-* perfective mode prefixes
l NEU	neuter derivative with *ghe-* imperfective or *ghe-* perfective mode prefixes
∅ NEU	neuter derivative with ∅ imperfective or *ghe-* perfective mode prefixes
aa NEU	neuter derivative with *aa-* imperfective or *ghe-* perfective mode prefixes
ONO	onomatopoetic
PERS	persistive
PRMB	perambulative
REP	repetitive
REV	reversative
SML	semelfactive

TRNS	transitional

Superaspects
CUST	customary
DIST	distributive
MULT	multiple
PROG	progressive

Postaspectual Derivations
CONA	conative
ERR	errative
INCP	inceptive
NEG	negative

Theme Categories
CONV	conversive
DESC	descriptive
EXT	extension
MOT	motion
OPER	operative
STAT	stative
SUCC	successive

Verb Prefixes
AREA	areal subject, direct object, or postpositional object *(hʉ-)*
CL	classifier
CLASSIF	classificatory verb
COMP	complementizer
D	D-effect
DS	component of an aspect-dependent derivational prefix string
DU	dual
G	gender
INCR	incorporated noun or adjective
INDF	indefinite subject or object *(k'e-)*
INDT P	indeterminate postpositional object *(de-)*
ITER	iterative
M	mode prefix
NOM	nominalizing suffix
O	direct object
P	postpositional object
PL	plural
POSS	possessive prefix
PP	postposition
RECP	reciprocal
REFL	reflexive
S	subject
SG	singular
T	thematic prefix
#	disjunct boundary

1
Introduction

1.1. Objectives

Koyukon presents a tremendously complicated aspectual system. Even among Athabaskan languages, remarkable for the richness of their aspectual inventories and the diversity of expression possible from these inventories, Koyukon has the most elaborate and richly varied possibilities for morphologically marked derivational aspect. The primary goal of this study, then, is to present, for the first time, a clear and detailed account of that system. The investigation includes three large sections. The first is an examination of the aspectual system, which involves sorting out a complex network of four modes, fifteen aspects, four superaspects, four post-aspectual derivations, and some 300 aspect-dependent derivational prefix strings. In the second part, I analyze the organization of verb theme categories, an organization directly linked to aspectual categories. The third part provides an assessment of the function of the aspectual system as a whole in discourse.

Providing such a detailed account entails furnishing an exhaustive analysis of both the morphological and the semantic correlates of temporal expression, as well as analysis of the organization, distribution, and function of that expression. In accomplishing that aim, it will become necessary to address some issues in the general study of linguistic aspect. Three issues in particular are critical in the description of the aspectual system of Koyukon and in the study of aspect in general: (1) semantic and morphological factors in the categorization of temporal notions, (2) the interaction of derivational and lexical means of expressing temporal distinctions, and (3) the relationship of aspect as a discourse-level phenomenon with its source and function on the sentential or lexical level.

It is my hope that this research will provide insight into the synergistic relationship of semantics and morphology and offer suggestions for new avenues of research on the cognitive bases of linguistic categorization.

1.2. Review of the literature on aspect

The fundamental question addressed in most of the recent studies of linguistic aspect is twofold: What is aspect and what are its primary semantic components?

Most authors explain aspect (in contrast to tense) as a means of describing the temporal characteristics of a situation without reference to the speech event. Comrie, for example, defines aspect as "different ways of viewing the internal temporal constituency of a situation"—as opposed to tense, which "locates the time of a situation relative to the situation of the utterance" (1976:2–3). Friedrich provides a similar definition of tense and aspect: tense, he says, refers to "the relative anteriority or posteriority of an action with reference to the speech situation. Temporal values inherent in the activity or state itself, on the other hand, are coded by aspect categories" (1974:35). Hopper, too, says that while tense has "a concrete relationship to the observer—the observer's own time-line—aspect depends on an absolute, observer-independent shaping of a state or action" (1979:4). Chung and Timberlake's definition, on the other hand, allows for more overlap between tense and aspect: "aspect characterizes the dynamicity or closure of an event with respect to a point or interval in time." They suggest, in fact, that "tense and aspect could be subsumed under a single category of tense-aspect which characterizes the relationship between an event and salient points on the temporal dimension" (1985:256).

Much of the recent work on aspect has been conducted from a functional viewpoint. Hopper claims that aspect has "a core function which is discourse-derived and in some sense universal, and a set of additive functions which are not universal (though some of them may be common) and which represent grammaticized semantic extensions of the discourse function" (1979:4). Givón, in his study of the emergence of aspect in creoles, also takes a functional approach, describing three communicational functions of aspect: "(1) Knowing the temporal order of occurrence of past events, (2) Being able to distinguish between sensory input and one's own imagination, (3) Being able to tell whether an event has occurred once or has protracted itself" (1979:155).

There have also been several typological studies of aspect. Dahl (1985), for example, collected data with a questionnaire containing sentences and short texts in English that native informants were asked to translate. In some cases the informants were linguists themselves; in other cases secondary sources were used to analyze informant responses. Bybee (1985) also presents a typological study of tense and aspect systems in which the data are taken largely from published reference grammars. In addition to suffering the inevitable risks of relying on secondary sources, these studies look at only fragments of the language and thus face the danger of missing important factors and significant relationships evident only in an examination of the functioning of a system as a whole. As Talmy says, "most previous typological and universal work has treated language's lexical elements as atomic givens, without involving the semantic components that comprise them. Accordingly, such studies have been limited to treating the properties that such whole forms can manifest." It is crucial, as he puts it, to go "beyond treating a single semantic component at a time, to treating a concurrent set of components. . . . That is . . . whole-system properties of semantic-surface relations" (1985:121). It is this larger picture of the place of aspect within the semantics of a whole language system that is the goal of my study.

Whatever their approach, most authors regard certain basic temporal distinctions as primary within an aspectual system. The distinctions between perfective and imperfective, state and non-state, durativity and boundedness are often cited as aspectual primitives. Givón's three communicational functions, for example, presuppose three basic aspectual distinctions: between perfective and imperfective, between realis and irrealis, and between nondurative and durative. Friedrich (1974:36), in his work on aspect in Homeric Greek, describes two other oppositions that he claims are basic aspectual features: completive versus non-completive and stative versus nonstative.

Comrie's study looks at aspect from the standpoint of general linguistics, presenting a survey of semantic aspectual distinctions, irrespective of their grammatical or lexical manifestation, found in a variety of languages and language families. In this thorough and helpful study, "general semantic distinctions are introduced and illustrated by means of language-particular categories that correspond more or less closely to the semantic distinctions established" (1976:10). Although he does not posit any particular aspectual categories as universal or basic, he chooses perfective, imperfective, habitual, continuous, and progressive as general categories on which to focus in his first chapter.

Chung and Timberlake offer a descriptive framework for tense, aspect, and mood. Their framework centers on the notion of event, which they define as consisting of three components: "a predicate; an interval of time on which the predicate occurs, which we call the event frame; and a situation or set of conditions under which the predicate occurs, which we call the event world" (1985:203). Within this framework, aspect is defined as characterizing "the relationship of a predicate to the time interval over which it occurs" (213). They claim that the notion of change is the central element in aspect and point to dynamicity, closure, iterativity, and durativity as the fundamental parameters for aspect.

Dahl's premise is that "the overwhelming majority of all categories found in the TMA [tense, mode, aspect] systems of the world's languages are chosen from a restricted set of category types" (1985: 31). The aspectual categories he claims as basic, according to his examination of sixty-four languages, include perfective/imperfective, progressive, conclusive, habitual, habitual-generic, and habitual-past.

In order to determine which aspectual categories were primary in Koyukon, it was necessary to explore the structure of semantic categories themselves. Dahl argues that "the most salient 'universals', or better, basic units of the general theory of TMA systems are . . . categories rather than features" (1985:33). That assertion of the primacy of categories, as opposed to features, brings up a central discussion in the literature on cognitive structures, one involving a theory of prototype semantics. Hopper and Thompson claim that the work on prototypicality by Rosch (1973, 1977, 1978) and others

> presents the hypothesis that human categorization is not arbitrary, but proceeds from central to peripheral instances of categories. Central instances of a category are "prototypical" for that category; and such instances appear to be more salient for speakers, according to a wide range of tests. [1984:707]

Dahl enters this discussion by introducing the terms *impreciseness* and *focusing* with regard to categories—in preference to the more general idea of prototypicality. He describes a focused category as one with a definable focus or foci and an imprecise category as one that has unclear or borderline members. He then discusses "multidimensional" impreciseness, referring to those cases where there is more than one criterion for deciding category membership. Those criteria may be considered autonomous and unordered, but categories can be "sharpened" so that one criterion becomes dominant relative to another. Focused categories are sharpened in that way. For example, he contends that both 'perfective' and 'past' are criterial features of the category perfective, but that 'perfective' is the "clearly dominant" parameter. He concludes that "the concept of a dominant parameter is often relevant in the description of TMA categories" (1985:3–10).

The view of aspect as comprising categories and of those categories as imprecise, focused, fuzzy, or prototype sets, is the underlying premise in the present study. The composition and use of those aspectual categories is the main focus of the research presented here. Chapter 5 in particular discusses the categorization of verbs according to aspectual criteria. In doing so, it also explores in some detail the interaction of lexical and derivational factors in aspectual meaning.

Many scholars have examined the role of lexical aspect in categorizing verb types (e.g., Vendler on English, 1957, 1967; Jacobsen on Japanese, 1984; Smith on English, 1983; and Navajo, 1989; Tai on Chinese, 1984). The basis for those particular studies is Vendler's proposal that verbs can be classified according to four aspectual situation types.

Vendler (1967) identified four classes, or situation types, of verbs: activities, accomplishments, achievements, and states. Achievements include those verbs that refer to single, punctual actions. States, of course, refer to static conditions such as 'knowing', 'having', or 'loving'. Dowty (1979) pointed out the need to consider the whole predicate rather than just the verb in order to distinguish activities—such as 'running', 'walking', or 'eating'—that include no reference to end points, from accomplishments—such as 'running a mile' or 'walking to school'—that are characterized by reference to a set end point or goal. Vendler considers states and achievements as belonging to one "genus" while activities and accomplishments pair to form a different genus. Activities and states also form a pair since they share the property of not referring to a bounded period of time.

Comrie also discusses "how the inherent meaning of certain lexical items and syntactic combinations of lexical items can determine semantic aspectual characteristics, and how these in turn interact with the aspectual categories of individual languages" (1976:4). He examines durative versus punctual situations, telic versus atelic situations, and static versus dynamic or processual situations.

Chung and Timberlake, too, refer to the interaction of lexical, derivational, and propositional factors in aspect. They distinguish four "nested levels" of aspectual meaning:

(a) the verb and its inherent aspectual properties; (b) the predicate, defined here in the narrow sense of a verb plus its major syntactic arguments (subject and objects); (c) the proposition, the predicate in relation to the event frame: and (d) the narrative/ textual, the proposition in the context of a connected set of propositions. [1985:214]

The present study examines all four of the levels described by Chung and Timberlake, looking first at the multiplicity of derivational aspect possible in Koyukon, proceeding to an examination of aspectual categorization on the level of the verb theme, and, finally, exploring the use of the aspectual system in narrative.

1.3. Plan of the study

In chapter 2, I offer a general view of the language, including its geographical boundaries and linguistic relationships, its phonemic and morphophonemic inventory, and a sketch of its verbal structure. More detailed consideration of those topics must be the focus of a second study; it was my intention here to supply only that information that is essential and relevant to the analysis of the aspectual system.

Chapters 3 and 4 are devoted to a thorough description of the Koyukon aspectual system. Chapter 3 concentrates on mode and aspect, the main components of the system. Chapter 4 proceeds to fill out this picture of the system with descriptions of aspect-dependent derivational strings, superaspect, and postaspectual derivations. The two chapters illustrate the difficulties that a system with such a large inventory of aspectual types poses for the analyst. Semantic overlapping and morphophonemic homophony are present throughout the system, and chapter 4 suggests that categorization here must be analyzed as a product of a combination of morphophonological attributes and semantic prototypes.

In chapter 5, I describe seven verb theme categories whose organization and boundaries are determined by semantic and morphological factors related to aspect. I survey various prototype and feature-based approaches to the study of cognitive categorization, comparing the facts of the aspectually-motivated verbal categorization schema of Koyukon with previous research into the classification of both verbal and nominal systems. I also take a closer look at the relationship between lexical and derivational means of expressing temporal notions. The Koyukon data support the view that derivational potential is driven, to a great extent, by lexical meaning.

This point is taken up again in chapter 6, on the role of aspect and theme category in discourse. Here I present a detailed analysis of a traditional Koyukon story in order to illustrate how the major elements of the aspectual system function within a narrative. The claim that aspect is fundamentally a discourse-level structuring device is considered in light of the demonstrated significance of lexical factors in the distribution of derivational aspect.

Chapter 7 offers conclusions and indicates some of the most important areas for further research.

1.4. Data and methodology

The bulk of the data used in this study comes from the *Koyukon Athabaskan Dictionary* (Jones, Axelrod, and Jetté, forthcoming), a project closely related to the present study. The dictionary is based on the superb manuscript dictionary (ca. 1915) of Father Jules Jetté, S.J. His dictionary, including various ethnological descriptions of the culture, is a masterpiece of both grammatical and cultural insight. Within the hundreds of pages of his beautiful longhand script is a wealth of information, including some archaic words and expressions no longer available from modern speakers. Although Jetté was a genius in the collection and analysis of language data, his ear was not sophisticated enough to distinguish the differences between the stop series (plain, aspirated, and glottalized) or among the vowels of Koyukon. In 1974 Eliza Jones began the task of retranscribing Jetté's entries into an accurate form and in a more modern orthography. That retranscription became the basis for a new dictionary—expanded, updated, and organized according to current principles of Athabaskan linguistic and lexicographic scholarship.

The *Koyukon Athabaskan Dictionary* was included as part of the larger Alaska Native Languages Dictionary Project, begun in March 1978 at the Alaska Native Language Center under the direction of Dr. Michael Krauss. During the spring of 1980, the center began the initial typesetting of a draft prepared by Jones and James Kari. That stage was completed by the following summer, and in the fall of 1981 Jones and I began the long process of editing and reorganizing the entries. By the summer of 1984, the 1981 typescript had been completely reviewed and edited and I had produced a computerized version of the basic skeleton for the verb entries, including all verb roots, stem sets, and themes. Work on the dictionary resumed in the fall of 1988, and at present we have well over half of the entire Koyukon corpus in near-final draft form.

Over the last fifteen years, an enormous amount of data drawn from traditional stories and historical narrative, as well as from more contemporary usage, has been added to Jetté's original work. New data collected in the course of preparing the present study have been incorporated into the dictionary as well. It now represents the largest corpus of lexical data yet gathered for any Alaskan Athabaskan language. The principal contributor and compiler has been Eliza Jones, but numerous other speakers from across the Koyukon region have participated. Primary contributors include Catherine Attla (Huslia), Charlie Brush (Nulato), Mary Dick (Tanana), Agnes Moore (Tanana), Johnson Moses (Allakaket), Josephine Mountain (Nulato), Madeline Solomon (Galena), Fred Stickman (Nulato), Henry Titus (Ruby), and Susie Williams (Hughes).

The computerization of the project has been a complicated process. The verb theme list that I completed in 1984 was prepared using a preliminary version of the *Lexware* lexicography programs written by Dr. Robert Hsu of the University of Hawaii. Several dictionaries of "exotic" languages, including Kari's *Ahtna Dictionary* (1990) have been successfully prepared with Hsu's software. The Koyukon dictionary, however, involves a greater degree of complexity and richness of detail than any of the previous dictionaries prepared using *Lexware*. In 1989 I worked closely with Hsu to develop a program tailored specifically to the intricacy and sophistication of the Koyukon data and format. Using that system, I enter data in a phrase-by-phrase manner, tagging each line according to its content and function. The *Lexware* programs allow sorting and compiling of the tagged lines along a variety of parameters.

The format for entering data reflects the theory of Athabaskan aspectual verb theme categories. Roots that participate in verbal derivations are entered preceding an inventory of all stems derived from that root. Each aspect is associated with a unique set of four stems, one for each mode. Themes are the basic verb entries, and follow the stem set lines. Each theme is followed by a line indicating its theme category and then by a gloss line. That, in turn, is followed by an abundant and representative sampling of verb forms derived from the theme, including all semantically idiomatic, or nonpredictable, derivatives of the theme. Each derived verb form is entered, followed first by a gloss line, and then by a complete morphological analysis that elucidates the form's derivational history.

Of the some 2000 root and affix entries, the dictionary contains approximately 600 roots that participate in verbal derivations. The entries for those roots constitute the data for chapters 3, 4, and 5 on aspect, and theme categories and are the source for statistics regarding frequency and distribution analyses. The *Lexware* programs were applied to this corpus to generate lists of stem sets according to aspect and of themes according to aspectual category that appear in Axelrod (1990).

The story examined in chapter 6 (in the discussion on the function of aspect in discourse) is drawn from *Sitsiy Yugh Noholnik Ts'in: 'As My Grandfather Told It'* (Attla 1983), a volume of stories told by Catherine Attla.

The orthography used throughout this study is the product of revisions that Eliza Jones, Michael Krauss, and I made in October 1988.

2
The Koyukon Language

Koyukon is an Athabaskan language of Alaska. The Athabaskan languages, along with Tlingit and Eyak, make up the Na Dene language family.[1] There are three major geographical groupings of Athabaskan languages:

- those languages spoken from western Alaska east through Canada to Hudson's Bay, from Eskimo territory southeast to the Great Plains, and southwest into British Columbia;
- Pacific Coast Athabaskan and Kwalhioqua-Tlatskanai;
- Navajo and Apache (the latter including three to five languages).

Koyukon is part of the first group; it is spoken in the area surrounding the Koyukuk River and its confluence with the Yukon. The languages closest to Koyukon geographically are Gwich'in, to the northeast; Tanana, to the east; Dena'ina, to the south; and Upper Kuskokwim and Holikachuk, to the southwest. Both Holikachuk, to the south, and Tanana, to the east, are partially intelligible to Koyukon speakers. However, the Alaskan and Canadian Athabaskan languages constitute a language and dialect continuum, with linguistic distance difficult to define.

Koyukon is a moribund language—approximately 650 speakers remain (Krauss, 1982), all over the age of twenty (Krauss 1980). The language has three main dialects: Lower, Central, and Upper Koyukon. Lower Koyukon is spoken in the villages of Kaltag and Nulato, and Upper Koyukon is spoken in the villages of Tanana, Rampart, Manley Hot Springs, and Stevens Village. The languages of South Fork and of Bearpaw and Minchumina are often classed as belonging to Upper Koyukon, but may constitute separate dialects. Central Koyukon can be divided into two subgroups: Central Koyukuk (including that variety spoken in Huslia, Hughes, and Allakaket) and Central Yukon (spoken in Koyukuk, Galena, Ruby, Kokrines, and by some speakers in Rampart, Tanana, and Huslia).

Eliza Jones, the principal source of the data presented in this study, is a speaker of Central Yukon Koyukon, although the study

---

1. Haida is considered by some to be another branch of this family and by others to be a language isolate.

considers data from all three dialects. Data not common to all dialects are marked with the abbreviations C (or CY, CK), U, or L. Data common to all dialects are written as they are pronounced in the Central dialect (and minor phonological variation in other dialects can be inferred).

2.1. Phonetics and morphophonology

This section provides only a summary of the sound system and major morphophonemic rules of Koyukon in order to facilitate the reader's understanding of the examples and analysis presented in chapters 3 through 5. For a more thorough examination of morphophonemic rules affecting the prefix complex of Koyukon, see Thompson (1977). Fuller analyses of stem suffixation processes can be found in Kari (1979) and Leer (1979). For detailed review of comparative Athabaskan phonology see Krauss (1964) and Krauss and Leer (1981).

2.1.1. The phonemes of Koyukon

The phonemes of Central Koyukon are shown in table 2.1. Phonetic equivalents are presented in square brackets when they are different from the orthographic symbols.

Lower Koyukon differs from this inventory in that /m/ (/*w/)is never [b]. The front velars have fronted to a palatal articulation in Upper Koyukon, so we find /ǰ/ and /č/ where the Lower and Central dialects have /g/ and /k/, and /š/ rather than /yh/. In Hughes and Allakaket, /y/ is pronounced as a velar fricative except when adjacent to a high front vowel or schwa. In Hughes, Allakaket, and in all Upper dialect communities, the rounded schwa /ʉ/ (*α) has merged with (and been replaced by) /u/. Koyukon shows only vestigial tone, only for some speakers.

2.1.2. Morphophonemics

The phonemes of the Koyukon verb prefix complex are subject to a great deal of syncope, merger, lengthening, and reduction. Because it is the verb stems that are most critical in the study of verbal aspect though, this section will present only the most frequent rules that operate to alter stem shape. Again, the reader is advised to consult Thompson (1977) for an analysis of the morphophonology of the prefix complex.

The following rules will be important in understanding the discussion of aspectual verb stem variation in chapters 3 and 4.

Table 2.1. Phonemes of Central Koyukon

CONSONANTS

	Labial	Apico-Alveolar		Front Velar	Back Velar	Glottal
		NONCONTINUANTS				
Stops						
Plain	b [p]	d [t]	dl [ƛ]	dz [c]	g [k]	gg [q]	' [ʔ]
Aspirated		t [tʰ]	tl [ƛʰ]	ts [cʰ]	k [kʰ]	kk [qʰ]
Glottalized		t'	tl' [ƛ']	ts' [c']	k'	kk' [q']
		CONTINUANTS				
Fricatives						
Voiceless		ł	s	yh [x̱]	h [x]	h
Voiced		l	z	y	gh [ɣ]	
Nasals						
Voiceless		nh [n̥]				
Voiced	m	n				

VOWELS

	FRONT		BACK	
Long	ee [i]	aa [æ]	o [ɔ]	oo [u]
Short	e [ə]		ʉ [ŏ]	u [ʊ]

Verb stem spirantization. A spirantization of root-final affricates and velars, this phenomenon is triggered by an obstruent suffix. For example, the root -*t'otl* 'cut' becomes -*t'oł* in the stem associated with the durative imperfective, future, and optative. Here are some other durative imperfective stems from obstruent-final roots:

ROOT	GLOSS	DUR IMPF STEM
'otl	chew	'oł
ts'oots	suck	ts'oos
zaak	carve	zaah
lokk	PL die	loh

Note that the plain alveolar stop /t/ never undergoes spirantization:

loot	scrape	loot

Verb stem vowel reduction. Aspectual derivations frequently cause a long vowel to become its corresponding reduced vowel:

ee, aa	→	e
o	→	tt
oo	→	u

For example, the root *-tlaatl* 'chop' becomes *-tleł* via vowel reduction and spirantization in the stem associated with the semelfactive aspect. There is occasionally an irregular relationship between the full vowel and its corresponding reduced vowel, so while *-kkot* 'patch', for instance, reduces to the expected *-kkut* in the semelfactive, *-t'otl* 'cut' has the reduced form *-t'uł*. An explanation for that phenomenon is beyond the scope of this brief discussion.

Vowel lengthening. In momentaneous stems of reduced vowel roots, there is often a lengthening of the root vowel in the imperfective and optative. In these cases, the reduced vowel lengthens as follows (with occasional irregularities):

e	→	aa, ee
tt	→	o
u	→	oo

The following momentaneous stem set of the root *-kkuyhtl* 'become crushed (animate subj.)' provides an example.

Imperfective	Perfective	Future	Optative
kkooyhtl	kkuyhtl	kkuyhtl	kkooyhtl

Suffixation of -k *and* -yh. A phonotactic constraint on final clusters in Koyukon requires that lateral consonants come last. The suffixes *-k* and *-yh* therefore appear preceding a root-final lateral affricate. The root *-daatl*, for example, becomes *-deyhtl* in the repetitive aspect by means of metathesis: *-daatl* + k → *-deł* + k (base form) → *dekł* (via metathesis) → *deyhł* (via spirantization) → *deyhtl* (via affrication).

2.2. Structure of the verb

The Koyukon verb is made up of a stem plus prefixes. The stem is composed of a root plus suffixes (and possibly ablaut, or lengthening) indicating mode and aspect. Prefixes indicate person, status, gender, mode, adverbials, and transitivity. The prefix complex of

Athabaskan languages can be analyzed as a template comprised of
basic positions or zones (see Kari 1988). The Koyukon prefix complex can be divided into roughly thirty separate, ordered prefix
positions preceding the stem. Table 2.2, adapted from Kari (1990),
will give a general idea of the ordering of elements.

Positions 0 and -1 represent the stem: the root occupies position
0 and the aspect and mode suffixes, position -1. To the right of that,
in positions -2 through -4 are negative suffixes (-2) and clause and
relative enclitics.

Position 1, to the immediate left of the stem, is occupied by the
four classifier prefixes (see Krauss 1969): ∅, l, de, and le. The second prefix position can be filled by the first person singular (s-) and
second person singular (ne-) and plural (-ʉh) subject pronouns. The
third person singular subject pronoun, ∅, is also in this position.

The four prefix positions contained in zone 3 are the conjugation
prefixes. The perfective prefix, ne-/∅, is in position 3A. This prefix
appears in neuter imperfective and active perfective derivations and
is the perfective marker proper (Krauss and Leer 1981).[2] Position
3B is occupied by mode prefixes. The le- perfective and negative
prefixes are marked in position 3C, and the ee- and aa- mode and
negative prefixes are in position 3D.

The qualifer prefixes—areal, thematic, directive, conative, ana-
tomical and gender, and inceptive prefixes—occupy the positions of
the fourth zone.[3]

The fifth zone is occupied by the pronominal prefixes. The third
person singular prefix is in position 5A. The so-called deictic subject
prefixes precede it: first person plural in 5B and third person plural
in 5C. To the left of those positions are the indefinite subject (5D)
and object (5F) prefixes,[4] with the direct object prefixes occupying
position 5E.

2. See chap. 3 (section 3.1.2) for a discussion of the difference between
this perfective marker and the imperfective and perfective mode prefixes.

3. This zone could be expanded to nine or ten positions. In particular,
there is evidence that the four prefixes listed in position 4F actually occupy
four separate positions: hʉ- 'areal', followed by the thematic prefixes he-,
oo-, ghe-. The epenthetic prefix, ee-, could also be considered as occupying
a separate position between 4C, 'inceptive', and 4D, 'gender'. I have collapsed these positions here for the sake of brevity.

4. The other two prefixes listed in position 5F are third person subject
prefixes which occur only in combination with third person direct object
prefixes in position 5E.

Table 2.2 Koyukon Prefixes

Postpositional Object (10)

B (3y)	+	A (pob)
he		be
		ye
		se
		ne
		k'e
		denaa
		hʉ
		yʉh
		neeł
		ede
		de
		∅

Derivational/Thematic (9) + iter (8) + dist (7) + inc (6) #

B (pp)	+	A (der/th)	+	8 iter	+	7 dist	+	6 inc	#
e		to		no		ne		to	
yee		do						tlee	
ghʉ		ts'e						beł	
aa		yen						yenee	
gho		kk'o						neget	
(...)		tlee						tseh	
		soo						(....)	
		taa							

Pronominal (5)

F (3y)	+	E (dob)	+	D (idf)	+	C (3p)	+	B (1p)	+	A (3s)	=
be		∅		k'e		he		ts'		ye	
he		be									
k'e		se									
		ne									
		denaa									
		hʉ									
		yʉh									
		neeł									
		ho									

Qualifier (4)

F (ar/qual)	+	E (con)	+	D (qua)	+	C (icp)	+	B (qual)	+	A (qual)
hʉ		oo		de		te		ne		le
he								∅		
oo										
ghe										

Conjugation (3)

D (trm)	+	C (spn)	+	B (mode)	+	A (prf)	+	subj (2)	[clas (1)
ee		l/ł		∅		∅		s	∅
aa				ne		ne		ne	ł
				ghe				ʉh	de
				ghu				∅	le

Stem (0)

root	+ vsf₁ (-1)	+ vsf₂ (-2)	+ vsf₃ (-3)	vsf₄ (-4)
CV(V)X	∅	aa	zo	ne
CV(V)(R)(')	ł	ee	ło	denh
	n	yu		(y)ee
	yh			nenh
	h			(h)aanh
	t			
	'			

Symbolized by #, the disjunct boundary divides those prefixes that are phonologically more intimately bound to the verb stem from those less tightly bound to the stem. Incorporated stems precede the disjunct boundary in position 6. Only a few of the possible incorporated noun and adjective stems are provided in the list given in the chart. In the seventh and eighth positions are the distributive and iterative prefixes, respectively.

Bound adverbials and postpositions are in positions A and B of zone 9. Postpositional objects precede them in zone 10.[5] The list given in the chart represents only a fraction of the actual number of adverbial and postpositional prefixes possible in these positions. These prefixes are the ones that will be discussed under the heading of aspect-dependent derivational prefix strings in section 2.3 and, more thoroughly, in chapter 4.

Some of the prefixes I have been discussing are obligatory in the sense that the particular position they occupy must be filled by one of the possible variants of that prefix class in every derivative of the verb. These obligatory prefixes are the person, mode, and classifier prefixes. Other prefixes (i.e., gender, adverbial, status) are optional —depending on the meaning of the derivative, the positions these prefixes occupy may or may not be filled. Sometimes one or more of the qualifier prefixes are thematic—that is, they are lexicalized and are present in every derivation of a particular verb. The classifier prefix is always thematic.[6] The thematic prefixes in combination with the root of the verb are referred to as the verb theme.

2.2.1. The verb theme

Sets of verb forms in Koyukon can be derived from an abstract underlying structure, or verb theme, that includes the verb root, classifier, thematic prefixes (if any), and a mark for transitivity (i.e., presence or absence of a direct object position). Verb forms derived from these themes have—in addition to the root and thematic, or lexical, prefixes—inflectional prefixes (person, gender, etc.) and

---

5. The third person prefix in position 10B, like those in position 5F, occurs only in combination with a third person prefix in position 10A.

6. The thematic classifier can be modified, however, in derivations altering the voice or transitivity of a verb. Specifically, the causative derivation changes any thematic classifier to *l-*. Passive, benefactive, reflexive, reciprocal, and certain other derivations entail a voicing of the classifier (i.e., *l-* becoming *le-*, ∅ becoming *de-*), a phenomenon known as D-effect.

derivational prefixes (mode, aspect, etc.).[7] As noted before, these prefixes are arranged in relatively fixed positions preceding the stem (i.e., the aspectually modified root).

The Koyukon theme is the underlying skeleton of the verb to which prefixes or strings of prefixes and suffixal elements are added in producing an utterance. The theme itself has a meaning and is the basic unit of the Athabaskan verbal lexicon (Rice 1989:797).

Consider the root *-tlaakk/tlukk,*[8] a classificatory verb that refers to the existence, position, movement, or handling of a mushy, soft, sticky, wet, or messy object. The root participates in sixteen different themes, including the following three:

(1) *G+de+tlaakk*

 'mushy, wet, sticky, messy, disorderly object (e.g., dough, wet clothes, mud, unconscious or drunk person) is in position'

(2) *O+G+∅+tlaakk*

 'handle, hold mushy, wet, sticky, messy, disorderly O'

(3) *P+e#O+∅+tlukk*

 'throw, slam animate or mushy, wet, messy O against P'

Notice that all three themes have a root and a classifier prefix to the immediate left of the root. The *G* in the first two themes indicates that derivatives are marked for gender. Gender in Athabaskan refers to classes based on shape, size, weight, and composition.[9] The last two themes include an *O*, which indicates that they

7. Mode can be considered inflectional, but because it is linked so closely with aspect, which is a derivational category, I refer to mode as derivational as well.

8. This verb has full vowel stems with the vowel *aa-* but reduced vowel stems with the vowel *u-*, rather than the expected *e-*, probably due to a Pre-Proto-Athabaskan root-final labialized back velar obstruent. Leer (in Young and Morgan 1987:290) has reconstructed the Proto-Athabaskan (PA) form for the root as **tleK'* from Pre-Proto-Athabaskan (PPA) **tleK'ʷ*. He posits a separate PA "successive" root, **tlʉK'* from PPA *tlɨK'ʷ*. The verb is therefore cited with the two root variants separated by a slash.

9. For example, the *de-* gender prefix is used with subjects (of intransitive verbs that require gender marking) and objects (of transitive verbs that require gender marking) that refer to wood, pelts, furniture, and containers. The *ne-* gender prefix is used with subjects and objects that refer to small round objects like berries and thimbles or to the face. Both prefixes are used in combination, *dene-*, when referring to heavy objects like cab-

are transitive themes: all derivatives have a direct object. The final theme also has P+e# to indicate that its derivatives all have the *e*-postposition plus a postpositional object (P). Each of the three themes also has a specific meaning associated with it.

The following are derivational products of these themes, with the additional meaning provided by person, mode and aspect prefixes and suffixes:[10]

(1a)   *eletlekk*
       ∅   + *le*   + *de*   + *tlekk*
       G   + M   + CL   + mushy + NEU IMPF
       'It (dough, mud, wet clothing) is there, in position.'

(2a)   *yedeneetlaakk*
       ye   + *de* + *ne* + ∅   + *tlaakk*
       3SG O   + G   + M   + CL   + mushy + MOM PERF
       'S/he arrived carrying it (wet pelt).'

(3a)   *heyeeltluh*
       hʉ   + *e*   # *ye*   + *le* + ∅   + *tluh*
       AREA   + PP   # 3SG O   + M   + CL   + mushy + SML PERF
       'S/he threw her/him/it against a surface, slammed her/him/it down on a surface.'

2.3. The aspectual system

This overview of the aspectual system of the language serves as an introduction to the more detailed examination in chapters 3 and 4.

2.3.1. Mode and aspect

Aspect in Koyukon is expressed by a complex, multidimensional system. Two major categories combine in expressing the temporal contour of the state or activity described by the verb. We call one of these two categories mode and the other aspect. I have called these two categories basic because they are obligatory—every verb must be marked for both mode and aspect. This morphological marking is an intersecting one—that is, mode and aspect are marked by prefixal and suffixal elements that encode both categories.

There are four modes: imperfective, perfective, future, and opta-

bages or animal heads.
    10. See the list of abbreviations (p. x) for a guide to reading the morpheme-by-morpheme glosses of examples.

tive. Mode, then, includes a basic aspectual distinction of completion (perfective) versus noncompletion (imperfective) along the same
plane as categories that have traditionally been viewed as tense
(future)[11] and mood (optative). All four, however, have true modal
function in that they provide the means to express the distinction
between realis and irrealis. Within its capacity to mark an utterance as realis, mode further conveys an aspectual distinction between imperfective and perfective; along with marking an utterance
as irrealis, it further indicates a distinction between intention (future) and desire or obligation (optative).

The Athabaskan modes are marked by one or more prefixes in
zone 3 of the prefix chart (table 2.2). The optative is marked by a
ghu- prefix and the future by *te-* (in position 4C) plus *ghe-* (position
3B) prefixes in all aspects. Imperfective and perfective are marked
by one of several possible prefixes depending on the aspect. For
example, verbs of the momentaneous aspect may have a *ne-* perfective mode prefix, as in example (2a) (presented in section 2.2.1), and
a *ne-* imperfective prefix, as in (2b):[12]

(2a) *yedeneetlaakk*
    ye   + *de*   + *ne*   + ∅   + *tlaakk*
    3SG O   + G   + M   + CL   + mushy + MOM PERF
    'S/he arrived carrying it (wet pelt).'

(2b) *yedaatlaah*
    ye   + *de*   + *ne*   + ∅   + *tlaah*
    3SG O   + G   + M   + CL   + mushy + MOM IMPF
    'S/he is arriving carrying it (wet pelt).'

Momentaneous derivations are also possible with a ∅, *le-*, or
ghe- perfective prefix, and a ∅ or *le-* imperfective prefix. Verbs in
the semelfactive and conclusive aspects, on the other hand, may
have only ∅ imperfective and *le-* perfective mode prefixes, as in the
semelfactive example in (3a), *heyeeltluh* 's/he threw her/him/it

11. However, Friedrich (1974), among others, calls the future a quasi-
mood.
12. The difference between the surface forms of the prefixal portion of
these two verbs is due to the presence of the *ne-* perfective prefix (position
3A of the chart presented in table 2.2) in example (2). I have chosen not to
include this prefix in the morpheme-by-morpheme glosses because I felt it
would complicate rather than clarify the explanation of the aspectual system.

against a surface', while verbs in the durative or consecutive aspects may have only ∅ imperfective and *ghe-* perfective prefixes.

The second basic temporal category is aspect. The fifteen aspects in Koyukon can be classed into three general groups. The first group includes those aspects that refer to an entity's state, condition, position, or existence. State aspects include the neuter and the transitional. The second and third groups are made up of aspects used in the expression of activities or events. The second group, motion aspects, refer specifically to the path or manner of an activity through time or space: the momentaneous, perambulative, continuative, persistive, and reversative. The third group, the activity aspects, contains those aspects that refer to the durativity, cyclicity, or punctuality of an activity: the durative, consecutive, repetitive, directive-repetitive, semelfactive, bisective, conclusive, and onomatopoetic.

Table 2.3. The Koyukon Modes and Aspects

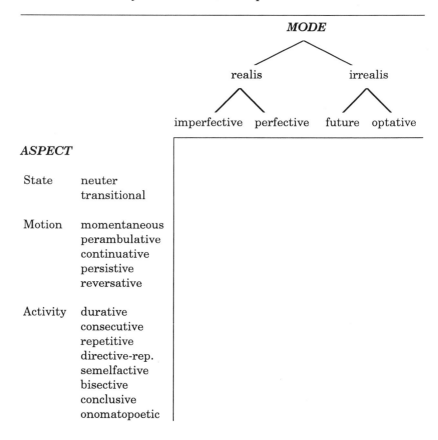

Aspect is marked morphologically by suffixation, vowel lengthening, or ablaut of the verb stem, or by a combination of all three strategies. Each aspect has a particular stem shape for each of the four modes. Examples (2a) and (2b) above showed that imperfective and perfective momentaneous forms are distinguished in part by different stem shapes. The mode and aspect system can be diagramed to illustrate this intersection of mode and aspect (see table 2.3). Notice that mode in this figure forms a horizontal axis and aspect a vertical axis.

Table 2.4 fills in the diagram of table 2.3, illustrating the stem shapes for all four modes of the aspects that are possible for the root *-tlaakk/tlukk* 'classificatory: mushy object':

Table 2.4. Stem Sets of *-tlaakk/tlukk*

	IMPF	PERF	FUT	OPT
NEUTER	*tlaakk*	*tlaakk*	*tlaakk*	*tlaakk*
MOMENTANEOUS	*tlaah*	*tlaakk*	*tluhtl*	*tlaah*
PERAMBULATIVE	*tlaah*	*tlaakk*	*tluh*	*tluh*
CONTINUATIVE	*tlaah*	*tlaakk*	*tlaah*	*tlaah*
PERSISTIVE	*tluh*	*tluh*	*tluh*	*tluh*
DURATIVE	*tlaah*	*tlaah*	*tlaah*	*tlaah*
CONSECUTIVE	*tlukk*	*tlukk*	*tlukk*	*tlukk*
SEMELFACTIVE	*tluh*	*tluh*	*tluh*	*tluh*
CONCLUSIVE	*tlukk*	*tlukk*	*tlukk*	*tlukk*

The mode prefixes required for each aspect help to disambiguate forms with homophonous stems; conversely, the different stems possible for each mode help to disambiguate aspects that require the same mode prefix.

2.3.2. The full aspectual system

Three more aspectual categories—aspect-dependent derivational prefix strings, superaspect, and post-aspectual derivations—combine with mode and aspect to make up the full aspectual system of Koyukon. These three categories, discussed at length in chaper 4, are not obligatory, as mode and aspect are, but they are fundamental constituents of temporal expression in the language.

A derivational prefix string is composed of one or more prefixes that combine to add a particular meaning to the theme.[13] Derivational strings may be aspect-dependent (i.e., they may occur only with a particular mode prefix and aspect), or they may be non-aspect-dependent (i.e., they may appear with a verb regardless of mode and aspect). Non-aspect-dependent derivational strings include the reflexive, causative, passive, and benefactive. The meanings of aspect-dependent derivational strings are generally adverbial. As Friedrich says, "The possibility of cooccurrence (or selectional combination) between verbal and adverbial subcategories is the *universal* criterion for aspect" (1974:4).

There are some 300 aspect-dependent derivational strings in Koyukon, each of which adds a particular meaning to the derivational product. All choose (or trigger) specific imperfective and perfective mode prefixes and aspectual stem forms. One aspect-dependent derivational string that may be added to the theme shown in (2) above *(O+G+Ø +tlaakk* 'handle, hold mushy, wet, sticky, messy, disorderly O') is *tlee#* plus *ne-* imperfective or *ne-* perfective mode prefixes plus momentaneous stem, which means '(go) out the door'. Note that the required mode prefixes and aspect are included as part of the string. Compare (2a), repeated here for convenience, with the inflected form containing this string in (2c).

(2a)   *yedeneetlaakk*
     ye   *+ de* *+ ne* *+ Ø*   *+ tlaakk*
     3SG O + G + M + CL + mushy + MOM
     'S/he arrived carrying it (wet pelt).'

(2c)   *tleeyedaaneetlaakk*
     tlee # *ye*   *+ de* *+ ne* *+ Ø*   *+ tlaakk*
     DS # 3SG O + G + M + CL + mushy + MOM
     'S/he took it (wet pelt) out the door.'

Another example of an aspect-dependent derivational string is *do#* plus *le-* imperfective or *le-* perfective mode prefixes plus momentaneous stem, which means 'elevated'. The following derivative, also from the theme in (2), contains this string:

---

13. The Binary Branching Hypothesis as discussed by Scalise (1985) states that a word formation rule attaches one and only one affix at a time, (i.e., the internal structure of a derived word will always be binary). Due to the pervasive nature of discontinuous dependencies in Koyukon, it may be more insightful to think of the affixation process as similar to the superimposition of transparency diagrams one atop the other rather than as a binary or nesting structure.

(2d) *doyeltlaakk*
    do # *ye*   + *le* + ∅ + *tlaakk*
    DS # 3SG O + M + CL + mushy + MOM
    'S/he hung it up (freshly cut fish, wet clothes, etc.).'

The second nonobligatory aspectual category is superaspect. There are four superaspects: distributive, multiple, customary, and progressive. The distributive is used to express a plurality of locations or objects associated with an activity, while the multiple denotes a multitude of subject or object referents. The customary conveys the habitual or frequent character of the activity, and the progressive expresses the incomplete nature of an activity or focuses on its duration. These derivations, like aspect, have unique stem sets and prefix morphology and express aspectual meaning. Superaspects are unlike aspects in Koyukon, however, in that they occur in combination with the fifteen aspects and may also occur with each other. They are, in effect, superimposed on regular aspectual derivations. Consider again examples (2c) and (2d), which illustrate the addition of aspect-dependent derivational strings. The example in (2e), below, illustrates the addition of the customary superaspect to the form in (2c).

(2c) *tleeyedaaneetlaakk*
    tlee # *ye*   + *de* + *ne* + ∅   + *tlaakk*
    DS # 3SG O + G   + M   + CL + mushy + MOM
    'S/he took it (wet pelt) out the door.'

(2e) *tleeyedetluh*
    tlee # *ye*   + *de* + ∅ + ∅   + *tluh*
    DS # 3SG O + G   + M   + CL + mushy + CUST
    'S/he customarily takes them (wet pelts) out the door.'

The example in (2f) illustrates the addition of the customary and the distributive superaspects to the form in (2d).

(2d) *doyeltlaakk*
    do # *ye*   + *le* + ∅   + *tlaakk*
    DS # 3SG O + M + CL + mushy + MOM
    'S/he hung it up (freshly cut fish, wet clothes).'

(2f) *donyetluh*
    do + *ne*   # *ye*   + ∅ + ∅ + *tluh*
    DS + DIST # 3SG O + M + CL + mushy + CUST
    'S/he customarily hangs them up (freshly cut fish, wet clothes) here
      and there.'

We know the form in (2f) is underlyingly a momentaneous form with *ne-* imperfective and perfective mode prefixes because we see the *do#* of that aspect-dependent derivational string. We know (2f) is a product of the distributive derivation as well because we see the *ne#* distributive disjunct prefix. Finally, we know it is derived for the customary superaspect (and that this derivation was a final step) because it has the characteristic stem shape of the customary.

The last category within the Koyukon aspectual system comprises the four postaspectual derivations: conative, inceptive, errative, and negative. These very productive derivations have characteristics in common both with aspect-dependent derivational strings and with superaspect. They choose or trigger the use of specific mode prefixes and may require other prefixes as well (in this respect they are like the aspect-dependent derivational strings). They are like superaspect in that they can be added onto any regular aspectual derivation, but unlike it in they are not associated with regular stem variation patterns.

All four postaspectual derivations convey an irrealis sense: the conative refers to trying to do something, the inceptive refers to beginning to do something, the errative refers to doing something incorrectly or excessively, and the negative refers to not doing something. The example in (2g) shows the conative postaspectual derivation applied to the example shown above in (2c):

(2g)   *tleeyoodeenaaltlaakk*
       tlee # *ye*   + *oo*   + *de* + *ne*   + *le* + ∅   + *tlaakk*
       DS   # 3SG O + CONA + G   + CONA + M   + CL + mushy + MOM
       'S/he tried to take it (wet pelt) out the door.'

Example (2h) shows the both conative postaspectual derivation and the distributive superaspect superimposed on the form in example (2d):

(2h)   *donyoonaaltlaakk*
       do + *ne*   # *ye*   + *oo*+*ne* + *le* + ∅   + *tlaakk*
       DS + DIST # 3SG O + CONA   + M   + CL + mushy + DIST
       'S/he tried to hang them up here and there.'

The examples above offer a hint of the wealth of temporal expression made possible by the multidimensionality of the Koyukon aspectual system. Chapters 3 and 4 provide a detailed presentation of all five of the system's components.

2.4. Verb theme categories

Just as different verbs can be grouped and assigned to a given theme on the basis of shared formal characteristics (i.e., root and basic prefixes occurring in all derivatives), so verb themes can be grouped into larger categories on the basis of shared formal and semantic characteristics. These larger categories are the verb theme categories. The discussion that follows is based largely on the principles and terminology introduced in Kari (1979).

There are seven major verb theme categories in Koyukon: stative, descriptive, extension, motion, operative, conversive, and successive. Each is characterized by a particular aspect—that is, the primary (or least marked) derivative of each is of a particular aspect or mode and aspect combination. Because each verb theme category is associated with a particular aspect or group of aspects, each can also be characterized as having a particular semantic core. For example, the first three verb theme categories listed above have primary aspectual derivations that are neuter and describe states. Each category is associated with neuter derivatives that have particular imperfective mode prefixes. Stative themes have primary neuter derivatives with an *le-* imperfective prefix and refer to physical position or location. Descriptive themes have primary neuter derivatives with a ∅ imperfective prefix and describe the physical characteristics of objects, in much the same way that adjectives do in English. Extension themes are primarily associated with *ne-* imperfective neuter derivatives and refer to something extended in a linear fashion (e.g., streams, trails).

The last four verb theme categories have active primary aspectual derivations and refer to processes or events. Each of these categories is characterized by a "diagnostic" aspect. The diagnostic aspect for the successive category, for example, is the semelfactive. Only successive themes have derivatives of the semelfactive aspect, though themes of this category may also have derivatives in all the other activity or motion aspects. Successive themes refer to punctual actions that can be performed once or as a series of single actions.

Conversive themes also describe activities but are telic, focusing not on the process but rather on the goal or completion of the action. The diagnostic aspect for the conversive theme category is the conclusive aspect, though the durative and motion aspects are also possible.

The durative is the diagnostic aspect for the operative category. Operative themes describe processes, activities that take place over a period of time. Themes of this category may also have motion aspect derivatives, but they never have semelfactive or conclusive derivatives.

Finally, the category of motion themes is characterized by derivatives of the momentaneous and other motion aspects only. Motion themes describe movement performed in a particular direction, manner, or time frame.

Distributional characteristics provide another way one can determine to which theme category a particular theme belongs. That is, one can look at what other verb themes the root appears in. We know, for example, that $\emptyset$ +taa 'lie' is a stative (positional) theme (rather than some other neuter theme category) not only from its meaning and derivational possibilities, but also because there is another theme paired with it, ne+$\emptyset$ +taa 'assume a lying position'. This type of stative theme always pairs with intransitive motion themes meaning 'assume ____ position', and no other neuter theme category does that. Similarly, classificatory stative themes always pair with classificatory motion themes—that is one of their defining characteristics.

Verb theme categories, then, are a means of abbreviating or symbolizing the structural, semantic, and distributional characteristics of a group of verb themes. It is important to note, though, that unlike themes, which are precise statements of the morphemes common to a group of inflected examples, theme categories are not precise descriptions of categories with clear-cut parameters. It has been stated that each category is characterized by a particular aspect and yet some aspects (e.g., neuter, momentaneous, durative) are not restricted to only one theme category. Similarly, aspect-dependent derivational strings, superaspect, and postaspectual derivatives are not restricted to only one category of verb theme. Finally, the semantic characteristics noted for each category represent only a general idea and not a strict guideline. There is quite a bit of semantic overlap between categories.

Some verbs, however, come to mind as prototypical examples of given theme categories, while other verbs are less clear semantic illustrations. For instance, prototypical themes of the processual operative category include 'to eat', 'to see', and 'to talk'. Prototypical examples of the telic conversive theme category include 'to make a single object', 'to kill a single object', and 'to sew, producing an article of clothing'. The punctual successive category has such prototypical themes as 'to bite', 'to chop', and 'to cut'. Other verbs,

such as 'to pluck feathers', might be considered by an English
speaker to be semantically appropriate to any of these three categories. One would need to know what aspectual derivations are possible for the verb in order to assign it to its actual theme category
(operative). Chapter 5 presents a detailed description of the organization of aspectual theme categories.

2.5. The literature on aspect in Athabaskan languages

It is not the intention here to provide an exhaustive survey of
everything written on these topics, but rather to provide a general
picture of both the background and the context for the current work.

The modern work on aspect in Athabaskan begins with that of
Edward Sapir. In his work on Navajo in the 1920s and 30s, Sapir
developed the concepts and terminology that form the basis for later
research (Sapir 1936, Sapir and Hoijer 1967). Sets of class notes
taken by Newman, Swadesh, and Haas during Sapir's lectures at
Yale from 1931 to 1936 have been collected by Michael Krauss at
the Alaska Native Language Center of the University of Alaska,
Fairbanks. Those notes reflect Sapir's insightful examination of
Athabaskan aspect and stem variation, presenting ideas not developed further (or, in some cases, recovered) until the 1970s.

Sapir saw two main categories of aspect in Athabaskan. One of
them included the neuter and transitional aspects. The second category encompassed the "durative, momentaneous, repetitive, semelfactive, continuative, distributive, diversive, reversative, repetitive,
conative, progressive, and transitional" aspects, but was divisible
into groups based on whether these aspects were "punctual" or "linear" (Swadesh 1932). For a careful review of the analysis of aspect
revealed in the Sapir class notes, see Kari (1979). Kari's review
concludes by saying that "Sapir's suggestive aspectual categories
were given only brief exemplification but no explicit structural and
semantic definition, and stem variation was assumed to be arbi-
trary and irregular" (55).

Other significant early work that contains reference to verb
stem variation and aspect in Athabaskan languages includes Morice's massive grammar of Carrier (1932), Li's work on Chipewyan
(1946), and Hoijer's work on Apachean (1945–49). Morice, unfortunately, was working without benefit of Sapir's insight and, although
his grammar gives abundant detail regarding varieties of the Carrier verb, he shows scant understanding of the systematic morphophonological processes of derivational aspect in Athabaskan. Li's

work on Chipewyan is more useful, supplying a table of stem sets according to the following "modes": neuter, momentaneous, continuative, customary, and progressive.

Hoijer (1946) provides plentiful exemplification of the prefixal components of the seven "mode and tense" paradigms he distinguished: imperfective, perfective, progressive, future, iterative, customary, and optative. He also (1948) identified form classes based on the number and kind of paradigms in which a base could be conjugated, as well as its transitivity, classifier, prefixes, and stem shape. Those classes, though, are a based on factors relating to voice rather than to aspect. Hoijer's (1949) study of the Apachean verb theme is perhaps the most relevant to the topic of this study. Here Hoijer discusses the verb theme and provides ample examples of the momentaneous, continuative, repetitive, semelfactive, diversative, reversative, distributive, conative, and transitional aspects. He gives little analysis of stem variation, however, saying that "Apachean languages have leveled their verb stems. . . . The fact that such leveling has taken place makes it somewhat more difficult to understand the few differences that remain" (13). In Sapir and Hoijer 1967, Hoijer dismisses the Navajo stem variation as suppletive.

More contemporary work on Athabaskan languages that includes discussion of aspectual phenomena includes Hale's (1956) thesis on Navajo and Golla's (1970) dissertation on Hupa. Hale's thesis gives a systematic view of the distribution of Navajo derivational prefixes according to mode and aspect. In Golla's exploration of the derivational processes of Hupa verbal morphology, he identifies classes of verb themes. Four of the theme systems Golla isolated were later adopted by Kari (1979), and subsequently in the present work.

In 1979 two fundamental works that dealt explicitly with verb stem variation, aspect, and aspectual verb theme categories were published by the Alaska Native Language Center. The two monographs had a significant impact on all work in this area to follow. The first of these works was Leer's 1979 monograph, *Proto-Athabaskan Verb Stem Variation. Part I: Phonology*. Leer's research constitutes a significant advance in the reconstruction of proto-Athabaskan and pre-proto-Athabaskan phonology. He defines an Athabaskan stem as a root plus or minus modification plus or minus suffix, and explains the historical phonological processes (spirantization, nasalization, ablaut, and the development of constriction) by which sets of verb stems can be derived from underlying roots.

The second important monograph from 1979 was Jim Kari's *Athabaskan Verb Theme Categories: Ahtna*. Although much of it was later updated and elaborated in his introduction to the *Ahtna Dictionary* (1990), this work still represents the most extensive published research exclusively on aspect and verb theme categories, and my own work draws heavily from it. Kari proposes a theory of the verb theme, "the structural and semantic common denominator that underlies all verb forms derived from it" (5). He then demonstrates how these themes can be grouped into "lexical verb theme categories that have definable semantic content and a common structure in their most basic derived forms" (5).

The monograph begins with an introduction to Ahtna phonology and morphology and then presents discussions of the verb theme categories, with detailed examination of particular aspects and superaspects only as that information becomes relevant. This approach, then, is quite different from the one I have adopted here. Kari distinguishes motion, conversive, and successive/operative theme categories for the active verbs. He thus posits a closer relationship of the successive and operative categories in Ahtna than I do for Koyukon. He describes five neuter theme categories—extension, positional, stative, dimensional, and descriptive—in contrast to the three I have delineated in Koyukon.

Kari also offers substantial analysis of conversive and operative theme subcategories and devotes special sections to classificatory themes and uncategorized verb themes. The monograph concludes with a richly detailed chapter on the phonology of verb stem variation.

Most of the work since 1979 on Athabaskan aspectual systems has followed the findings presented by Leer and Kari. The most important of the current work includes two dissertations, Hardy (1979) on Navajo stem variation,[14] and Midgette (1987) on the Navajo progressive.

Hardy's (1979) dissertation, *Navajo Aspectual Verb Stem Variation*, aimed to "establish an inventory of aspect categories for the Navajo verb, and to make clear the bases on which the inventory is defined" (1). His approach to the problem is both semantic and

---

14. This research was completed in the same year that Leer and Kari's monographs were published, but Hardy had access to manuscript versions of those works while preparing his dissertation.

structural, but his final definitions of the nine aspects he isolates
are based primarily on prefix and stem morphology:

> Purely semantic facts could be made the basis for a study of Na-
> vajo aspect, apart from any structural considerations. Such an
> approach would have the following disadvantages. First, making
> use of semantic information alone there is no basis for distinguish-
> ing such categories as imperfective, iterative, and progressive (ten-
> ses) from such categories as continuative, repetitive, and durative
> (aspects). Differences clearly exist, but they are not semantic ones.
> [38]

A second disadvantage, he claims, is the inability to exclude the
categories I have included in chapter 4 as aspect-dependent derivational prefix strings and postaspectual derivations: "Semantically
there is no way to exclude it, although from a structural viewpoint
it is not part of the aspect system of Navajo" (39). This dismissal of
the semantic criteria for defining aspect is a serious weakness in
Hardy's study.

Midgette's (1987) dissertation focuses on the Navajo progressive
mode in the discourse context. Although she redefines Navajo mode
as aspect, "inflectional systems determining the temporal shape of a
situation," and aspect as Aktionsart, "the temporal shape as specified lexically" (vii), she presents a clear and insightful summary of
Navajo verb theme categories and aspectual contrasts. Within the
framework of cognitive grammar, she examines the modal properties of the progressive in conversation and its use as a backgrounding device in narrative. Midgette's conclusion that "Aspect has to do
with the determination of the lexeme, as a lexical unit, while Mode
is a true inflectional system which shapes this unit for discourse
purposes" (58) corresponds to some degree with my own findings
regarding the use of the Koyukon aspectual system in discourse (to
be discussed in chap. 6).

This survey can not be concluded without mentioning Rice's
(1989) grammar of Slave and the work of Young and Morgan. Rice's
voluminous grammar provides an excellent and very valuable description of the aspectual system of Slave. Young and Morgan's
Analytical Lexicon of Navajo (1992) is organized on the principles of
verb theme categorization and, along with their revised grammar
and dictionary (1987), is the richest and most complete source of
information on the aspectual system of Navajo.

2.5.1. The literature on aspect in Koyukon

The Jesuit missionary Jules Jetté, in his enormously comprehensive and perceptive dictionary and grammar of Koyukon (1905, 1906), provided both an incomparably rich source of data and a most insightful analysis of the verbal system of the language. In his unpublished manuscript, *On the Language of the Ten'a* (1906), Jetté notes Koyukon stem variation, which he refers to as "tense-changes in the roots" (43). He recognized at least three separate aspectual stem sets for motion verbs, which correspond to what we now call the momentaneous, continuative, and perambulative aspects. He isolated several verb "phases," including one that corresponds to what we now call the customary superaspect (Jetté's "frequentative" and "habitual"). In his discussion of "derived multiples," he also showed how the multiple and distributive superaspects alter stem shape. Among the postaspectual derivations, Jetté noted the conative and, of course, the negative.

Eliza Jones's work on Koyukon stem variation grew out of her work with Krauss, Kari, and Leer in the 1970s at the Alaska Native Language Center. She prepared an incisive summary (1979) of the aspectual potential of the classificatory verbs, including all the possibilities of mode, aspect, superaspect, and postaspectual derivations. She has continued this approach in her work, first with Kari and later with me on the *Koyukon Athabaskan Dictionary*.

The collaborative effort of Chad Thompson, Eliza Jones, and myself on the *Han Zaadletl'ee Koyukon Language Curriculum Scope and Sequence* (1983) was intended, with accompanying lesson plans and a student workbook, to provide an overview of Koyukon grammar for the bilingual secondary school teacher. I included about fifteen chapters that deal specifically with aspect and theme category, including descriptions of the momentaneous, semelfactive, conclusive, durative, repetitive, persistive, perambulative, continuative, reversative, and neuter aspects. The first discussion of the consecutive aspect, at that time called the seriative, also appears in the work. In addition, I gave an introduction to the organization of the Koyukon verb theme categories and discussed the distinguishing characteristics of each of the major activity theme categories. These chapters represent a preliminary stage in my research into the Koyukon aspectual system but do contain much that remains unchanged in this present work.

2.6. Summary

Koyukon has a rich and elaborate aspectual system. Five major components of this system can be isolated: mode, aspect, aspect-dependent derivational strings, superaspect, and postaspectual derivations. The next chapter begins the fuller examination of the aspectual system of Koyukon with a discussion of its two fundamental constituents, mode and aspect. The description of the phonetic and morphophonemic components of the language provided in section 2.1, along with the overview of verb and theme structure in section 2.2, should make the following discussion easier to follow.

3
Mode and Aspect

3.1. The Koyukon modes

As outlined in chapter 2, mode in Koyukon constitutes one of the two major temporal categories in the Koyukon aspectual system. The four modes include what is generally regarded as the most basic aspectual distinction, that of perfective versus imperfective. However, that distinction is included in the same form (and function) class with categories that have traditionally been viewed as tense (future) and mood (optative). The Koyukon aspects, by contrast, include the means for characterizing an event in terms of durativity, punctuality, and cyclicity—categories also traditionally associated with aspectual systems—as well as the means to express more adverbial concepts such as 'back and forth in a zigzag manner', 'making a round trip', or 'breaking in two'. The category that most Athabaskanists call aspect, then, is reminiscent of Aktionsart, a category that characterizes the *manner* of the action.[1]

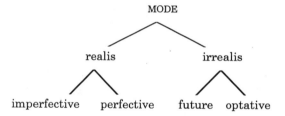

Figure 3.1. The Koyukon modes

Koyukon mode is perhaps best described as that category by means of which the distinction between realis and irrealis is expressed. Within its capacity to mark the nature of an utterance as

1. I choose not to take this use of the term *Aktionsart* any further. As noted in chapter 2, Midgette (1987) refers to Navajo mode as aspect and aspect as Aktionsart, both on alleged semantic grounds and also because it allows a distinction to be made between mode as an inflectional category and aspect as a derivational category (see also Comrie 1976:6–7, regarding this use of the two terms). Because of the close interrelationship of mode and aspect in Koyukon, it would be misleading to suggest that kind of structural distinction here.

realis, mode further expresses the aspectual distinction between imperfective and perfective. Within its capacity to mark irrealis, mode further expresses a distinction between intention (future) versus desire or obligation (optative).

3.1.1. Imperfective

The imperfective mode is used to describe an ongoing, unfinished activity or a static condition. The following are examples of verbs in the imperfective mode:

(1a) *ełyoł*
     ∅   + ł   + yoł
     M   + CL   + snow + DUR IMPF
     'It's snowing.'

(1b) *estseh*
     ∅   + s   + ∅   + tseh
     M   + 1SG S   + CL   + cry + DUR IMPF
     'I'm crying.'

The ∅ mode prefix is used for the imperfective of all aspects except the perambulative (which requires a *ne-* imperfective prefix) and some momentaneous derivatives (which require *ne-* or *le-* imperfective prefixes), and the neuter. Neuter imperfective morphology is derived from the momentaneous perfective and thus permits four other imperfective mode prefixes: *aa-*, *le- [*se-]*, *ghe-*, and *ne-* (see section 3.2.1).

3.1.2. Perfective

The perfective describes a completed activity or past state. Compare examples (2a) and (2b) with (1a) and (1b), above.

(2a) *noghełyotl*
     no   + ghe   + ł   + yotl
     ITER   + M   + CL   + snow + DUR PERF
     'There was a winter with heavy snowfall.' Lit. 'It snowed again.'

(2b) *ghestsaah*
     ghe   + s   + ∅   + tsaah
     M   + 1SG S   + CL   + cry + DUR PERF
     'I cried.'

There are four mode prefixes used in the perfective: ∅, *le-*, *ne-*, and *ghe*. Krauss and Leer point out that the true perfective prefix is the *ne-/∅* prefix (/*ŋ/) in position 3A of the prefix complex (as shown in table 2.2), and that those prefixes are, in fact, "conjugation" prefixes rather than perfective prefixes.

> The perfective marker proper, an *n~i* type prefix in modern Athabaskan which is manifested at least (originally) to the right of the subject pronouns, if manifested at all, is not to be confused with what have been called the "perfective prefixes," **s(ə)-, *gə- >* γə-, and **nə-*, which are more properly called conjugation prefixes. These three prefixes are in fact each found in both perfectives and non-perfectives, and thus do not in themselves distinguish the perfective. [1981:41]

Because the *ne-/∅* prefix also appears in neuter imperfective derivatives, however, in the following discussion I will refer to the four "conjugation" prefixes used to indicate the perfective mode as perfective prefixes.

Krauss proposes the following distinction between the Athabaskan perfective prefixes:

> The choice between *s-* [Koyukon *l-*], γ- *[gh-]* and *n-* perfective is expectably governed in part by the derivational prefixes, but insofar as the perfectives contrast, *n-* has the marked meaning 'to a point, completive', has the marked meaning 'from a point, inceptive', and *s-* is unmarked in this respect, 'static'. This would seem to be true of active as well as of neuter forms. [1969:82]

Young and Morgan provide a similar description of the perfective prefixes in Navajo:

> The *yi*-Perfective *[∅ -]* expresses simple completion of the action of the verb, without connotations of termination or of a durative-static sequel. . . . The *ni*-Perfective, like the *ni*-Imperfective, connotes the fact that the verbal action is terminal in effect, as in arriving, stopping, finishing. . . . Again, like the *si*-Imperfective, the modal prefix *si-* identifies the action of the verb as being of a type that assumes a durative-static status upon completion. [1987:104]

Unfortunately, those characterizations do not seem to hold for Koyukon. The *le-* perfective is used with semelfactive, bisective, conclusive, continuative, distributive, perambulative, most reversative, some transitional, and some momentaneous derivatives. The *ghe-* perfective is used with durative, consecutive, repetitive, directive-repetitive, persistive, progressive, customary, neuter, some reversative, and some momentaneous derivatives. The ∅ - is used in some transitional and some momentaneous derivatives, and the *ne-* perfective prefix is used exclusively with momentaneous derivatives. Table 3.1 provides a summary of the distribution of the perfective prefix variants.

Table 3.1. Perfective Mode Prefixes

le-	*ghe-*	∅	*ne-*
MOM	MOM	MOM	MOM
TRANS		TRANS	
REV	REV		
SML	DUR		
BIS	CONS		
CNCL	REP		
CONT	DIR-REP		
PRMB	PERS		
DIST	PROG		
	CUST		
	NEU		

It is difficult to imagine a single semantic characterization underlying each of these groupings. If we extract those aspects that appear in more than one column, as in table 3.2, however, we can see a tendency for the *le-* perfective to occur with those aspects and superaspects that describe punctual or unitary activities, while the *ghe-* perfective prefix occurs in derivatives that describe repeated, ongoing, or habitual activities or states.

Table 3.2. Semantics of the *le-* and *ghe-* Perfective Mode Prefixes

le-	*ghe-*
punctual, unitary	*repeated, ongoing, habitual*
SML	DUR
BIS	CONS
CNCL	REP
CONT	DIR-REP
PRMB	PERS
DIST	PROG
	CUST
	NEU

Because momentaneous derivatives occur with each of the four perfective prefixes, they are an important set to examine for an indication of the semantic range of each prefix.

In momentaneous derivatives, as Krauss (1969) points out, derivational prefixes other than the perfective prefix carry a great deal of the meaning and "choose" the perfective and imperfective prefixes that accompany them. The mode and aspect choosing derivational prefixes comprise the set of aspect-dependent derivational strings, discussed at length in section 4.1. All four perfectives may occur without any other conjunct or disjunct prefixes. In these cases, the n momentaneous[2] perfectives refer to terminative or completive activity, as in examples (3a–b):

(3a) *nesyo*
      ne + s   + ∅   + yo
      M   + 1SG S   + CL   + go + MOM PERF
      'I arrived.'

(3b) *neebaanh*
      ne + ∅   + baanh
      M   + CL   + swim + MOM PERF
      'S/he arrived swimming.'

Although this use of the *ne-* perfective in Koyukon momentaneous derivatives corresponds to both Krauss's and Young's characterizations, the *le-*, ∅, and *ghe-* perfectives in Koyukon differ from their descriptions. The *l* momentaneous perfectives, like the list of *le-* perfective aspects given in table 3.2, frequently refer to punctual or unitary activities. Consider the following examples:

(4a) *daałeneenh*
      de + le   + de   + neenh
      T   + M   + CL   + shiver + MOM PERF
      'S/he shivered once, had a shiver.'

2. Momentaneous verbs that take *ne-* perfective and ∅ imperfective prefixes are referred to as 'n momentaneous'; those that take *ghe-* perfective and ∅ imperfective prefixes are referred to as gh momentaneous; those that take *le-* perfective and ∅ imperfective are referred to as *l* momentaneous; those that take *le-* perfective and *le-* imperfective are referred to as *ll* momentaneous; and those that take ∅ perfective and ∅ imperfective are referred to as ∅ momentaneous.

(4b)   *daałeteh*
     de + *le* + *de* + *teh*
     T + M + CL + fly + MOM PERF
     'It (dust) flew up (in a gust).'

Like the transitional, which may also require a ∅ perfective prefix, the ∅ momentaneous perfective often refers to the entrance into a state or the inception of a process or activity, as in the following examples:

(5a)   *yeełtsonh*
     ye + ∅ + *ł* + *tsonh*
     3SG O + M + CL + smell + MOM PERF
     'S/he smelled it, caught its scent.'

(5b)   *deebaah*
     de + ∅ + ∅ + *baah*
     T + M + CL + cry + MOM PERF
     'S/he burst out crying.'

(5c)   *eelbenh*
     ∅ + ∅ + *benh*
     M + CL + water rises + MOM PERF
     'It (water) rose; it flooded.'

(5d)   *needebets*
     ne + ∅ + *de* + *bets*
     T + M + CL + flutter + MOM PERF
     'It (butterfly, small bird) flew off.'

As with other aspects that require a *ghe-* perfective prefix, *gh* momentaneous derivatives often refer to movement that involves some repetition or duration before its completion, as in the following examples:

(6a)   *naaghedenekk*
     no # *ghe* + *de* + *nekk*
     ITER # M + CL + flat, flexible object moves + MOM PERF
     'It (string, seam, cloth) unraveled.'

(6b)   *heyedolnekk*
     heye + *e* # *de* + *ghe* + *le* + *nekk*
     3SG P + PP # T + M + CL + swarm + MOM PERF
     'They ganged up on her/him.'

Most momentaneous derivatives do occur with more complex, mode-choosing derivational strings of prefixes that add meaning relating to the manner or direction of the activity. In a few cases the mode-choosing derivational prefixes are identical, though, leaving only the difference in the perfective prefix itself to account for differences in meaning. For example, in the following verbs we can compare the meaning difference between the aspect-dependent derivational prefix strings *P+gho#* plus *ne-* perfective prefix and momentaneous stem, which means 'catching, injuring on P', and *P+gho#* with *ghe-* perfective prefix and momentaneous stem, which means 'catching, snagging on P' (note that *ne-* and *ghe-* are the most commonly used momentaneous perfective prefixes):

(7a) *deghoneek'eł* (*n* momentaneous)
      de   + gho # ne + ∅   + k'eł
      INDT   + PP   # M   + CL + tear + MOM PERF
      'It (clothing) caught on something and tore as s/he ran straight into it.'

(7b) *deghogheek'eł* (*gh* momentaneous)
      de   + gho # ghe + ∅   + k'eł
      INDT   + PP   # M   + CL + tear + MOM PERF
      'It (clothing) caught on something and tore as s/he ran carelessly past it'

Both (7a) and (7b) express completed action. The *n* momentaneous in (7a) seems to be used to refer to a more directed action, while the *gh* momentaneous in (7b) refers to less deliberate action, action performed more tangentially with respect to the (postpositional) object.

After examining the list of some 300 aspect-dependent derivational prefix strings (included as an appendix to the Koyukon Athabaskan Dictionary), the clearest semantic characterization we can draw involves a link between the choice of perfective prefix and the direction of the activity referred to by the verbal form. The following generalizations regarding the perfective prefixes can be made:

- Strings indicating direction *into* something tend to take the *ghe-* perfective prefix (e.g., the string *P+yee#* plus *ghe-* perfective prefix and momentaneous stem means 'into P').
- Strings indicating movement going down vertically also take *ghe-* perfective (e.g., *no#* plus *ghe-* perfective prefix and momentaneous stem means 'down').

- Movement going down at an angle is associated with $\emptyset$ perfective (e.g., *do#de+ee+* plus $\emptyset$ perfective prefix and momentaneous stem means 'going down an incline, descending').
- Movement going up vertically is also associated with $\emptyset$ perfective (e.g., *ye#(ee+)* plus $\emptyset$ perfective prefix and momentaneous stem means 'going up vertically').
- Movement up at an angle is associated with *le-* perfective (e.g., *ho#* plus *le-* perfective prefix and momentaneous stem means 'up a slope').

3.1.3. Future

The future mode refers to a state, process, or activity that will occur at some future time. It predicts some state of affairs located temporally subsequent to the time of the utterance. Future derivatives take a *te-* prefix, which is equivalent to the inceptive *te-* prefix, plus a *ghe-* prefix, which is equivalent to the progressive *ghe-* prefix, plus the future stem.

(8a) *neghaaneyh*
 ne # ghe + aa   + $\emptyset$ + neyh
 T   # T   + M   + CL + be strong + NEU IMPF
 'S/he is powerful, very strong.'

(8b) *negheetoneyh*
 ne # ghe + te + ghe + $\emptyset$ + neyh
 T   # T   + M   + CL + be strong + NEU FUT
 'S/he is going to be powerful, very strong.'

(9) *gonh taak'etaaghetlkeltl*
 gonh taa # k'e   + te + ghe + s   + ł   + keltl
 there DS   # INDF   + M   + 1SG S + CL + tie + MOM + FUT
 'I will put in a fishnet here.'

(10) *gon ootaaghskkaat*
 gon   oo + te + ghe + s   + $\emptyset$ + kkaat
 there T + M   + 1SG S + CL + buy + DUR FUT
 'I will buy this one.'

3.1.4. Optative

Use of the Koyukon optative mode corresponds to the traditional definitions of optative and hortatory moods:[3] it indexes the speaker's attitude toward an event and is used to express a wish, to refer to activity the speaker would like to see take place, and to urge someone to do something. It carries the notions of futurity, volition, necessity, and desirability. Optative verbs are formed with the prefix *ghu-* plus the optative stem.[4]

(11a) *ghuson'*
    ghu + *s*   + ∅   + *hon'*
    M   + 1SG S   + CL   + eat + DUR OPT
    'I should eat; let me eat.'

(11b) *Huslia nets'oo'os*
    Huslia   *ne* # *ts'e*   + *ghu* + ∅   + *'os*
    Huslia   DS # 1PL S   + M   + CL   + DU go + MOM OPT
    'We should go to Huslia; let's go to Huslia.'

The optative, like the future, carries the notion of futurity. Where the future makes a prediction about an event or condition that will occur at some unspecified future time, however, the optative expresses a wish or instruction that the event or condition take place at a specific time in the future. Compare the following sentences with the adverb *daa'* 'later' in examples (12) and (13).

(12a) *k'etołyoyh daa'*
    k'e   + *te* + *ghe*   + *ł*   + *yoyh*
    INDF O   + M   + CL   + bake + CNCL FUT
    'S/he will bake something (half-dried fish) later.'

(12b) *k'eghoołyoyh daa'*
    k'e   + *ghu* + *ł* + *yoyh*
    INDF O   + M   + CL+ bake + CNCL OPT
    'S/he should bake something (half-dried fish) when it is time (to cook).'

(13a) *tołkon' daa'*
    te + *ghe* + *ł*   + *kon'*
    M   + CL   + rain + DUR FUT
    'It will rain later.'

---

3. See, for example, Hall (1964:157–58).

4. Phonological processes cause the *ghu-* prefix to change to *oo-* in conjunction with the third person singular and first and third person plural prefixes, to *ghoo-* with the second person singular prefix, and to *ooh-* with the second person plural prefix.

(13b) *go soo ghułkon' daa'*
  go soo   ghu + ł   + kon'
  hopefully M   + CL + rain + DUR OPT
  'I hope it rains then.'

Commands forbidding some activity are formed using the optative plus the enclitic -*yu* 'prohibitive'.

(14a) *sugh nohughoolnege yu*
  se   + ghu no # hu + ghu + ne   + le   + nege
  1SG P + PP   T   # T   + M   + 2SG S + CL + tell + DUR OPT
      NEG
  'Don't tell on me!'

(14b) *noholnek*
  no # hu + ghe + le   + nek
  T   # T   + M   + CL + tell + DUR PERF
  'S/he told, tattled.'

(15a) *beghedeeghoonol yu*
  be   + ghe # de + ghu + ne   + ∅   + nol
  3SG P + PP   # T   + M   + 2SG S + CL + touch + REV OPT NEG
  'Don't touch it!'

(15b) *bek'eghedaałnoghaa*
  bek'e   + ghe # de + ł   + noghaa
  INDF S/3SG P + PP   # T   + CL + touch + REV IMPF NEG
  'Nothing touches it.'

Prohibitives may also be made using the adverbial *nedaakoon*. With optative negative verbs, *nedaakoon* is followed by *soo'* and the resulting verb phrase implies an ethical prohibition ('you are not supposed to V') rather than the momentary prohibition implied by the usual second person optative negative ('do not V'). Note that these optative negatives with *nedaakoon* may be in third as well as second person. Prohibitives with *nedaakoon* may also be made with imperfective positive verbs. They differ in meaning from the optative prohibitives; they express a prohibition on activity currently being done. Compare the optative prohibitives in (16) with the imperfective ones in (17).

(16a) *tleeghoohol yu*
  tlee # ghu + ∅   + hol
  DS   # M   + CL + go + MOM OPT NEG
  'Do not go out at any time; you should never go out.'

(16b) *nedaakoon soo' hoozel yu*
    he   + *ghu* + ∅   + *ze*
    3PL S + M   + CL + shout + MOM OPT NEG
    'They should not shout at any time (while hunting).'

(17a) *nedaakoon kk'oneedoyh*
    kk'o # *ne* + *ne*   + *de* + *oyh*
    DS   # M   + 2SG S + CL + go + PRMB IMPF
    'You shouldn't be walking around.'

(17b) *nedaakoon heneehaayh*
    he + *ne* + ∅   + *haayh*
    T   + M   + CL + talk + REP IMPF
    'Don't talk! stop talking!'

Nonnegative commands are also made using either the second person imperfective verb, as in (18), or using an optative, as in (19). The imperfective command is used when the speaker wants the action to be carried out at the time of speaking, while the optative is used to command action at some future time.

(18a) *soho tl'oyee nok'eeneeł*
    se   + *oho* *tl'o* + *yee* *no*   # *k'e*   + ∅ + *ne*   + ∅
    + *neeł*
    1SG P + PP   P   + PP   ITER # INDF + M + 2SG S + CL
    + POUR + MOM IMPF
    'Pour some (coffee) for me again (now).'

(18b) *leedo haa'*
    le + *ne*   + ∅ + *do*   *haa'*
    M   + 2SG S + CL + sit + MOM IMPF POLITE
    'Sit down!'

(19a) *tlenok'edeghooteeł*
    tle # *no*   # *k'e* + *de* + *ghu* + *ne*   + *teeł*
    DS # ITER # DS + DS + M   + 2SG S + CLASSIF: elongated
    object + MOM OPT
    'Put some more wood in the fire (later)!'

(19b) *hełts'e yeh ghoodo'*
    hełts'e   *yeh*   *ghu* + *ne*   + ∅ + *do'*
    evening house M   + 2SG S + CL + sit + NEU OPT
    'Stay in this evening!'

Most of the preceding optative examples have expressed the notion of futurity. The optative may also be used, with the adverb *ts'ehaadenh*, to indicate an inability to perform the activity referred to by the verb. Note that this usage is also consonant with the characterization of the optative as an irrealis marker.

(20) *deghusnaah ts'ehaadenh*
      de + *ghu* + *s*   + ∅   + *naah*
      T   + M   + 1SG S   + CL   + happen + OPT
      'I am stuck, have no way to help myself, nowhere to stay.'

In most cases, however, the optative is used to convey a notion of future activity. The similarities between future and optative are striking not only in their future and irrealis meaning but also in their stem morphology. Stem shape according to mode and aspect will be described in some detail in section 3.2. By the end of that section, the similarity in stem shape between future and optative will have become apparent. In fact, it is only in the transitional and momentaneous aspects that the two modes have different stem shapes, and then only in stems derived from closed roots. Future and optative stems derived from open roots are always identical within each aspect. Because they do have different stem shapes in closed root transitional and momentaneous verbs though, and because they always have different prefixal components, it is best to consider these two modes as formally distinct.

3.2. The Koyukon aspects

As noted in chapter 1, Koyukon has fifteen distinct morphologically marked aspects. The examples in this section illustrate the semantic thrust of most of those aspects. Because the purpose of these examples is to demonstrate the general semantic range of the aspectual category rather than specific details of the individual aspects, morphological analysis is omitted here. More specific information regarding the morphological character and semantic domain of each aspect is provided in sections 3.2.1–15. The forms in (21) are all derivational products of the verb root -'o, the classificatory verb referring to compact objects, and the forms in (22) have the verb root -*tlaatl* 'chop'.

Examples (21a) through (21m) illustrate neuter and motion aspects. *Neuter* derivatives, shown in (21a) and (21b), refer to the state, condition, or position of a referent.

(21a) *ts'eh le'onh* (neuter)
  'A hat is there, in position.'

(21b) *bekk'aay hʉnaal'onh* (neuter)
  'S/he is shy, ashamed.'

The entrance into the state referred to by neuter derivatives is most often described using the transitional aspect:

(21c) *bekk'aay hʉnaadle'ot* (l transitional)
  'S/he became ashamed, embarrassed.'

The directed or purposeful movement of a subject or object is described with the momentaneous.

(21d) *yeenee'onh* (momentaneous, *ne-* perfective)
  'S/he arrived carrying it.'

(21e) *yee'onh* (momentaneous, ∅ - perfective)
  'S/he found it.'

(21f) *kk'eł yetaal'onh* (momentaneous, *le-* perfective)
  'S/he threw it away.'

(21g) *doyeel'onh* (momentaneous, *le-* perfective/*le-* imperfective)
  'S/he put it up.'

(21h) *noyeghee'onh* (momentaneous, *ghe-* perfective)
  'S/he took it down.'

The preceding five examples show momentaneous derivatives referring to the appearance of an object or to its movement in a particular direction. Examples (21i) through (21m) illustrate aspects that describe specific and characteristic kinds of movement. Like the momentaneous, those aspects refer to motion, but they focus more on the manner and quality of the motion than on its direction. The perambulative is used to describe motion carried out in a wandering or elliptical path.

(21i) *kk'otlee'eet'oyh* (perambulative)
  'S/he/it is moving her/his/it's head around, looking in all directions.'

The *persistive*, shown in (21j), allows back and forth movement to be described and indicates that the movement is done repeatedly and usually against the resistance of some constraint. The *repetitive* in (21k) also refers to repeated back and forth movement, but does not imply any constraint on it.

(21j) *netlee'et'oh* (persistive)
       'S/he is moving her/his head back and forth.'

(21k) *yeyeghee'ok* (repetitive)
       'S/he raised it repeatedly, lifted it up and down.'

The *continuative* is used to describe movement carried out in a smooth path from a beginning point to an outlying point and back again.

(21l) *eeyet neyeel'onh* (continuative)
       'S/he took it to there and back; s/he made a round
       trip to there with it.'

The *reversative* is often used to describe a turning over, or reversing motion—as the flipping of a pancake.

(21m) *k'ets'e noyedaal'onh* (reversative)
       'S/he turned it over, turned it upside down.'

Examples (22a) through (22g), with the root *-tlaatl* 'chop', illustrate aspects used to describe activities. Activity verbs are distinguished from the motion verbs exemplified in (21c) through (21l) in that the aspects here express the duration, cyclicity, punctuality, and telicity of the action rather than the path of the movement. The *semelfactive*, typified in example (22a) is used to describe a single, abrupt action, while the *consecutive*, in (22b), describes repeated single, abrupt actions.

(22a) *yeeltleł* (semelfactive)
       'S/he chopped it once, gave it a chop.'

(22b) *yegheetletl* (consecutive)
       'S/he chopped it repeatedly.'

The *directive-repetitive*, as shown in (22c), is similar to the consecutive but is used to describe a situation in which the object (i.e., the recipient of the action) is not affected or altered by the action. The activity is carried out toward the object, but contact is not made.

(22c) *yootlaał* (directive-repetitive)
'S/he chops at it repeatedly.'

The *bisective* refers to a single action in which contact is made and which results in a division of the object-recipient into two parts.

(22d) *yenaaltleł* (bisective)
'S/he chopped it in two.'

Example (22e) illustrates another use of the momentaneous: to express a completion of the activity, a situation in which the activity of chopping is done until it can be done no further. The *conclusive*, in (22f), also expresses the completion of the activity, but in this case carries the implication of the attainment of a specific goal.

(22e) *neeyeeneetlaatl* (momentaneous, *ne-* perfective)
'S/he chopped it all up.'

(22f) *yeghedaaltlaatl* (conclusive)
'S/he hewed it into a shape.'

The *durative*, exemplified in (22g), expresses an ongoing or habitual activity.

(22g) *yegheetlaatl* (durative)
'S/he was chopping it (for a while).'

As the examples in (21) and (22) illustrate, aspect allows fine distinctions to be made regarding the manner, quality, quantity, and texture of an activity. The choice of aspect (by itself and in combination with aspect-dependent derivational strings) allows for very different views of the action with alteration of its temporal nature (duration, iterativity, etc.) and its transitivity (i.e., the extent to which an object is affected by the action).

The next fifteen sections provide a formal (i.e., morphological and distributional) and semantic description of each aspect; each description involves an examination of four factors, the first of which is stem set. Following Kari (1979), verbs are considered to be

of a particular aspect if they have the morphological stem set variation (the pattern of stem shape according to mode) associated with
that set.[5] The stem form, then, reflects both the category of mode
and the category of aspect (in much the same way that Latin verb
endings reflect more than one category, i.e., person, number, voice,
tense, aspect, and mood).

A root is modified according to aspect and mode by the following
processes: spirantization, suffixation, ablaut, and vowel lengthening
or reduction. Leer (1979) presents a clear and quite detailed diachronic theory of Athabaskan verb stem variation. One of the most
important processes discussed in his study involves the interaction
of suffixation and spirantization. According to Leer (1979:41) the
process of spirantization (introduced in section 2.1.2) operates on
"(1) stems with full vowels not followed by a suffix, and (2) on stems
followed by an obstruent suffix" (41). He reconstructs the obstruent
suffixes of Pre-Proto-Athabaskan as *-ł, *-x̣, *-k, *-x, and *-t. The
only nonobstruent suffix is the perfective suffix, *-ŋ. Leer says that
this latter suffix, when added to obstruent-closed roots,

> had the effect of voicing stem-final fricatives and preventing spir-
> antization, but later dropped off, possibly already in PA, so that
> with modern languages, the perfective suffix is describable as a
> morphophoneme. In the momentaneous imperfective-optative
> stem, where there was no such suffix, spirantization occurred.
> [38–39]

In other words, there is spirantization of all root-final obstruents
unless the PA *-ŋ perfective suffix is present or in stems with a
reduced vowel and a -∅ suffix. Stems from obstruent-final roots
with full vowels and -∅ suffix have spirantized final obstruents.
The obstruent suffixes produce both vowel reduction and spirantization.

The descriptions presented here are based solely on synchronic
data from a corpus of some 600 verb roots in Koyukon. I include an
account of the regular stem variation pattern for each aspect and
note all exceptions, leaving diachronic and comparative explanation
of those patterns for future research.

Prefixal components—the set of mode prefixes (and often, adver-

---

5. The continuative imperfective is taken as the basic stem and is used
as the citation form for the root, based on the diachronic evidence presented
in Leer (1979).

bial disjunct prefixes as well) associated with each aspect—constitute the second factor involved in describing each aspect. The third factor is the meaning conveyed by the aspect; the fourth is the aspect's distributional potential—that is, what other aspectual derivations of the theme are possible. I will include only brief descriptions of distributional potential and productivity here, leaving further discussion for chapter 5, Verb Theme Categories.

3.2.1. Neuter

After the momentaneous, the neuter has the widest distributional range of all the Koyukon aspects. Of the roughly 600 verb roots in the corpus, 280 (about 47 percent) allow neuter derivatives. The neuter is used to refer to the existence, condition, or position of an animate or inanimate object. Derivatives may convey adjectival notions regarding the size, shape, or appearance of an object; indicate location; or express a state of being, such as 'to be alive' or 'to know something'. The following examples should give some idea of the range of expressions for which the neuter aspect is used.

(23a) *Fairbanks lesdo*
　　　Fairbanks le + s　　　+ ∅　+ do
　　　　　　　　　M　+ 1SG S　+ CL　+ sit + NEU
　　　'I live in Fairbanks.'

(23b) *ts'eh le'onh*
　　　ts'eh le　+ ∅　+ 'onh
　　　hat　　M　+ CL　+ CLASSIF: compact + NEU
　　　'The hat is there.'

(23c) *kusge daałetl'ets*
　　　kusge de　+ le　+ de　+ tl'ets
　　　cat　　T　+ M　+ CL　+ black + NEU
　　　'The cat is black.'

(23d) *nohooltseen'*
　　　no # hʉ　+ ne　+ le　　+ tseen'
　　　DS # T　　+ M　+ CL　+ make + NEU
　　　'It (dam, fence) is built across. . . .'

(23e) *k'oołdzes*
　　　k'e+oo　+ ∅　+ ł　　+ dzes
　　　T　　　+ M　+ CL　+ dance + NEU
　　　'S/he likes to dance, s/he is a talented dancer.'

Open roots (those of the shape CV) have stems with a glottal suffix
in the perfective, future, and optative. The neuter imperfective stem
has an *-nh* suffix; this stem is, in fact, derived from the momentaneous perfective stem (see section 3.2.3). Krauss and Leer describe the relationship between neuter imperfective and active perfective morphology:

> We attribute the *n~i* type perfective prefix, and the perfective
> suffix *-ŋ*, not only to active perfectives but also to neuter imper-
> fectives. A "stative" such as *sə-te·-ŋ* 'he is lying (prone)' is in form
> a perfective, like the corresponding Eyak *sə-teh-ł* 'he lay down, he
> is lying', though synchronically it must be termed a neuter *imper-
> fective*, at least in languages which have full modal inflection for
> neuters (having also e.g. neuter perfective *ɣ-ŋ-te·* 'he was lying
> (prone)'). Likewise, a *ŋə*-adjectival neuter such as *ŋəle·-n* 'he is'
> is in form clearly a perfective, but is termed a neuter imperfective
> in view of the neuter perfective *ɣə-ŋ-le·* 'he was'. [1981:41–42]

A typical stem set to illustrate the pattern for open-root neuter
verbs is shown below.[6]

baa 'swim'

IMPF	PERF	FUT	OPT
baanh	*baa'*	*baa'*	*baa'*

Roots closed with a nasal show the same stem suffixation pattern. Stems derived from roots with reduced vowels also show vowel
lengthening in the perfective, future, and optative.

don 'hole extends'

donh	*don'*	*don'*	*don'*

len 'water flows'

lenh	*leen'*	*leen'*	*leen'*

Obstruent-closed roots have the *-ŋ* suffix in all modes, producing
unspirantized, unvaried stem sets: stems for all four modes are
identical in shape with that of the root.

daakk 'PL experience events'

daakk	*daakk*	*daakk*	*daakk*

6. Stem sets presented here and elsewhere in this chapter are always
shown in the following order: (1) imperfective, (2) perfective, (3) future, and
(4) optative.

bets 'be wide'
    bets   *bets*   *bets*   *bets*

3.2.2. Transitional

Transitional forms refer to a change of state or to the entrance
into a state. Compare the following neuter and transitional derivatives of the theme *de+∅+ts'eh* 'have one's mouth open, agape':

(24a) *daalts'eh* (neuter)
     de + le + ∅   + ts'eh
     T   + M + CL + mouth open + NEU
     'S/he has her/his mouth open.'

(24b) *deets'aah* (transitional)
     de + ∅ + ∅   + *ts'aah*
     T   + M + CL + mouth open + TRNS
     'S/he opened her/his mouth.'

Transitional derivatives are possible with either a ∅ - perfective
mode prefix, as in the preceding example, or a *le-* perfective prefix,
as in the following example.

(25a) *oolnaał* (transitional)
     oo + *le* + ∅   + *naał*
     DS + M + CL + long + TRNS
     'It became long.'

(25b) *nenaał* (neuter)
     ne + ∅ + ∅   + *naał*
     DS + M + CL + long + NEU
     'It is long.'

Approximately ninety verb roots (15 percent of the corpus) permit transitional derivatives. Most open roots have stems with a *-t*
suffix in the perfective and an *-h* suffix in the imperfective, future,
and optative. An example of this stem suffixation pattern follows:

nee 'consider, expect'
    neeh   *neet*   *neeh*   *neeh*

This pattern also obtains in the stem sets of some nasal-closed
roots, though there is even less regularity in that category.

len 'SG, DU thinks thus'
    leeh   *leet*   *leeh*   *leeh*

A second pattern shows open and nasal-closed roots with the *-h* suffix on imperfective stems and often on future and optative stems as well, but with a glottal suffix in the perfective. The difference between these two patterns correlates with the use of the ∅ - perfective prefix versus the *oo-* conjunct prefix plus *le-* perfective prefix: stem sets with *-t* in the perfective have derived forms with the *oo-* plus *le-* perfective prefix. Transitional derivatives referring to becoming a certain color always have the ∅ - perfective prefix, as in the following example:

(26)   *eelbaa'*
       ∅ + *le*   + *baa'*
       M+ CL   + gray + TRNS
       'It turned gray.'

This is, however, the only clear semantic difference to be found between the two types of transitional. This, coupled with the the fact that no distinctions can be seen in stems derived from obstruent-closed roots, has led me to classify both types of 'entrance into a state' aspectual derivation as the single aspect transitional.

Obstruent-closed roots with a full vowel have unspirantized perfective stems. Imperfective and optative stems show spirantization of the final obstruent. Future stems have a *-ł* suffix, which produces vowel reduction and spirantization. The *-ł* suffix then appears after the spirantized final as the affricate *-tl*. Stems of the root *ghaats* 'accumulate from melting' are typical of this pattern:

ghaats 'accumulate from melting'
       ghaas   *ghaats*   *ghestl*   *ghaas*

Obstruent-closed roots with a reduced vowel have stems that follow this same pattern, except that there is an additional lengthening of the root vowel in the imperfective, perfective, and optative stems:

tsetl 'bruise; ferment'
       tseeł   *tseetl*   *tsełtl*   *tseeł*

When the final obstruent in a closed root with either full or reduced vowel is the alveolar stop *t*, the stem suffixation produces stem shapes corresponding to the following set:

tset 'hair is messy'
       tseet   *tseet*   *tseł*   *tseet*

3.2.3. Momentaneous

In momentaneous derivatives (as stated in section 3.1 .2) derivational prefixes other than the perfective prefix carry a great deal of the verb's meaning and "choose" the perfective and imperfective prefixes that accompany them. Those derivational prefixes that choose mode and aspect comprise the set of aspect-dependent derivational strings (discussed at length in chap. 4, section 4.1). The combination of derivational prefixes and aspectually derived stem in momentaneous derivatives is often used to refer to the direction or manner of movement. The momentaneous may also be used to talk about the execution or cessation of an activity, without reference to notions of iterativity or telicity. The following examples, all derived from the theme $O+G+\emptyset+ton$ 'handle elongated O' with the root *ton* 'classificatory: rigid elongated or flat object' are typical of momentaneous derivatives.

(27a) *yeeneetonh*

    ye   *+ ne*   *+ ∅*   *+ tonh*

    3SG O + M   + CL   + rigid + MOM

    'S/he carried it, arrived with it.'

(27b) *eeyet neeyeeneetonh*

    eeyet   *nee* # *ye*   *+ ne*   *+ ∅*   *+ tonh*

    there   DS   # 3SG O + M   + CL   + rigid + MOM

    'S/he took it there.'

(27c) *neek'ok'eneetonh*

    nee+k'o # *k'e*   *+ ne*   *+ ∅*   *+ tonh*

    DS   # INDF O + M   + CL   + rigid + MOM

    'S/he steered off from shore.'

(27d) *ts'aayeeneetonh*

    ts'aa # *ye*   *+ ne*   *+ ∅*   *+ tonh*

    DS   # 3SG O + M   + CL   + rigid + MOM

    'S/he brought it out into the open.'

(27e) *tleeyeeneetonh*

    tlee # *ye*   *+ ne*   *+ ∅*   *+ tonh*

    DS   # 3SG O + M   + CL   + rigid + MOM

    'S/he took it out of the house.'

(27f) *toyegheetonh*

    to # *ye*   *+ ghe*   *+ ∅*   *+ tonh*

    DS # 3SG O + M   + CL   + rigid + MOM

    'S/he put it in the water, launched it.'

(27g) *hoyedaagheetonh*
       ho # *ye*   + *de* + *ghe* + ∅ + *tonh*
       DS # 3SG O + G   + M   + CL + rigid + MOM
       'S/he took it (sliver) out, took it (stick) out (of the ground).'

(27h) *kk'eł yetaaltonh*
       kk'eł   *ye*   + *te* + *le* + ∅   + *tonh*
       away   3SG O   + DS   + M   + CL   + rigid + MOM
       'S/he threw it away.'

Momentaneous derivatives are attested for 283 (47 percent) of the total corpus of verb roots. The momentaneous is by far the most productive and frequent of the Koyukon nonstate aspects.

Open roots most often have stems with a *-yh* suffix in the imperfective, an *-nh* suffix in the perfective, and a *-ł* suffix in the future and optative. Nasal-closed roots show the same stem suffixation pattern and have, additionally, vowel lengthening of reduced root vowels in the imperfective, optative, and future. The following stem sets illustrate these patterns:

>   *'o* 'classificatory: compact object'
>   *'oyh*   *'onh*   *'oł*   *'oł*
>
>   *neen* 'tremble'
>   *neeyh*   *neenh*   *neeł*   *neeł*
>
>   *ben* 'paint, smear'
>   *beeyh*   *benh*   *beeł*   *beeł*

Momentaneous perfective stems from obstruent-closed roots show no spirantization because of the $*-\eta$ suffix. Leer (1979:38–39) posits lengthening[7] with subsequent spirantization in momentaneous imperfective and optative stems and, in future stems, a $*-ł$ suffix accompanied by vowel reduction and subsequent spirantization. Imperfective and optative stems, then, show spirantization of the final obstruent. Future stems have the *-ł* suffix, which appears after the spirantized final as the affricate, *-tl*. Stems of the root *baats* 'cook by boiling' are typical of the momentaneous pattern:

>   *baats* 'cook by boiling'
>   *baas*   *baats*   *bestl*   *baas*

---

7. For a discussion of lengthened stems in the momentaneous imperfective and optative, see Leer (1979:41).

Stems from obstruent-closed roots with reduced vowel follow the same pattern except that here we can see the vowel lengthening in the imperfective and optative stems. Notice that the stem variation pattern here is different from that of the transitional in having no lengthening in the perfective stem. Compare the transitional stem set for *tsetl* 'bruise; ferment' presented above with the momentaneous stem set for *yetl* 'seize' below:

yetl 'seize'
  yeeł   yetl   yełtl   yeeł

3.2.4. Perambulative

The perambulative is used to describe motion carried out in a wandering or elliptical path, or motion carried out so as to cover an area. It is characterized morphologically by the disjunct prefix *kk'o-*. Derivatives have *le-* perfective and *ne-* imperfective mode prefixes. The perambulative also triggers the classifier voicing phenomenon known as D-effect in intransitive verbs. Thus, in perambulative derivatives of verb themes that do not take a direct object, a *ł-* will change to *le-* and a ∅ classifier to *de-*. In intransitive themes that already have *le-* or *de-* classifiers, there is no change. Consider the following examples:

(28a) *kk'o'eedetsaah* (perambulative)
    kk'o # *ne* + *de* + *tsaah*
    DS   # M   + CL   + cry + PRMB
    'S/he is going around crying, walking around here and there while crying.'

(28b) *etseh* (durative)
    ∅   + ∅   + *tseh*
    M   + CL   + cry + DUR
    'S/he's crying.'

(29a) *kk'ots'eededaał* (perambulative)
    kk'o # *ts'e*   + *ne* + *de* + *daał*
    DS   # 1PL S   + M   + CL   + PL go + PRMB
    'We are traveling around.'

(29b) *ts'eneedaatl* (*n* momentaneous)
    ts'e   + *ne* + ∅   + *daatl*
    1PL S   + M   + CL   + PL go + MOM
    'We arrived.'

(29c) *ts'odeł* (progressive)
    ts'e   + *ghe*   + ∅   + *deł*
    1PL S   + M   + CL   + PL go + PROG
    'We are going along.'

The perambulative is also found thematized in themes such as *kk'o#de+neek* 'work quickly':

(30) *kk'o'eedeneeyh*
    kk'o # *ne* + *de* + *neeyh*
    DS   # M   + CL   + move hands + PRMB
    'S/he is working quickly.'

Of the total corpus, 111 verb roots (18 percent), permit perambulative derivatives. Open and sonorant-closed roots have stems with a -*yh* suffix in the imperfective, -*nh* suffix in the perfective, and -*k* suffix in future and optative. There is vowel lengthening in the imperfective, future, and optative stems.[8]

   'o 'classificatory: compact object'
      'oyh   *'onh*   *'ok*   *'ok*

   ken 'move with force'
      keeyh   *kenh*   *keek*   *keek*

Of the approximately twenty-seven total open and sonorant-closed roots that permit perambulative derivatives, nine show ablaut.

    tso/tsaa 'tire'
      tsaayh   *tsonh*   *tsaak*   *tsaak*

    'aan 'do; see'
      'eeyh   *'aanh*   *'eek*   *'eek*

Full-vowel obstruent-closed roots have reduced vowels in future and optative stems. Reduced-vowel obstruent-closed roots have vowel lengthening in imperfective stems. Final obstruents are spirant-

---

8. Note the following exceptions. The root *lo/laa* 'classificatory: plural objects' is unsuffixed in the imperfective. The roots *no* 'be alive, move' and *(h)on* 'eat' have glottal suffix in the perfective. The root *(y)o/(h)aa* 'SG, DU talks' has glottal suffix in future and optative stems. The roots *nen/leek* 'compact object moves independently' and *tsen'* 'be possessive' have very irregular stem sets: *leeyh, nenh, leyh, leyh* and *tseeyh, tseek, tseek, tseek*.

ized in imperfective stems; perfective stems are unspirantized, reflecting the presence of the *ŋ perfective suffix.

Stem sets from obstruent-closed roots show complex reflexes of the *-k* suffix in the future and optative. Roots with final *-t* have future and optative stems with final *-k:*

> *koot* 'classificatory: food'
>
> | *koot* | *koot* | *kek* | *kek* |
> |---|---|---|---|
>
> *let* 'SG experiences event'
>
> | *leet* | *let* | *lek* | *lek* |
> |---|---|---|---|

Roots with final *-s* or *-ts* have future and optative stems with final *-sk:*[9]

> *ggaats* 'go wide-eyed'
>
> | *ggaas* | *ggaats* | *ggesk* | *ggesk* |
> |---|---|---|---|
>
> *bets* 'be wide'
>
> | *bees* | *bets* | *besk* | *besk* |
> |---|---|---|---|

Most roots with final *-ł* or *-tl* have future and optative stems closed with *-yhtl:*[10]

> *baatl* 'revolve'
>
> | *baał* | *baatl* | *beyhtl* | *beyhtl* |
> |---|---|---|---|
>
> *gheł* 'flee'
>
> | *ghaał* | *gheł* | *gheyhtl* | *gheyhtl* |
> |---|---|---|---|

Roots closed with a velar or uvular have stems with spirantized finals:

> *daakk* 'PL experience events'
>
> | *daah* | *daakk* | *deh* | *deh* |
> |---|---|---|---|

9. The only exceptions are the roots *-'ots* 'DU go by foot' which has the stem set, *'os, 'ots, 'us, 'us,* and the root *-ghos* 'go aimlessly', which has the stem set *ghos, ghos, ghus, ghus.*

10. Five (roughly 29 percent), of these stems have irregular future and optative stems. These include *daatl/detl* 'PL go' *(daał, daatl, deyhtl, daał),* *ggotl/ggutl* 'rip, jerk' *(ggoł, ggotl, gguyhtl, ggoł),* and *tsotl/tsutl* 'flexible object moves' *(tsoł, tsuł, tsuł, tsuł).* The last two roots of this group never show vowel reduction in any Athabaskan language: *looł* 'drag' *(looł, looł, loołk, loołk)* and *tl'ootl* 'braid' *(tl'ooł, tl'ootl, tl'oołk, tl'oołk).*

3.2.5. Continuative

The continuative refers to a smooth, back-and-forth movement.
Sixty-five verb roots (10 percent of the total corpus) allow continuative stem sets. Derivatives have *le-* perfective and *∅-* imperfective
mode prefixes. Derivatives with a *ne-* disjunct prefix are frequently
attested:

(31a) *neyedenaal'onh*
       ne # ye   + de + ne   + le   + ∅   + 'onh
       DS # 3SG O + T   + M   + CL   + CLASSIF: compact + CONT
       'S/he did beadwork on it; s/he beaded it.'

(31b) *nek'edenaatldek*
       ne # k'e   + de + ne   + le   + ł   + dek
       DS # INDF O + T   + M   + CL   + write + CONT
       'S/he wrote something.'

(31c) *eeyet nelbaanh*
       ne # le   + ∅   + baanh
       DS # M   + CL   + swim + CONT
       'S/he swam there and back, made a round trip to there swimming.'

Continuative derivatives are possible with other aspect-dependent prefix strings as well—often unbound adverbs, as in the following:

(32)   *hutugh k'eldlo*
       hu + tughu   k'e   + le   + ∅   + lo
       P   + among INDF O + M   + CL   + CLASSIF: plural objects + CONT
       'S/he served the group (food).'

Open roots have no suffix on imperfective stems, an *-nh* suffix
on perfective stems,[11] and a *-ł* suffix on future and optative
stems.[12] That pattern is illustrated in the following example:

11. Some roots never take perfective suffixes—e.g., *(y)o* 'SG goes' and
lo/laa 'classificatory: plural objects'. The roots are products of ablaut,
defined for Athabaskan (Leer 1979:28) as that process by which PPA root-
final sonorants (i.e., **y* and **w*) were "absorbed" into root vowels (when
those vowels were reduced rather than full).
12. Three other roots have aberrant stem sets: *(y)o/(h)aa* 'SG, DU talks'
(haa, yo, yo', yo'), tsee 'make SG, DU O' *(tsee', tsee', tsee', tsee'),* and *'een/'ee*
'steal, sneak' *('enh~'ee', 'eenh, 'ee', 'ee').*

baa 'swim'

| *baa* | *baanh* | *baał* | *baał* |

Nasal-closed roots have unvaried stem sets with reduced vowel and no suffix:[13]

'aan 'do; see'

| *'enh* | *'enh* | *'enh* | *'enh* |

Obstruent-closed roots with full vowel retain the full vowel and have spirantized finals in the imperfective, optative, and future:[14]

'aatl 'PL swim, float'

| *'aał* | *'aatl* | *'aał* | *'aał* |

Obstruent-closed roots with reduced vowel have unsuffixed, unvaried stem sets:[15]

bets 'be wide'

| *bets* | *bets* | *bets* | *bets* |

3.2.6. Persistive

The persistive aspect allows back-and-forth movement to be described, and, further, indicates that the movement is done repeatedly and usually against the resistance of some constraint. This aspect is frequently used with a *ne-* disjunct prefix and the classifier voicing phenomenon called D-effect. The examples below show the use of the persistive with this string and without it:

(33a) *nekaadetl'eh*

| *ne* | # *kaa* | # ∅ | + *de* | + *tl'eh* |
| DS | # tail | # M | + CL | + squirm, crawl + PERS |

'It (dog) is wagging its tail.'

---

13. There are two exceptional roots in this category. The root *kk'on/ kk'un* 'burn' has a perfective stem with non-reduced vowel: *kk'unh, kk'onh, kk'unh, kk'unh.* The root *ton* 'classificatory: elongated or flat object' has a full vowel in the perfective stem and an ablauted vowel with *-ł* suffix in the future and optative: *tenh, tonh, teeł, teeł.*

14. The only exception is the root *tsaah/tseh* 'cry', which has a future stem that looks much like a momentaneous future, *tsehtl,* in free variation with the regular continuative future stem, *tsaah.*

15. There are two exceptional roots in this category. The root *kkuyh* 'vomit' has a lengthened vowel in all modes: *kkooyh, kkooyh, kkooyh, kkooyh.* The root *'ʉh/'ʉt* differs from the typical continuative pattern in having an *-ł* suffix in the future: *'ʉt, 'ʉt, 'ʉł, 'ʉt.*

(33b) *ne'edetl'et*
 ne   # ∅   + de + tl'et
 DS # M   + CL   + splash + PERS
 'It (liquid in container) is sloshing back and forth.'

(33c) *yek'edenetkeeh*
 ye + e   # k'e + de + ne + ∅   + l   + keeh
 P   + PP # T   + T   + T   + M   + CL + press + PERS
 'S/he is ironing it (pitch seam on boat).'

(33d) *nethook'etkeeh*
 neet + e   # hoo   # k'e + ∅   + l   + keeh
 P   + PP # teeth # T   + M   + CL + press + PERS
 'S/he is grinding her/his teeth.'

Forty-two of the verb roots (7 percent) in the corpus permit persistive derivatives. Such derivatives have a *ghe-* perfective prefix or *∅ -* imperfective prefix and stems which demonstrate the presence of an *-h* suffix in all four modes.

Open roots have unvaried stem sets with *-h* suffix, as in the following example:

 'o 'classificatory: compact object'
 'oh   *'oh*   *'oh*   *'oh*

Only two nasal-final roots allow persistive derivatives. Their stem sets are unvaried, with *-h* suffix and lengthened or umlauted vowel:

 ken 'move with force'
 keeh   *keeh*   *keeh*   *keeh*

 ton 'classificatory: elongated or flat object'
 teeh   *teeh*   *teeh*   *teeh*

Obstruent-closed roots with full vowel have unvaried stem sets with reduced vowel and spirantized final obstruent. Obstruent-closed roots with reduced vowel also have unvaried stem sets with spirantized finals:

 daakk 'PL experience events'
 deh   *deh*   *deh*   *deh*

 nekk 'flat, flexible object moves independently'
 neh   *neh*   *neh*   *neh*

Stem sets from glottal-closed roots are unsuffixed and unvaried:

> *tsee'* 'supernatural event occurs'
> *tsee'*   *tsee'*   *tsee'*   *tsee'*

3.2.7. Reversative

The reversative acquired its name from its primary use in Navajo, to describe a turning over, or reversing motion—as the flipping of a pancake. It is used in Koyukon as well to express that meaning, but also has many other uses. Structurally, reversative derivatives have ∅- imperfective and *le-* or *ghe-* perfective prefixes. Many of the *le-* perfective derivatives occur with the adverb *k'ets'e* and a *no#* disjunct and *de-* conjunct prefix as well.

(34a) *k'ets'e noyedaatldaatl*
       k'ets'e   no   # ye   + de   + le   + ł   + daatl
       over   DS   # 3SG O + T   + M   + CL   + PL move + REV
       'S/he quickly turned them (hotcakes) over.'

(34b) *k'ets'e noyedaatlkooł*
       k'ets'e   no   # ye   + de   + le   + ł   + kooł
       over   DS   # 3SG O + DS   + M   + CL   + CLASSIF: flat, flexible object
               + REV
       'S/he turned it (paper) over; s/he turned it (pelt) inside out.'

Forty-one roots (roughly 7 percent of the corpus) permit reversative derivatives. Open and nasal-final roots have stems with full vowel and *-h* suffix in the imperfective, future, and optative (except *-no* 'be alive, move', which has *-ł* in future and optative and *-baa* 'swim', which has *-ł* in the future). Open roots have perfective stems with *-nh* suffix.[16] Nasal-final roots have perfective stems with *-nh* final.[17] Nasal-final roots also typically show umlaut and an *-h* suffix in imperfective, future, and optative stems. Example stem sets follow:

> *laa* 'be, become'
> *laah*   *laanh*   *laah*   *laah*

---

16. Five roots that derive via ablaut and therefore never have perfective suffixes (see fn. 11) prove exceptions to this: *-do* 'SG, DU sit, stay, dwell', *-lo* 'classificatory: plural objects', *-tl'ee* 'PL sit, stay, dwell', *-zee* 'find bear in den', *-yo* 'punish'.

17. With four exceptions: *-'aan* 'possess; use; learn', *-den* 'be skilled', *-k'aa/k'aan* 'observe taboo', *-yaa/yaan* 'be fat', all of which have *-n* final.

zon/zen 'chisel ice'
   zeeh   *zonh*   *zeeh*   *zeeh*

Full-vowel obstruent-closed roots have imperfective, future, and optative stems with reduced vowel and spirantized final. Perfective stems are unspirantized, reflecting the *-ŋ suffix. Obstruent-closed roots with reduced vowels have unsuffixed, unvaried stem sets.

daatl/detl 'PL go, PL move independently'
   deł   *daatl*   *deł*   *deł*

bet 'be greedy'
   bet   *bet*   *bet*   *bet*

Semantically, the reversative is used to express a variety of meanings in addition to 'reversal', which is illustrated in the examples above. Jones (p.c.) suggests that the aspect conveys a sense of difficulty, of resistance to the event or movement described, but although it is quite distinctive in formal terms, this aspect seems to be far less coherent semantically than the other aspects. There are approximately 27 themes whose primary (or sole) derivatives are of the reversative aspect with *le-* perfective (or ∅ - imperfective) prefix. In addition, there are seven themes whose primary derivatives are reversative in aspect and have a *ghe-* perfective prefix (or ∅ - imperfective prefix). The meanings of these themes include those presented in table 3.3.

3.2.8. Durative

Durative forms refer to activities carried out over an extended period or to activities performed as a general means of employment. For example:

(35a) *hutl gheeghonh* (durative)
   hutl   *ghe*   + ∅   + *ghonh*
   sled   M   + CL   + make PL O + DUR
   'S/he made sleds (all day); s/he was a sled maker.'

(35b) *gheetsaah* (durative)
   ghee   + ∅   + *tsaah*
   M   + CL   + cry + DUR
   'S/he cried.'

(35c) *k'oongheet'aan'* (durative)
   k'e   + *oo* + *ne* + *ghe* + ∅   + *t'aan'*
   INDF O   + T   + T   + M   + CL   + gather + DUR
   'S/he picked something (berries); s/he was a berry picker.'

Table 3.3. Reversative Themes

le- PERFECTIVE	*ghe*- PERFECTIVE
'be born'	'sing P'
'grow'	'learn P'
'singular die'	'work O (wet hide)'
'acquire a habit'	'touch P'
'catch fish'	'undress O'
'catch a game animal'	'undress oneself'
'find bear in den'	'animal becomes aloof'
'rob, kidnap'	
'set snare'	
'try, test, attempt'	
'search'	
'count'	
'exercise O'	
'make O busy'	
'punish'	
'(trail) is difficult to follow'	
'fail to understand'	
'sew in spite of illness'	
'tie'	
'make Indian ice cream'	
'sweep'	
'wash, bathe'	

NOTE: O = direct object; P = postpositional object (see chapter 2).

Activities that require some duration of time and that have no in-herent goal or completion point are often referred to with the durative. Verbs describing seeing, smelling, eating, drinking, crying, singing, playing, scraping skins, or scaling fish are found most frequently in the durative. Verbs describing the weather (e.g., raining, snowing, blowing) are also commonly found in durative derivatives.

The durative is associated with the most varied and complex stem set patterning of any aspect. Of the 600 or so verb roots in the corpus, 167 (27 percent) permit durative derivatives. The primary pattern (86 percent of the total sets) is as follows:

Reduced-vowel obstruent-closed roots, without exception, have unspirantized and unvaried stem sets. The unspirantized final in the perfective stem reflects the $*$-η suffix, and the unspirantized finals in the nonperfective stems reflect a $\emptyset$ suffix. (Remember that a reduced-vowel root with $\emptyset$ - suffix is the only other situation that will result in a nonspirantized final obstruent.) The suffixation pattern is thus: $\emptyset$ $*$-η $\emptyset$ $\emptyset$.

dzets 'strike with fist'
  dzets   *dzets*   *dzets*   *dzets*

netl 'throb'
  netl   *netl*   *netl*   *netl*

Most full-vowel obstruent-closed roots have a spirantized final in the imperfective, future, and optative stems.[18] Thus, the suffixation pattern here is again ∅ *-ŋ ∅ ∅.

daatl 'PL go'
  daał   *daatl*   *daał*   *daał*

kk'ok 'scream'
  kk'oyh   *kk'ok*   *kk'oyh*   *kk'oyh*

lol 'yawn'
  loł   *loł*   *loł*   *loł*

Most open roots have stems with a glottal suffix in the perfective,

18. Sixteen verb roots present exceptions to this pattern:
Five full-vowel closed roots *(baats* 'boil', *ghots* 'scrape and eat cambium', *kootl/ketl* 'molt', *ts'eek* 'ice crystals fall', and *zeetl* (C) 'bail water') do not show the expected spirantization and have instead unsuffixed, unvaried stem sets:

baats 'boil'
  baats   *baats*   *baats*   *baats*

Eight other roots (*daakk* 'pl. experience event', *dokk* 'vanish', *ghaats* 'accumulate from melting', *gheek* 'lay, stack boards', *totl/tutl* 'stamp, kick', *tlaakk* 'classificatory: mushy object', *tsotl/tsutl* 'flexible object moves', *ts'ookk* 'give high-pitched scream') show an unexpected spirantization of the stem-final obstruent in the perfective and have, consequently, unsuffixed unvaried stem sets:

daakk 'PL experience event'
  daah   *daah*   *daah*   *daah*

Three spirant-final verb roots (*ghos/ghus* 'make clamor', *tsaah/tseh* 'cry', *zeeł/zeł* 'shout') show an unexpected vowel reduction in the imperfective, future, and optative stems. They are cited with both vowels in root listings. Note that this is the only group of exceptions that show some semantic similarity: all refer to oral noise.

ghos/ghus 'make clamor'
  ghus   *ghos*   *ghus*   *ghus*

future, and optative: ∅ ' ' '.[19]

> *tlaa* 'dog barks'
> | *tlaa* | *tlaa'* | *tlaa'* | *tlaa'* |
>
> *dlee* 'orate'
> | *dlee* | *dlee'* | *dlee'* | *dlee'* |

Full-vowel nasal-final roots usually have a glottal suffix in perfective, future, and optative stems, so again the pattern is ∅ ' ' '.[20]

> *kon* 'rain'
> | *konh* | *kon'* | *kon'* | *kon'* |

Reduced-vowel nasal-final roots, without exception, have unspirantized and unvaried stem sets. The suffixation pattern is thus ∅ *-ŋ̲ ∅ ∅.

> *ben* 'paint'
> | *benh* | *benh* | *benh* | *benh* |
>
> *dzen* 'score with knife'
> | *dzenh* | *dzenh* | *dzenh* | *dzenh* |

19. There are four exceptions to this pattern out of a total of only thirteen open-root durative stem sets:

ghaa 'kill SG (animate)'
| *ghaa* | *ghaa'* | *ghaał* | *ghaał* |

'o 'classificatory: compact object'
| *'o* | *'o'* | *'oł* | *'oł* |

kkaa 'dig'
| *kkaa* | *kkaanh* | *kkaał* | *kkaał* |

kko 'grind'
| *kk'o* | *kk'onh* | *kk'oł* | *kk'oł* |

Note that the first three are among the most productive verb roots in the language.

20. There are three exceptions to this pattern out of a total of seven full-vowel nasal-final roots:

ghon 'make, kill PL'
| *ghonh* | *ghonh* | *ghon'* | *ghon'* |

neen 'tremble'
| *neenh* | *neenh* | *neenh* | *neenh* |

kkun 'make offering to shaman'
| *kkoyh* | *kkoyh* | *kkoyh* | *kkoyh* |

Nasal-final roots with final glottal stop have unsuffixed, unvaried stem sets:

t'aan' 'gather'
   t'aan'   *t'aan'*   *t'aan'*   *t'aan'*

kkun' 'quarrel'
   kkun'   *kkun'*   *kkun'*   *kkun'*

3.2.9. Consecutive

Durative and consecutive[21] stems both require a $\emptyset$- imperfective or *ghe-* perfective mode prefix and may or may not have the same shape. With full-vowel roots the consecutive stem has a reduced vowel, while the durative retains the full vowel of the root.[22] Kari (1979) dismissed the rare occurrence of this *ghe-* perfective with reduced vowel in Ahtna as a secondary durative form. Based on the data from Koyukon, I determined it to be a separate aspect.[23]

Fifty-one verb roots in the corpus (8.5 percent) have consecutive stem sets, and these sets are always unvaried. Root-final obstruents are not spirantized.[24] The following stem sets illustrate the consecutive pattern:

tseetl 'splash'
   tsetl   *tsetl*   *tsetl*   *tsetl*

dzets 'strike with fist'
   dzets   *dzets*   *dzets*   *dzets*

The one glottal-closed root that has a consecutive stem set is *ts'oo'* 'kiss' which has the stem *-ts'oo'* in all modes. The only nasal-closed

21. In previous descriptions of this aspect, I called it the seriative. In order to avoid confusion with the Navajo seriative, a derivational type quite different both in form and meaning, Kari and I agreed to change the name of this aspect in Koyukon and Ahtna to consecutive.

22. Further research is necessary to determine which processes would be involved in producing stems with a nonspirantized final obstruent and reduced vowel.

23. See Thompson, Axelrod, and Jones (1983).

24. With two exceptions: *dokk* 'vanish', which has the stem *-dɯh* in all modes (cf. the durative stem set from this root, which also has a spirantized final in all modes: *-doh)*, and *gok* 'become split', which has the stem *-guyh* in all modes.

root with a consecutive stem set is *dzen* 'score with knife', and it has an unsuffixed, unvaried stem set. The only open root to show consecutive stems is *tlaa* 'bark', which has the stem *-tlaa'* in all modes.

With reduced-vowel roots, consecutive and durative stems are homophonous. However, two clearly different meanings are associated with the single form. One meaning refers to extended periods of undifferentiated activity and, by analogy to the distinction that obtains in full-vowel roots, I call the forms associated with that meaning durative; the other meaning refers to repeated single instances of activity, and I call the forms associated with that meaning consecutive. In full-vowel roots, the meaning distinction is accompanied by a form distinction. Compare the consecutive derivative of the theme *O+G+∅+t'otl* 'cut O with an edged tool' in (36a) with the durative derivative in (36b):

(36a) *k'egheet'utl* (consecutive)
     k'e   + *ghe*   + ∅   + *t'utl*
     INDF O   + M   + CL   + cut + CONS
     'S/he made a series of cuts in something; s/he cut cards
       repeatedly.'

(36b) *k'egheet'otl* (durative)
     k'e   + *ghe*   + ∅   + *t'otl*
     INDF O   + M   + CL   + cut + DUR
     'S/he cut something (fish for drying); s/he operated on her/him.'

The consecutive is usually found with verb themes that refer to punctual activities like cutting that are primarily expressed with the semelfactive aspect, indicating a single, abrupt action. The notion of repeated single actions with these themes is often expressed by some form of the repetitive aspect rather than by the consecutive. The difference in meaning between consecutive and repetitive is often hard to define. The examples in (37) from the theme *O+∅+ts'ek* 'pinch O' illustrate the difference in meaning between consecutive and directive-repetitive, a frequently used aspect in this type of theme.

(37a) *yeelts'eyh* (semelfactive)
     ye   + *le*   + ∅   + *ts'eyh*
     3SG O   + M   + CL   + pinch + SML
     'S/he pinched her/him once.'

(37b) *yegheets'ek* (consecutive)
     ye   + *ghe*   + ∅   + *ts'ek*
     3SG O   + M   + CL   + pinch + CONS
     'S/he pinched it (piecrust) repeatedly.'

(37c) *yoots'eeyh* (directive-repetitive)

ye	+ *oo*	+ ∅	+ ∅	+ *ts'eeyh*
3SG O	+ DS	+ M	+ CL	+ pinch + DIR-REP

'S/he is pinching her/him repeatedly.'

The consecutive is used in (37b) to refer to the pinching of a piecrust because, unlike human flesh, pastry dough retains the effect of the pinch. Note, though, that the consecutive is rare with this theme because piecrust is generally pinched around the pan, a motion so integral to the activity that it is more naturally expressed with the aspect-dependent derivational string *P+baaghe##no# ll* momentaneous 'around the edge of P', as in (37d):

(37d) *yebaaghe naa'etlts'ek* (*ll* momentaneous)

ye	+ *baaghe*	*no*	# *le*	+ *ł*	+ *ts'ek*
3SG P	+ PP	DS	# M	+ CL	+ pinch + MOM

'S/he pinched it all around the edge.'

With other verbs, however—such as 'poking', 'punching', and 'kicking', in which the effectiveness of the action relative to the object argument is a parameter involved in the meaning—the consecutive is used (in contrast with the directive-repetitive; see section 3.2.11) to express the accomplishment of the goal or contact. Compare the examples in (38) from the theme *O+G+ł+ggootl* 'crunch O, bite O with a crunch, chew O with a crunching noise', and those in (39) from the theme *O+G+∅+totl* 'kick O (with sole of foot), stamp on O':

(38a) *yegheełggotl* (durative)

ye	+ *ghe*	+ *ł*	+ *ggotl*
3SG O	+ M	+ CL	+ crunch + DUR

'S/he was crunching it, chewing it with a crunching noise.'

(38b) *yeetlgguł* (semelfactive)

ye	+ *le*	+ *ł*	+ *gguł*
3SG O	+ M	+ CL	+ crunch + SML

'S/he crunched it once, bit it with a crunch once.'

(38c) *yełggutl* (consecutive)

ye	+ ∅	+ *ł*	+ *ggutl*
3SG O	+ M	+ CL	+ crunch + CONS

'S/he crunches on it again and again.'

(38d) *yootggoot* (directive-repetitive)

ye	+ oo	+ ∅	+ ł	+ ggoot
3SG O	+ DS	+ M	+ CL	+ crunch + DIR-REP

'It (dog) snapped at her/him repeatedly.'

(39a) *yegheetutl* (consecutive)

ye	+ ghe	+ ∅	+ tutl
3SG O	+ M	+ CL	+ stamp + CONS

'S/he stamped on it; s/he kicked her/him repeatedly.'

(39b) *yootot* (directive-repetitive)

ye	+ oo	+ ∅	+ ∅	+ tot
3SG O	+ DS	+ M	+ CL	+ stamp + DIR-REP

'S/he is kicking at her/him.'

The difference in meaning between the consecutive and the repetitive is also related to the notion of completion, though the area of overlap between the semantic ranges of these two aspects is a bit more extensive. They are rarely, if ever, used in derived forms of the same theme. The following examples are perhaps the clearest illustration of the meaning difference. Example (40) is from the theme $O+G+∅+kk'os$ 'chew O (hard, resistant substance)', and (41) is from the theme $O+G+∅+'otl$ 'chew O (e.g., meat)'.

(40) *dzaah gheekk'usk* (repetitive)

dzaah	ghe	+ ∅	+ kk'usk
gum	M	+ CL	+ chew + REP

'S/he was chewing gum.'

(41) *nelaan ghee'utl* (consecutive)

nelaan	ghe	+ ∅	+ 'utl
meat	M	+ CL	+ chew + CONS

'S/he bit the meat repeatedly.'

3.2.10. Repetitive

Like the consecutive, the repetitive refers to repeated actions, though the consecutive seems to convey a sense of the abruptness of those actions that is missing in the meaning of repetitive derivatives. Some typical repetitive derivatives are:

(42a) *dzoghoteey he'ettsek*

dzoghoteey	hu	+ e	# ∅	+ ł	+ tsek
door	AREA	+ PP	# M	+ CL	+ move hands quickly + REP

'S/he is pushing on the door with force repeatedly.'

(42b) *nodootlk'etts'ehk*
    nodootl # *k'e* + ∅ + *ł*   + *ts'eh*
    eyelash # T   + M + CL + bat eyelashes + REP
    'S/he is batting, fluttering her/his eyelashes.'

Thirty-three verb roots (roughly 5 percent of the corpus) allow repetitive stem sets. Open roots have a *-k* suffix in perfective, future, and optative stems and a *-yh* suffix in the imperfective, as in the following typical set:

    taa 'SG, DU animate lies'
    taayh   *taak*   *taak*   *taak*

Only one nasal-closed root has a repetitive stem set, *ton* 'classificatory: elongated or flat object' and it shows the imperfective *-yh* suffix and *-k* perfective, optative, and future suffix along with vowel ablaut:

    ton 'classificatory: elongated or flat object'
    teeyh   *teek*   *teek*   *teek*

Obstruent-closed roots have reduced-vowel, unvaried stems with *-k* suffix. This suffix produces spirantization of velar and uvular root-final consonants, a *-yh* preceding a root-final *-tl*, or a final *-k* when the root-final consonant is *-t*.[25]

    daakk 'PL experience events'
    deh   *deh*   *deh*   *deh*

    daatl/detl 'PL go, PL move independently'
    deyhtl   *deyhtl*   *deyhtl*   *deyhtl*

    tset 'move hand quickly'
    tsek   *tsek*   *tsek*   *tsek*

Six verb roots have an alternative repetitive stem set pattern. Imperfective, optative, and future stems from these obstruent-closed roots have stem sets with a *-k* suffix, producing a reduced vowel and the same stem-final alternations seen in perfective, fu-

---

25. There is only one exception to this pattern: *kk'os* 'stiffen', which has an unvaried stem set with reduced vowel but no evidence of the *-k* suffix: *kk'us, kk'us, kk'us, kk'us.* It may be best to reanalyze this set as a consecutive one.

ture, and optative stems of the regular repetitive pattern. The six
roots are: *t'oot* 'suck', *dzeets* 'dance', *lol* 'dream', *luk* 'catch in snare',
neek 'act with the hand', and *neek* 'sense, feel'.

t'oot 'suck'
t'uk   t'oot   t'uk   t'uk

dzeets 'dance'
dzes   dzeets   dzes   dzes

Only one non-obstruent-closed root has a stem set in this aspect:
'een/'ee 'sneak, steal'. With this root, however, we see a *-yh* rather
than a *-k* suffix in imperfective, future, and optative stems:

'een/'ee 'sneak, steal'
eeyh   eenh   eeyh   eeyh

The form of the repetitive aspect that occurs with four of these
seven roots is exceptional for another reason: it requires an *le-*
perfective mode prefix rather than the usual repetitive *ghe-*
perfective prefix. The four roots that show this pattern are *'een/'ee*
'sneak, steal', *lol* 'dream', *neek* 'act with the hand', and *neek* 'sense,
feel'. Some examples of repetitive derivatives from these roots are:

(43a) *sooge enaaleneek*
    sooge   e # ne + le + de + neek
    marten PP # T   + M + CL + sense + REP
    'S/he was unsuccessful at (trapping) marten.'

(43b) *deyooghenaatlneek*
    de + e # ye   + oo + ghe + ne + le + le   + neek
    DS   # 3SG O + DS   + M + CL + move hand + REP
    'S/he pleated it; s/he gathered it (in sewing).'

(43c) *naanolslol*
    ne   + aa # no # le + s   + ∅ + lol
    2SG P + PP # T # M + 1SG S + CL + dream + REP
    'I dreamed about you.'

There is some temptation to refer to this group with a different
aspectual label due to the different stem suffixation pattern. The
temptation is even stronger in the case of the four roots with derivatives that take a different perfective prefix as well. Because the
group is so small, however, and because we never see a verb root

admitting both patterns, it is more sensible to think of it as a group of exceptions. The four exceptions may represent mixed stem sets, with regular repetitive imperfective, optative, and future stems but with perfective stems (and mode prefix) "borrowed" from the momentaneous.

3.2.11. Directive-repetitive

The directive-repetitive, as shown in (44), is similar to the consecutive but is used to describe a situation in which the object (i.e., the recipient of the action) is not affected or altered by the action. The activity is carried out toward it, but no contact is made.

The directive-repetitive is also quite similar to derivatives with an aspect-dependent derivational string with *n* momentaneous and an *oo-* conjunct prefix, known as the directive. The *oo-* prefix, which is also an obligatory component of the directive-repetitive aspect, seems to carry the meaning of movement toward an object, but without that movement accomplishing the goal or making the contact. This prefix is also a constituent of the conative post-aspectual derivation (see chap. 4, section 4.3.1). Compare the following examples of the directive-repetitive and the *n* momentaneous directive. Note that the semantic distinction between those two aspectual derivations rests in the repeated nature of the action expressed by the directive-repetitive.

(44a) *too aahaa yoogheeneeł* (directive-repetitive)
   too   aahaa ye   + oo + ghe + ∅ + neeł
   water with   3SG O + DS + M   + CL + spill + DIR-REP
   'S/he threw water at her/him repeatedly (without its
      necessarily reaching her/him).'

(44b) *too aahaa yooneeneeł* (*n* momentaneous, directive)
   too   aahaa ye   + oo + ne + ∅ + neeł
   water with   3SG O + DS + M   + CL + spill + MOM
   'S/he threw water at him.'

(45a) *yoogheeltl'eeł* (directive-repetitive)
   ye   + oo + ghe + le   + tl'eeł
   3SG O + DS + M   + CL + move with force + DIR-REP
   'S/he charged at it repeatedly.'

(45b) *yoonaaltl'eł* (*n* momentaneous, directive)
   ye   + oo + ne + le + tl'eł
   3SG O + DS + M + CL + move with force + MOM
   'S/he attacked her/him, rushed her/him.'

Twenty-four verb roots (4 percent of the corpus) have directive-repetitive stem sets. These stem sets, in addition to the semantic contrasts, are critical to distinguishing the directive-repetitive from the consecutive or the *n* momentaneous directive. All directive-repetitive stem sets are unvaried. Obstruent-closed roots with full vowels have stems with spirantized final obstruents.[26] Obstruent-closed roots with reduced vowels have lengthened stems with spirantization.[27] Typical stem sets are:

> *tlaatl* 'chop'
>   *tlaał*   *tlaał*   *tlaał*   *tlaał*
>
> *dzets* 'strike with fist'
>   *dzees*   *dzees*   *dzees*   *dzees*

No nasal-closed roots allow directive-repetitive derivatives; only one open root does: *(y)o/(h)aa* 'SG, DU talks' and its stems show ablaut and have *-yh* suffix in the imperfective, glottal suffix in the perfective, and a *-k* suffix in the perfective:[28]

> *(y)o/(h)aa* 'SG, DU talks'
>   *haayh*   *yo'*   *haak*   *haak*

3.2.12. Semelfactive

Seventy verb roots (roughly 12 percent) allow semelfactive derivatives. These derivatives express abrupt single instances of an activity. Many of these verbs refer to activity performed with an instrument, as in the following:

(46) *yeelt'uł*
     ye   *+ le* *+ ∅*   *+ t'uł*
     3SG O + M + CL + cut + SML
     'S/he cut it once.'

---

26. With one exception: *t'oot* 'suck', which has a reduced vowel in its durative stems.

27. With one exception: *-gheł* 'elongated object moves', which fails to lengthen.

28. Stems derived from this root vary according to the classifier prefix preceding it. Stems shown above are those that occur with a ∅ classifier. Only with this classifier are there alternate future and optative stems with glottal suffix.

(47)   *yeeltleł*
       ye   + *le* + ∅   + *tleł*
       3SG O   + M   + CL + chop + SML
       'S/he chopped it once, gave it a chop.'

(48)   *yeelggut*
       ye   + *le* + ∅   + *ggut*
       3SG O   + M   + CL + poke + SML
       'S/he poked it, pricked it once.'

Other semelfactive forms, however express single instances of an action not involving an instrument.

(49)   *yeetlggut*
       ye   + *le* + *l*   + *ggut*
       3SG O   + M   + CL + crunch + SML
       'S/he bit it with a crunch once; s/he crunched it once.'

(50a) *lek'eł*
       le + ∅   + *k'eł*
       M + CL + tear + SML
       'It ripped, burst out.'

(50b) *tl'eeyh lek'eł*
       tl'eeyh   le + ∅   + *k'eł*
       mosquitoes   M + CL + tear + SML
       'Mosquitoes burst out in swarms.'

(51)   *daadlekkuł*
       de + *le* + *le*   + *kkuł*
       T + M   + CL + cough + SML
       'S/he coughed once.'

The semantic range of the semelfactive occasionally overlaps with that of the *l* momentaneous and the ∅ momentaneous, both of which may be used to refer to single abrupt actions. Compare the semelfactive derivative of the theme ∅ +*tsaah* 'cry' in (53) with the (∅ – perfective) momentaneous derivative in (52):

(52)   *eetsaah* (∅ momentaneous)
       ∅ + ∅   + *tsaah*
       M + CL + cry + MOM
       'S/he cried out.'

(53) *letseh* (semelfactive)
　　　le + ∅ + *tseh*
　　　M + CL + cry + SML
　　　'People really mourned his death.' Lit., 'People cried out for him
　　　once.'

Although both verbs express a single, abrupt action, the semelfactive aspect of the form in (53) emphasizes the unitary nature of the
(logically plural) subject as well as of the (logically prolonged and
varied) activity; it also emphasizes the intensity of that activity.[29]

　　The semelfactive can also be used to provide greater focus on
the suddenness of an action than the *l* momentaneous. Compare the
semelfactive example in (54) with the *l* momentaneous example in
(55), both from the theme ∅ +*dokk* 'vanish, disappear'. Jones (p.c.)
reports that in (54) the emphasis is on the abruptness of the disap-
pearance, with the verb indicating that the action happened "just
like that!"

(54) *yeetldɩh* (semelfactive)
　　　ye　+ *le* + *l*　+ *dɩh*
　　　3SG O + M + CL + disappear + SML
　　　'S/he caused it to disappear all of a sudden; s/he stole it.'

(55) *yetaatldokk* (*l* momentaneous)
　　　ye　+ *te* + *le* + *l*　+ *dokk*
　　　3SG O + DS + M + CL + disappear + MOM
　　　'S/he caused it to disappear; s/he stole it.'

　　Semelfactive verbs are usually perfective and require a *le-* perfective mode prefix. Stems derived from obstruent or nasal-closed
roots have reduced vowel and spirantization of a final obstruent,
reflecting some obstruent suffix in all modes. The following stem
sets are typical:

　　　tlaatl 'chop'
　　　　tlel　　　*tlel*　　　*tlel*　　　*tlel*

　　　dek 'shoot arrow'
　　　　deyh　　　*deyh*　　　*deyh*　　　*deyh*

　　　dzen 'score with knife'
　　　　dzenh　　　*dzenh*　　　*dzenh*　　　*dzenh*

29. This is the only case so far documented of a verb theme having
both a ∅ momentaneous and a semelfactive derivative.

The only attested open root with semelfactive derivatives, *tlaa* '(dog) barks', has an unvaried stem set with full vowel and glottal suffix. The infrequent instances of imperfective semelfactive derived forms have a $\emptyset$ - mode prefix and a meaning extremely similar to that of the customary superaspect.

(56) *eet'uł* (semelfactive imperfective)
      $\emptyset$ + $\emptyset$ + *t'uł*
      M + CL + cut + SML
      'S/he customarily cuts it, gives it a cut every now and then.'

3.2.13. Bisective

Only twenty-five verb roots in the corpus (about 4 percent) permit bisective derivations. Derivatives refer to single actions in which contact is made, resulting in a division of the object-recipient into two (usually equal) parts. Compare the meanings of the bisective examples in the (a) forms below with the semelfactive or momentaneous examples in the (b) forms.

(57a) *naadleduh*
      ne + *le* + *le* + *duh*
      DS + M + CL + burst + BIS
      'It (bone, brick) snapped in half.'

(57b) *dleduh*
      le + *le* + *duh*
      M + CL + burst + SML
      'It (sack of flour) burst.'

(58a) *yenaatltsut*
      ye + *ne* + *le* + *ł* + *tsut*
      3SG O + DS + M + CL + cut + BIS
      'S/he quickly cut it in two.'

(58b) *yeetltsut*
      ye + *le* + *ł* + *tsut*
      3SG O + M + CL + cut + SML
      'S/he slashed it (with a knife); s/he snipped it (with scissors).'

(59a) *naadledun'*
      ne + *le* + *le* + *dun'*
      DS + M + CL + break + BIS
      'It (bone, dish) broke in half.'

(59b) *nee'eeldun'*
    nee # *ne* + *le* + *dun'*
    DS # M + CL + break + MOM
    'It (bone, cookie) cracked all up.'

    Notice that bisective derivatives require a *ne–* conjunct prefix and take *le–* perfective and $\emptyset$ – imperfective mode prefixes.

    Bisective stem variation is highly regular: stem sets are always unvaried. Closed roots have stems with spirantized final and reduced vowel[30] and nasal-final roots have stems with voiceless nasal final and reduced vowel. The only open root to permit a bisective derivation is *–kk'o/kk'ol* 'grind', which has the bisective stems *–kk'u* and *–kk'unh* in free variation. Examples of bisective stem sets include:

tlaatl 'chop'
    tleł   *tleł*   *tleł*   *tleł*

guts 'bite'
    gus   *gus*   *gus*   *gus*

tsen 'break'
    tsenh   *tsenh*   *tsenh*   *tsenh*

    Because the stem variation associated with the bisective is virtually identical with that of the semelfactive, and because the two aspects are often found with verbs referring to cutting or breaking, it has been suggested (Kari, p.c.) that the bisective is merely a semelfactive aspect-dependent derivational string. That is, it is a prefix string (having, in this case, just the one conjunct prefix *ne–*) that is "added" to a semelfactive derivative giving the supplementary meaning of 'in half'. In fact, this analysis is unsatisfactory because it fails to account for the distributional facts of bisective derivatives. While bisective forms often occur in themes that also permit semelfactive derivatives, the correspondence is not exact. Of the seventy verb roots that allow semelfactive derivatives, only fourteen also allow bisective derivatives; of the twenty-five roots that allow bisective derivatives, eleven do not allow semelfactive derivatives. On distributional grounds, then, we must consider the bisective to be a separate aspect.

---

30. Except for the root *–leeł* 'twist', which does not reduce.

3.2.14. Conclusive

The conclusive aspect refers to telic activities—those that focus on a particular goal. It expresses the completion of an activity and carries the implication of the attainment of a specific objective. Compare the conclusive derivatives in the (a) forms below with the momentaneous or durative derivatives in the (b) forms.

(60a) *nok'eghenaatlt'usk* (conclusive)

no	# *k'e*	+ *ghe*	+ *ne*	+ *le*	+ *ł*	+ *t'usk*
DS	# INDF O	+ DS	+ DS	+ M	+ CL	+ slap + CNCL

'S/he made something (bread).' Lit. 'S/he slapped something (dough) into a shape.'

(60b) *doyedaaneełt'usk* (*n* momentaneous)

do	# *ye*	+ *de*	+ *ne*	+ *ł*	+ *t'usk*
DS	# 3SGO	+ DS	+ M	+ CL	+ slap + MOM

'S/he slapped her/him repeatedly.'

(61a) *k'eghedaatltseenh* (conclusive)

k'e	+ *ghe*	+ *de*	+ *le*	+ *ł*	+ *tseenh*
INDF O	+ DS		+ M	+ CL	+ make SG + CNCL

'S/he carved something (wood) into a shape.'

(61b) *hułtsee* (durative)

hu	+ ∅	+ *ł*	+ *tsee*
AREA	+ M	+ CL	+ make SG + DUR

'S/he is whittling, planing.'

(62a) *denaadledlut* (conclusive)

de + *ne*	+ *le*	+ *le*	+ *dlut*
T	+ M	+ CL	+ boil + CNCL

'It came to a boil.'

(62b) *denoldlut* (durative)

de + *ne*	+ *ghe*	+ *le*	+ *dlut*
T	+ M	+ CL	+ boil + DUR

'It was boiling.'

Activities typically expressed by conclusive derivatives include those that result in a change of shape or texture of an object, such as drying, hardening, sealing; or getting wet, crushed, frozen, cooked, or dressed. Other activities typically expressed by the conclusive are those with a well-defined goal or endpoint, such as making a singular object, packaging an object, defeating a foe, shaping or painting an object, urinating, defecating, and vomiting.

Derivatives have $\emptyset$ - imperfective or *le-* perfective mode prefixes. Ninety-three verb roots (15 percent of the corpus) have conclusive stem sets. Stems derived from open roots have no suffix in the imperfective, *-nh* in the perfective, and *-l* in the future and optative.

    tsee 'make SG, DU O'
     tsee   *tseenh*   *tseel*   *tseel*

Nasal-closed roots and obstruent-closed roots with reduced vowels have unspirantized, unvaried stem sets reflecting the suffixation pattern $\emptyset$ *-ŋ̣ $\emptyset$ $\emptyset$.

    ten 'freeze'
     tenh   *tenh*   *tenh*   *tenh*

    lets 'urinate'
     lets   *lets*   *lets*   *lets*

Most obstruent-closed roots with full vowels (25 out of 34) have this same suffixation pattern resulting in stems with spirantized finals in the imperfective, future, and optative.

    ts'oots 'dry up'
     ts'oos   *ts'oots*   *ts'oos*   *ts'oos*

Nine full-vowel obstruent-closed roots, however, are "non-spirantizing": they have unspirantized stems in all modes.

    baats 'boil' ("non-spirantizing")
     baats   *baats*   *baats*   *baats*

3.2.15. Onomatopoetic

Onomatopoetic verbs express the production of a sound or noise generated by an object, instrument, or animal. Like English 'buzz', 'crack', and 'meow', they refer to sounds that resemble the sounds of the verb stems themselves. The onomatopoetic is unusual in having unspirantized, unvaried stem sets, regardless of the shape of the root.[31]

Seventy-four roots (12 percent of the corpus) allow (or have ex-

---

31. The one exception to this is the root *t'otl/tutl* 'cut', which has the varied stem set *t'ol, t'otl, t'ol, t'ol*.

clusively) onomatopoetic derivatives. Derivatives always have a *de-* conjunct prefix, required on any verb expressing oral sound. Most derivatives also have *le-* classifier. They have a $\emptyset$ - imperfective mode marker and may have either *ghe-* or *le-* perfective mode prefix. With the *ghe-* perfective prefix, a derivative refers to a duration or repetition of the sound. With the *le-* perfective prefix, a derivative refers to a single, abrupt instance of the sound. In this way the onomatopoetic is very reminiscent of the meaning contrast between the semelfactive and the consecutive or durative aspects. In fact, onomatopoetic stems can also be found with aspect-dependent derivational prefix strings and mode markers usually associated with the momentaneous and with the perambulative. For that reason it may be best not to think of onomatopoetic as a genuine aspect. I include it here for lack of a better place to put such a productive derivation type.

Of two general types of onomatopoetic derivatives the first refers to animal calls or to such sounds as an echo, a bang, or choking. Verbs of this type are derived from themes of the form *de+le+*STEM:

(63a) *delggukk*
    de + $\emptyset$ + *le* + *ggukk*
    T + M + CL + gull cry + ONO
    'It (gull) is crying.'

(63b) *dolggukk*
    de + *ghe* + *le* + *ggukk*
    T + M   + CL + gull cry + ONO
    'It (gull) was crying.'

(63c) *daadleggukk*
    de + *le* + *le* + *ggukk*
    T + M + CL + gull cry + ONO
    'It (gull) gave a sudden cry.'

(64a) *delkk'ekk*
    de + $\emptyset$ + *le* + *kk'ekk*
    T + M + CL + choke + ONO
    'S/he is making a choking sound.'

(64b) *dolkk'ekk*
    de + *ghe* + *le* + *kk'ekk*
    T + M   + CL + choke + ONO
    'S/he was making choking sounds.'

(64c) *daadlekk'ekk*
    de + *le* + *le*   + *kk'ekk*
    T   + M + CL + choke + ONO
    'S/he made a sudden choking sound.'

The second type of onomatopoetic verb describes a sound, such as ripping or crunching, produced by a particular inanimate. The inanimate is expressed as a postpositional object with *aa-* postposition. Themes from which such verbs are derived have the form *P+aa#de+le*+STEM. Most of these themes have both derivatives that express the impersonal concept 'sound of X comes from P'[32] and derivatives that express the personal 'S makes P produce sound of X', though a few have only one derivative or the other.

(65a) *baadelkket* (impersonal)
    be   + *aa* # *de* + ∅ + *le* + *kket*
    3SG P + PP # T   + M + CL + snap + ONO
    'A snapping, cracking sound came from it (joint).'

(65b) *yaadelkket* (personal)
    ye   + *aa* # *de* + ∅ + *le* + *kket*
    3SG P + PP # T   + M + CL + snap + ONO
    'S/he is making a snapping noise with it.'

3.3. Summary

The information presented in the preceding fifteen sections regarding stem set variation may seem a bit overwhelming. The essential point to bear in mind is that there are different suffixation patterns that, in conjunction with prefix morphology, act to signal differences in aspect. The following table presents an easy reference to stem suffixation patterns on open roots only. A list of stem sets for all aspects of all 600-odd roots is available in Axelrod (1990).

32. Like passive derivatives, these forms have an indeterminate subject (i.e., they cannot be inflected for subject) and so the third singular pronominal postpositional object has the "superior" unmarked form *be-* rather than *ye-*. Because the meaning relationship between the personal and impersonal onomatopoetic forms is somewhat different from that between active forms and their passive derivatives, I have chosen to label the two onomatopoetic forms personal and impersonal rather than active and passive and not to designate one as the derivative of the other.

The Semantics of Time

Table 3.4. Aspectual Stem Suffixation in Open Roots

	IMPF	PERF	FUT	OPT
Neuter	$-nh$	$-{}'$	$-{}'$	$-{}'$
Transitional	$-h$	$-t$~-${}'$	$-h$	$-h$
Momentaneous	$-yh$	$-nh$	$-l$	$-l$
Perambulative	$-yh$	$-nh$	$-k$	$-k$
Continuative	$-\emptyset$	$-nh$	$-l$	$-l$
Persistive	$-h$	$-h$	$-h$	$-h$
Reversative	$-h$	$-nh$	$-h$	$-h$
Durative	$-\emptyset$	$-{}'$	$-{}'$	$-{}'$
Consecutive	$-{}'$	$-{}'$	$-{}'$	$-{}'$
Repetitive	$-yh$	$-k$	$-k$	$-k$
Directive-Rep.	$-yh$	$-{}'$	$-k$	$-k$
Semelfactive	$-{}'$	$-{}'$	$-{}'$	$-{}'$
Bisective	$-\emptyset$~-nh	$-\emptyset$~-nh	$-\emptyset$~-nh	$-\emptyset$~-nh
Conclusive	$-\emptyset$	$-nh$	$-l$	$-l$

Notice that the irrealis modes (future and optative) have identical stems in open roots derived for each of the aspects.

Finally, it should be clear from the preceding sections that the Koyukon aspects can be divided into three general groups: *state*, focusing on a state, condition, position, or attribute; *motion*, referring to the movement of some entity from one locus to another; and *activity*, referring to an action or event. As pointed out in section 3.2, activity verbs are distinguished from motion verbs in that the activity aspects express the duration, cyclicity, punctuality, and telicity of the action rather than the path of the movement. The following table summarizes that tripartite division:

Table 3.5. The Koyukon Aspects

STATE	MOTION	ACTIVITY
neuter	momentaneous	durative
transitional	perambulative	consecutive
	continuative	repetitive
	persistive	directive-repetitive
	reversative	semelfactive
		bisective
		conclusive

The significance of this division will become clear in the discussion of aspectual verb theme categories in chapter 5, where it is shown how aspects cluster with respect to the category of a particular theme. For that discussion also bear in mind that the activity verbs can be divided into two subgroups: those that require a *ghe-* perfective mode prefix (durative, consecutive, repetitive, and directive-repetitive) and those that require a *le-* perfective mode prefix (semelfactive, bisective, and conclusive).

The next chapter describes three categories which are important constituents of the full Koyukon aspectual system but which are not obligatory, as mode and aspect are. The nonobligatory aspectual categories are aspect-dependent derivational strings, superaspect, and postaspectual derivations.

4
The Aspectual System

4.1. Aspect-dependent derivational strings

Derivational prefix strings in Koyukon are composed of one or more prefixes that combine to add a particular meaning to derivatives of a theme. Derivational strings may be non-aspect-dependent (i.e., strings that appear with a verb regardless of its mode and aspect) or aspect-dependent (i.e., they may occur only with a particular mode prefix and aspect). Approximately 330 aspect-dependent derivational prefix strings have been isolated. Their form is that of a discontinuous template in conjunction with mode and aspect, and their specific meaning obtains when they are linked to the particular mode and aspect markers they "choose." These strings have meanings that are generally adverbial—modifying the state, process, or activity referred to by specifying the manner, direction, or time frame involved.

Aspect-dependent derivational strings have distinct, isolatable meanings that they add to derivatives of a theme. They will alter the meaning of the verb in exactly the same way regardless of what the verb is. For example, with the theme ∅+*kkaa* 'paddle' or ∅+'*ots* 'DU go by foot', application of the aspect-dependent derivational string *ts'aa#* + *n* momentaneous adds the meaning 'out into the open' to derivatives of the theme.

(1a) *neekkaanh*
     ne + ∅ + *kkaanh*
     M + CL + paddle + MOM
     'S/he arrived paddling.'

(1b) *ts'aaneekkaanh*
     ts'aa # *ne* + ∅ + *kkaanh*
     DS # M + CL + paddle + MOM
     'S/he paddled out into the open.'

(2a) *henee'ots*
     he + *ne* + ∅ + '*ots*
     3PL S + M + CL + DU go + MOM
     'They (two) arrived walking.'

(2b) *ts'aahenee'ots*
     ts'aa # *he* + *ne* + ∅ + '*ots*
     DS # 3PL S + M + CL + DU go + MOM
     'They (two) walked out into the open.'

84

Some verb roots and themes in Koyukon have more abstract meanings than 'paddle' or 'DU go'. Those themes usually have a more limited set of derivational strings that can apply to them. Applying those strings produces derivatives with specific meanings which are not related to the theme in as regular a manner as are the derivatives discussed above. An example of such a theme is ∅ + *let*, a motion theme[1] usually glossed as 'SG, DU experiences event'. With the addition of derivational and inflectional prefixes, derivatives of this theme have a wide range of meanings, including 'be sad', 'be scared', 'grow up', 'spend time', 'die', 'drown', and 'spring break-up comes'. With the aspect-dependent derivational string illustrated above, *ts'aa#* + *n* momentaneous 'out into the open', derivatives have the meaning 'wake up':

(3) *ts'aaneelet*
    ts'aa # *ne* + ∅ + *let*
    DS # M + CL + SG event + MOM
    'S/he woke up.'

Roughly 90 percent of the 330 aspect-dependent derivational strings choose the momentaneous or neuter aspects or both. Most of these strings may occur with either momentaneous or neuter derivatives with a particular momentaneous perfective or neuter imperfective mode prefix. For example, the strings P+*do#* 'entering through P (doorway), into P' and *do#de+* 'in a pile' may occur with either an *n* momentaneous derivative *or* a neuter derivative with *ne-* imperfective prefix (hereafter referred to as *n* neuter):

(4a) *hedoyeenee'onh* (*n* momentaneous)
    hʉ + *do* # *ye* + *ne* + ∅ + *'onh*
    AREA + DS # 3SG O + M + CL + CLASSIF: compact + MOM
    'S/he brought it in.'

(4b) *hedodaanee'o* (*n* neuter)
    hʉ + *do* # *de* + *ne* + ∅ + *'o*
    AREA + DS # G + M + CL + line extends + NEU
    'It (pole) is extending inside.'

1. The criteria employed in determining the category of a verb theme are detailed in chapter 5.

(5a)   *doyedaaneełk'eł* (*n* momentaneous)
       do # *ye*   + *de* + *ne* + *ł*   + *k'eł*
       DS # 3SG O   + DS   + M   + CL   + tear + MOM
       'S/he tore it up into a pile.'

(5b)   *dodaat'onh* (*n* neuter)
       do # *de* + *ne* + *de* + *'onh*
       DS # DS   + M   + CL   + CLASSIF: compact + NEU
       'Many (cubes) are in a pile.'

The above examples represent the majority of cases, in which the primarily momentaneous string may be used with neuter derivatives (with equivalent mode prefix) of themes referring to extension or position. In other cases, though, a string may require a neuter imperfective prefix that is different from the momentaneous perfective prefix it chooses. Such a string is P+*doggu*##*k'e*+*de*+ 'covering P with something (lid, cloth)', which occurs with *gh* momentaneous derivatives or *n* neuter derivatives:

(6a)   *yedoggu k'edegheełkool* (*gh* momentaneous)
       ye   + *doggu* *k'e*+*de* + *ghe* + *ł*   + *kool*
       3SG P   + DS   DS   + M   + CL   + CLASSIF: flexible + MOM
       'S/he covered it with something (cloth).'

(6b)   *yedoggu k'edaaneełkool* (*n* neuter)
       ye   + *doggu* *k'e*+*de* + *ne* + *ł*   + *kool*
       3SG P   + DS   DS   + M   + CL   + CLASSIF: flexible + NEU
       'It is covered with something (cloth).'

Other strings are attested only with momentaneous or only with neuter derivatives.

Of the momentaneous and neuter aspect-dependent derivational strings, ninety-eight are tied to *gh* momentaneous derivatives (or *gh* neuter derivatives, in cases where the string occurs with no paired momentaneous examples); fifty-six are *n* momentaneous strings (or occur with the *n* neuter with no paired momentaneous examples); forty-nine are *∅* momentaneous strings (or *∅* neuter); forty-four are *l* momentaneous strings, thirty-eight are *ll* momentaneous strings, and six strings occur only with *l* neuter derivatives.

The nonmomentaneous aspect-dependent derivational strings include eight continuative strings (three of which may also occur with the *l* neuter), six conclusive strings, three persistive strings, three repetitive and two durative strings (and one that can occur with either durative or repetitive), two semelfactive strings, one reversative string, one *le-* onomatopoetic string, and one transitional string (although this last string is also used with *n* momentaneous derivatives). There are also a perambulative and a bisective string, which are somewhat different from the other aspect-dependent derivational strings in that they are obligatory. The perambulative and bisective never occur without the derivational prefixes of those strings.

Most of the aspect-dependent derivational strings may occur in combination with one or more superaspects as well. The most commonly attested of these are the distributive, customary, and progressive. The use of some strings is limited to certain theme types.

In the examples in (22) in chapter 3, I pointed out that aspect has a relationship with transitivity: some aspects are used to express the extent to which an object is affected by the activity. The aspect-dependent derivational strings interact with transitivity as well. Some aspect-dependent prefix strings, like the non-aspect-dependent derivational prefix strings (e.g., causative, benefactive, reflexive), alter the transitivity of a theme's derivative either by triggering deletion of a direct object, thus making the derivative intransitive, or, less frequently, by adding an object to produce a transitive derivative of an otherwise intransitive theme. Compare the following derivatives of the theme $O+G+\emptyset+tlaatl$ 'chop O'. The (a) example is a regular durative derivative of the theme; the (b) example has the aspect-dependent derivational string $P + gh\textit{u}\# + n$ momentaneous 'through P'; and the (c) example reflects the aspect-dependent derivational string $ts'e\# + gh$ momentaneous 'through the ice'. The aspect-dependent derivational strings illustrated in the (b) and (c) examples always produce an intransitive derivative, regardless of the transitivity value of the theme.

(7a) *yegheetlaatl*
ye + *ghe* + ∅ + *tlaatl*
3SG O + M + CL + chop + DUR
'S/he was chopping it.'

(7b) *yugh neetlaatl*
ye + *ghu* # *ne* + ∅ + *tlaatl*
3SG P + DS # M + CL + chop + MOM
'S/he chopped a hole through it.'

(7c) *ts'egheetlaatl*
      ts'e # *ghe* + ∅   + *tlaatl*
      DS   # M   + CL   + chop + MOM
      'S/he chopped a hole through the ice.'

4.2. Superaspect

Superaspect is the term coined by Kari (1979) to refer to derivations which are like aspect in that they have a unique stem set and prefix morphology and express an aspectual (or aspect like adverbial) meaning but which are unlike the aspects described above in that they can co-occur with other aspects, and with each other, producing a layering of meaning.

There are four superaspects in Koyukon: the distributive, the multiple, the customary, and the progressive. The four superaspects can combine with any of the fifteen aspects, but each superaspect has its own stem set variation for every verb root and its own mode prefixes; superaspect stem variation and mode prefixes take precedence over those associated with the aspect with which it combines. Consequently, unless the superaspect supplements a form with an aspect-dependent derivational prefix string, it can be difficult to determine on morphological grounds which regular aspectual derivation underlies a form that has been derived further for superaspect.

Compare the following examples in (8) from the theme *beł#ne+ le+daakk* 'fall asleep'. The (a) example is a plain momentaneous derivative with *le-* perfective prefix. The (b) example shows the *l* momentaneous form derived further with the *distributive* superaspect, adding a 'here and there' import to the meaning. The (c) example shows the addition of the *multiple* superaspect to the *l* momentaneous example in (a), adding the meaning of plural subjects. The (d) example shows the *customary* superaspect with its consequent meaning of habitual occurrence. The (e) example shows the *progressive* superaspect.

(8a) *bełnaadledaakk* (*l* momentaneous)
      beł   # *ne*   + *le*   + *le*   + *daakk*
      T (sleep) # T   + M   + CL   + experience + MOM
      'S/he fell asleep.'

(8b) *nebełheenaadledaakk* (distributive)
      ne   # *beł* # *he*   + *ne*   + *le*   + *le*   + *daakk*
      DIST   # T   # 3PL S   + T   + M   + CL   + experience + DIST
      'They (many) fell asleep here and there.'

(8c) *yenbełheenaadledaakk* (multiple)
   yen　# *beł*　# *he*　+ *ne*　+ *le*　+ *le*　+ *daakk*
   MULT　# T　　# 3PL S　+ T　　+ M　　+ CL　+ experience + MULT
   'They (group of people) fell asleep.'

(8d) *nobeł'eetenledeh* (customary)
   no　# *beł*　# *te*　+ *ne*　+ *ø*　+ *le*　+ *deh*
   ITER　# T　　# DS　+ T　　+ M　　+ CL　+ experience + CUST
   'S/he keeps falling asleep.'

(8e) *bełnoldehtl* (progressive)
   beł　# *ne*　+ *ghe*　+ *le*　+ *dehtl*
   T　　# T　　+ M　　+ CL　+ experience + PROG
   'S/he is going to sleep, falling asleep.'

Notice that the superaspects form a group that has semantic cohesiveness as well as morphological and distributional regularities. All four carry a notion of plurality. The distributive indicates a greater number of locations for the activity or a greater number of object referents; the multiple indicates a greater number of subject or object referents; the customary indicates a greater number of occasions for the activity; and the progressive indicates a greater time span for the activity.

(See sections 4.2.1 through 4.2.4 for a more detailed description of each of the four superaspects.)

4.2.1. Distributive

The distributive is used most often to express a repeated or "here and there" quality about the state or activity referred to by the verb. It may also be used to indicate a plurality of items described by the verb, when those items represent patients. In the following pairs the (b) examples (which are derived from the preceding (a) examples) illustrate the semantic range of the distributive.

(9a) *yeghuneełtsot* (with P+*ghu*# *n* MOM 'through P')
   ye　　+ *ghu*　# *ne*　+ *ł*　+ *tsot*
   3SG P　+ PP　# M　　+ CL　+ cut + MOM
   'S/he quickly cut a hole through it.'

(9b) *yeghun'etltsot* (distributive)
   ye　　+ *ghu*　# *ne*　# *le*　+ *ł*　+ *tsot*
   3SG P　+ PP　# DIST　# M　+ CL　+ cut + DIST
   'S/he cut several holes in it (hide — while skinning it hastily).'

(10a) *yedegheetset* (with P+*e*#*de*+ *gh* MOM 'releasing P')
    ye   + *e*   # *de* + *ghe* + ∅   + *tset*
    3SG P + PP # DS + M   + CL + handle + MOM
    'S/he released it; s/he stopped doing it.'

(10b) *yendaaltset* (distributive)
    ye   + *e*   # *ne*   # *de* + *le* + ∅   + *tset*
    3SG P + PP # DIST # DS + M   + CL + handle + DIST
    'S/he released them (at several points in time); s/he ceased them
    (different activities).'

(11a) *nohooneeltseen'* (with *no*# *n* MOM 'across')
    no # *hu̱* + *ne* + *l̦*   + *tseen'*
    DS # T   + M   + CL + build + MOM
    'It (beaver) built (a dam) across (the stream).'

(11b) *nu̱'u̱nhootltsee'* (distributive)
    no # *ne*   # *hu̱* + *le* + *l̦*   + *tsee'*
    DS # DIST # T   + M   + CL + build + DIST
    'It (beaver) built (dams) across (the stream) at several places.'

(12a) *l̦aats daal̦enokk* (l neuter)
    l̦aats   *de* + *le* + *de* + *nokk*
    sand   T   + M   + CL   + CLASSIF: granular + NEU
    'There is some sand there.'

(12b) *yeh nedaal̦enokk* (distributive)
    yeh   *ne*   # *de* + *le* + *de* + *nokk*
    house   DIST # T   + M   + CL   + CLASSIF: granular + DIST
    'It (dust) is in piles here and there in the house.'

The distributive always occurs with a disjunct prefix, *ne*-. It
requires a *le*- perfective prefix and a ∅ - imperfective mode prefix.
There are 107 verb roots in the corpus (roughly 17 percent), which
admit distributive stem sets. Of the nineteen attested distributive
stem sets from open roots, ten have perfective stems with a *-nh*
suffix; of the remaining nine, seven have glottal-suffixed perfective
stems and two have unsuffixed perfective stems. Imperfective stems
have a glottal suffix.[2] Fourteen of the nineteen open roots have future and optative stems with a glottal suffix and five have a *-l̦* suf-

---

2. The sole exception is the root *yo/yaa* 'grow', which has the irregular
stem set *yaah, yonh, yaah, yaah.*

fix on those stems.[3] The following stem sets illustrate these patterns:

tsee 'make SG O'
tsee'	*tseenh*	*tsee'*	*tsee'*

kko 'CLASSIF: object in container'
kko'	*kko'*	*kko'*	*kko'*

ghaa 'pack on back'
ghaa'	*ghaanh*	*ghaał*	*ghaał*

Distributive stems from nasal-final roots are even more irregular, with variation between unsuffixed, unvaried stem sets and sets with lengthening, ablaut, or glottal suffix. Closed roots with full vowels retain the full vowel in all modes and have spirantized finals in the imperfective, future, and optative. Closed roots with reduced vowels have unspirantized, unvaried stem sets.[4] The following stem sets from closed roots show these patterns:

'aatl 'PL swim, float'
'aał	*'aatl*	*'aał*	*'aał*

t'ekk 'glue'
t'ekk	*t'ekk*	*t'ekk*	*t'ekk*

4.2.2. Multiple

The multiple indicates that the subjects or objects referred to by the verb are particularly numerous. As shown in the preceding section, the distributive can likewise be used to express the numerousness of patients. Furthermore, these two superaspects may not co-occur (i.e., a single verb form cannot be derived for both the multiple and the distributive at the same time). There is, however, little semantic overlap between the multiple and the distributive. When one wants to remark on an unusual plurality of a subject of an active verb, whether transitive or intransitive, the multiple, rather than the distributive, is always used:

---

3. One root, *'o* 'linear extends', has both the glottal suffix and the *-ł* suffix in free variation in future and optative stems.

4. There are two exceptions: *nekk* 'continue', which has the stem set *neh, neh, neh, neh;* and *'uh/'ut* 'handle flat, flexible object quickly', which has the stem set *'ut, 'ut, 'uk, 'uk.*

(13a) *k'eldzes* (durative)
     k'e + ∅ + le + dzes
     T   + M + CL + dance + DUR
     'S/he is dancing.'

(13b) *nu'unk'eldzes* (distributive)
     no # ne   # k'e + ∅ + le   + dzes
     DS # DIST # T   + M + CL + dance + DIST
     'S/he danced across (the creek) here and there (i.e., s/he danced across the creek and then came to another one and danced across it, and so on).'

(13c) *yenk'eheeldzees* (multiple)
     yen # k'e + he   + ∅ + le   + dzees
     MULT # T   + 3PL S + M + CL + dance + MULT
     'They (many) are dancing.'

(14a) *kkun'gheetlaatl* (durative)
     kkun' ghe + ∅ + tlaatl
     wood   M   + CL + chop + DUR
     'S/he chopped wood.'

(14b) *kkun'nehutlaal* (distributive)
     kkun' ne   # he   + ∅ + ∅ + tlaal
     wood   DIST # 3PL S + M + CL + chop + DIST
     'They were chopping wood here and there.'

(14c) *kkun'yenheetlaatl* (multiple)
     kkun' yen   # he   + ∅ + ∅   + tlaatl
     wood   MULT # 3PL S + M + CL + chop + MULT
     'They (many) were chopping wood.'

When plurality is to be expressed about a patient (i.e., the object of a transitive verb or the subject of a neuter intransitive verb), the multiple is used to indicate quantity while the distributive is used to indicate the spatial distribution of that quantity. Compare the following examples with those in section 4.2.1:

(15a) *yeetltlukk* (conclusive)
     ye   + le + l   + tlukk
     3SG O + M + CL + soften + CNCL
     'S/he boiled it to softness.'

(15b) *yenyeeltlukk* (multiple)
     yen # ye   + ∅ + l   + tlukk
     MULT # 3SG O + M + CL + soften + MULT
     'S/he boiled them (many) to softness.'

(16a) *yeeldzaakk* (conclusive)
  ye   *+ le*   *+ ∅*   *+ dzaakk*
  3SG O   + M   + CL   + pitch + CNCL
  'S/he put pitch on it (canoe); s/he buttered it (bread).'

(16b) *beedoy yen'eedzaakk* (multiple)
  beedoy   *yen*   # ∅   *+ ∅*   *+ dzaakk*
  canoe   MULT   # M   + CL   + pitch + MULT
  'S/he put pitch on many canoes.'

(17a) *belo' dlenuts* (*l* neuter)
  be   *+ lo'*   *le*   *+ le*   *+ nuts*
  3SG   + hand   M   + CL   + swell + NEU
  'Her hand is swollen, remains swollen.'

(17b) *hebekkaa' yen'eelnoots* (multiple)
  hebe+kkaa'   *yen*   # ∅   *+ le*   *+ noots*
  3PL + feet   MULT   # M   + CL   + swell + MULT
  'Their feet are swollen.'

(18a) *kkaaken deets'aagge* (∅ neuter)
  kkaaken   *de* *+ ∅*   *+ ∅*   *+ ts'aagge*
  boot   G   + M   + CL   + narrow + NEU
  'The boot is narrow.'

(18b) *kkaaken yendeets'aagge* (multiple)
  kkaaken   *yen*   *# de* *+ ∅*   *+ ∅*   *+ ts'aagge*
  boot   MULT   # G   + M   + CL   + narrow + MULT
  'The (many) boots are narrow.'

(19a) *hooɬts'aanh* (∅ neuter)
  hʉ *+ ∅* *+ ɬ*   *+ ts'aanh*
  T   + M   + CL   + jealous + NEU
  'S/he is jealous.'

(19b) *yenhehooɬts'aanh* (multiple)
  yen   *# he*   *+ hʉ* *+ ∅* *+ ɬ*   *+ ts'aanh*
  MULT   # 3PL S   + T   + M   + CL + jealous + MULT
  'They (many) are jealous.'

Notice that in the last of these neuter examples, a third person plural pronominal subject prefix was required for the multiple while in the preceding two neuter examples, no such prefix was present. The presence or absence of a plural subject prefix in the multiple varies according to the theme. In transitive themes a plural subject prefix is obligatory to indicate plurality of the subject as opposed to plurality of the object. Compare the following examples:

(20a) *yenk'ehookkaat*

yen	# *k'e*	+ *he*	+ ∅	+ ∅	+ *kkaat*
MULT	# INDF	+ 3PLS	+ M	+ CL	+ buy + MULT

'They (many) are buying things.'

(20b) *yenyookkaat*

yen	# *ye*	+ ∅	+ ∅	+ *kkaat*
MULT	# 3SG O	+ M	+ CL	+ buy + MULT

'S/he bought them (many things).'

As can be observed from the previous examples, the multiple is marked by a disjunct prefix, *yen-*. Occasionally the *yen-* prefix may reduce to *ye-*: *yents'ohedeetlaagge* or *yets'ohedeetlaagge* 'they (many) are bad; they are bad people'.

The multiple requires a ∅ perfective or ∅ imperfective mode prefix. Eighty-eight verb roots (roughly 15 percent of the corpus) show multiple stem sets. Multiple stem sets derived from open roots have, in every case, a *-yh* suffix in the imperfective and usually show a *-k* suffix in the perfective, future, and optative stems.[5]

baa 'be gray'			
baayh	*baak*	*baak*	*baak*

Stem sets derived from nasal-closed roots also have the *-yh* suffix in the imperfective and *-k* in the future and optative. Roots with reduced vowels show lengthening (and some full-vowel roots show ablaut) in these stems as well. Perfective stems from nasal-closed roots have either an *-nh* suffix or a *-k* suffix (plus lenthening or ablaut).[6]

ten 'freeze'			
teeyh	*tenh*	*teek*	*teek*

ten 'sleep'			
teeyh	*teek*	*teek*	*teek*

5. There are four exceptions, all of which have a *-nh* suffix in the perfective stem. The exceptional stem sets are derived from the following roots: *kkaa* 'paddle' *(kkaayh, kkaanh, kkaayh, kkaayh)*, *no/naa* 'move camp' *(naayh, nonh, naa', naa')*, *tl'oo* 'dress; bind' *(tl'ooyh, tl'oonh, tl'ook, tl'ook)*, and *yo/yaa* 'grow' *(yaah, yonh, yaah, yaah)*.

6. Two exceptional roots, *(h)on* 'eat' and *noon* 'drink', have perfective stems with glottal suffix.

Closed roots usually have unspirantized perfective stems and imperfective, future, and optative stems with spirantized final. Roots with reduced vowels show lengthening in the imperfective, future, and optative:

> *dzeets* 'dance'
>   *dzees*   *dzeets*   *dzees*   *dzees*
>
> *k'uts* 'pluck'
>   *k'oos*   *k'uts*   *k'oos*   *k'oos*

4.2.3. Customary

The customary refers to activity that occurs occasionally or habitually. The following examples illustrate the semantic range of the customary.

(21a) *belo' dlenuts* (*l* neuter)
  be + *lo'*   *le* + *le*   + *nuts*
  3SG + hand   M   + CL   + swell + NEU
  'Her hand is swollen, remains swollen.'

(21b) *no'eelnus* (customary)
  no   # ∅ + *le*   + *nus*
  ITER   # M   + CL   + swell + CUST
  'It swells occasionally.'

(22a) *eededzaakk* (∅ transitional)
  ∅   + *de*   + *dzaakk*
  M   + CL   + dirty + TRNS
  'It became dirty.'

(22b) *no'eededzeh* (customary)
  no   # ∅ + *de*   + *dzeh*
  ITER   # M   + CL   + dirty + CUST
  'It keeps getting dirty; it gets dirty now and then.'

(23a) *heldlekel* (conclusive)
  hu + *e* # *l* # *le* + *le*   + *kel*
  T   + T   # T # M   + CL   + tie + CNCL
  'S/he put on a belt.'

(23b) *helnolekeyhtl* (customary)
  hu + *e* # *l* # *no* # ∅ + *le*   + *keyhtl*
  T   + T   # T # ITER   # M   + CL   + tie + CUST
  'S/he customarily puts on a belt.'

(24a) *etlts'eek* *(l* neuter)
   le + *ł* + *ts'eek*
   M + CL + hurt + NEU
   'It hurts, stings.'

(24b) *eełts'eyh*
   Ø + *ł* + *ts'eyh*
   M + CL + hurt + CUST
   'It stings, becomes painful now and then, hurts once in a while.'

(25a) *deyee k'edaatltl'ee* (reversative)
   de + *yee k'e* + *de* + *le* + *ł* + *tl'ee*
   INDT P + PP INDF O + T + M + CL + PL sit + REV
   'S/he caught fish in the fishnet.'

(25b) *deyee k'edegheełtl'eek* (customary)
   deyee k'e + *de* + *ghe* + *ł* + *tl'eek*
   INDF O + T + M + CL + PL sit + CUST
   'S/he customarily caught fish in the fishnet.'

The customary is frequently found in nominalizations, as in the following:

(26a) *deghaak'ets'eghedeełkooł* (with P +*gho*#*ghe*- Ø NEU 'hanging up on P')
   de + *gho* # *k'e* + *ts'e* + *ghe* + *de* + *Ø* + *ł* +
   kooł
   INDT P + DS # INDF O + 1PL S + DS + G + M + CL +
   CLASSIF: flexible + NEU
   'We keep something *(k'e-* 'flag') hanging up on something *(de-* 'pole').'

(26b) *deghonaaghedeelkeyhdle* (customary)
   de + *gho* # *no* # *ghe* + *de* + *Ø* + *le* + *keyhtl* + *ee*
   INDT P + DS # ITER # DS + G + M + CL + flex + CUST + NOM
   'flag' lit. 'that which is customarily hung'

The customary requires a *ghe*- perfective or *Ø* - imperfective mode prefix. The customary often occurs with the disjunct iterative prefix, *no*-, which carries the meaning 'again' or 'returning'. It also frequently appears with the *l* momentaneous string consisting of the single conjunct prefix *te*-, which carries the meaning of activity carried out in an outward and linear fashion. An example of a customary derivative with the iterative and *te-* conjunct prefix follows:

(27a) *noyegheedzok* (with *no#* *gh* momentaneous 'down')
      no # *ye*   + *ghe* + ∅   + *dzok*
      DS # 3SG O + M   + CL   + CLASSIF: multiple + MOM
      'S/he threw them (dishes) down.'

(27b) *nok'eetengheedzuyh* (L) (customary)
      no   # *k'e*   + *te*   + *ne* + *ghe* + *dzuyh*
      ITER # INDF O + DS   + DS   + M   + CLASSIF: multiple + CUST
      'S/he used to throw things; s/he played dice.'

(27c) *no'eetendedzuye* (nominalization)
      no   # *te*   + *ne*   + ∅   + *de*   + *dzuyh*   + *ee*
      ITER # DS   + DS   + M   + CL   + multiple + CUST + nom
      'dice' lit. 'those that are thrown repeatedly'

The customary is by far the most productive of the four super-aspects. Of the corpus of roughly 600 verb roots, 291 (49 percent) admit customary stem sets. Open roots have stems with a *-yh* suffix in the imperfective and a *-k* suffix in the perfective, future, and optative, as illustrated in the following:

      baa 'swim'
        baayh   *baak*   *baak*   *baak*

Nasal-final roots show the same suffixation pattern. In addition, nasal-final roots with reduced vowels exhibit vowel lengthening and those with full vowels may show ablaut:

      ben 'paint, smear'
        beeyh   *beek*   *beek*   *beek*

      gheen 'glitter'
        gheeyh   *gheek*   *gheek*   *gheek*

      (h)on 'eat'
        heeyh   *heek*   *heek*   *heek*

Obstruent-closed roots have unvaried stem sets. A *-k* suffix produces vowel reduction and manifests in much the same way as does the *-k* suffix of the perambulative future and optative (see chap. 3, section 3.2.4): it replaces a final *-t* with *-k*, suffixes as *-k* after a final *-s*, produces spirantization of final *-k* and *-kk*, and appears as a front velar fricative *(yh)* before final *-tl*. Roots closed with a final

-ts show spirantization, and the *-k* suffix may or may not appear overtly after the resulting final *-s*. The following stem sets illustrate customary suffixation of closed roots:

> *tlot* 'sit down'
>   *tluk*   *tluk*   *tluk*   *tluk*
>
> *kk'os* 'stiffen, thicken, stick'
>   *kk'ʉsk*   *kk'ʉsk*   *kk'ʉsk*   *kk'ʉsk*
>
> *neek* 'act with the hand'
>   *neyh*   *neyh*   *neyh*   *neyh*
>
> *nekk* 'swallow'
>   *neh*   *neh*   *neh*   *neh*
>
> *tseetl* 'splash'
>   *tseyhtl*   *tseyhtl*   *tseyhtl*   *tseyhtl*
>
> *dzets* 'strike with fist'
>   *dzes*   *dzes*   *dzes*   *dzes*
>
> *bets* 'wide'
>   *besk*   *besk*   *besk*   *besk*

4.2.4. Progressive

The status of the progressive in the aspectual system of Koyukon is controversial. My analysis of its distributional and semantic characteristics has led me to the conclusion that the progressive must be put into the same class as customary, distributive, and multiple; that is, although it is considered a mode in Navajo (Young 1980, 1987; Midgette 1988) and an aspect in Ahtna (Kari 1979, 1990), the progressive is most properly classed as a superaspect in Koyukon. The progressive meets the major criterial attribute of this class in its ability to co-occur with other aspects (except the perambulative) and aspect-dependent derivational strings, as in the following examples:

(28a) *neeneeyo*[7] (with *nee# n* MOM 'to a point')
  nee # *ne* + ∅ + *yo*
  DS # M + CL + SG go + MOM
  'S/he walked up to a point.'

7. This is a vowel initial root. Perfective stems with ∅ classifier show stem-initial *y-* (as a reflex of the PA *-ŋ perfective prefix), while nonperfective stems with ∅ classifier have an epenthetic stem-inital *h-*.

(28b) *neeghehoł* (progressive)
  nee # ghe + ∅ + hoł
  DS # M   + CL + SG go + MOM
  'S/he was walking up to a point.'

(29a) *eszoonh* (∅ neuter)
  ∅ + s   + ∅ + zoonh
  M + 1SG S + CL + good + NEU
  'I am good.'

(29b) *dzaan k'ozooł* (neuter, progressive)
  dzaan k'e + ghe + ∅ + zooł
  day   DS + M   + CL + good + PROG
  'S/he was good all day.'

(30a) *ooszooh* (transitional)
  oo + ∅ + s   + ∅ + zooh
  DS + M + 1SG S + CL + good + TRNS
  'I became good.'

(30b) *oogheszooł* (transitional, progressive)
  oo + ghe + s   + ∅ + zooł
  DS + M   + 1SG S + CL + good + PROG
  'I'm becoming better and better.'

The progressive can also occur with most other superaspects (although it cannot co-occur with the multiple):

(31) *nu'unk'eho'oł* (progressive, distributive)
  no + ne # k'e   + he   + ghe + ∅ + 'oł
  DS + DIST # INDF O + 3PL S + M   + CL + CLASSIF: compact
    object +PROG
  'Different people are carrying compact objects across.'

(32) *nu'unyegheeteek* (progressive, distributive, customary)
  no + ne # ye   + ghe + ∅ + teek
  DS + DIST # 3SG O + M   + CL + CLASSIF: elongated object +
    CUST
  'They're customarily carrying things across here and there.'

The progressive also qualifies as a Koyukon superaspect because it has a unique stem set. It differs from the other superaspects, however, in that it has a stem only for one mode, the imperfective. The progressive is marked by a *ghe-* mode prefix and an *-ł* suffix. On nasal-closed roots, the suffix triggers vowel lengthening and on obstruent-closed roots, it produces vowel reduction and spirantization. The *-ł* suffix appears as the affricate *-tl* after the result-ing root-final spirant:

> *baa* 'swim'
> *baał*

> *ggun* 'dry'
> *ggoł*

> *ghaatl* 'be dark, calm'
> *ghełtl*

> *ghaats* 'accumulate from melting'
> *ghestl*

> *tl'eet* 'splash'
> *tl'eł*

Although only 165 (28 percent), of the verbs in the corpus show progressive stem sets, this does not reflect the true productivity or frequency of this superaspect. Except for a few cases of ablaut and suppletion, progressive stem derivation is a quite regular process and Jones (p.c.) may have neglected to note the stem set in some dictionary entries because of this very regularity and predictability.

According to Li (1946:405), the Chipewyan progressive "refers to an activity which is kept on particularly while one is moving along." This is often true in Koyukon, as the following example illustrates:

(33a) *ets'ooh* (durative)
 ∅ + ∅ + *ts'ooh*
 M + CL + scream + DUR
 'It (mink) is screeching; s/he (child) is squealing.'

(33b) *ghets'oohtl, ghets'uhtl* (progressive)
 ghe + ∅ + *ts'oohtl˜ts'uhtl*
 M + CL + scream + PROG
 'She/he/it is going along squealing.'

The progressive is used to express other meanings as well. It often functions as an alternative to the imperfective in motion verbs and, in fact, is found more frequently in texts and conversations to describe incomplete or ongoing activities or states than is the imper-fective. The following pairs of examples provide some idea of the subtle difference between imperfective and progressive with momentaneous forms. In all three pairs, the progressive focuses attention on the movement involved and locates the referent along the path of that movement. The imperfective, on the other hand, provides a more neutral statement of the incompleted movement.

(34a) *no'eedebaayh* (n momentaneous imperfective)
    no   # *ne* + *de* + *baayh*
    ITER # M   + CL + swim + MOM
    'S/he's returning (and is anywhere along the route).'

(34b) *naaghedebaał* (progressive)
    no   # *ghe* + *de* + *baał*
    ITER # M   + CL + swim + PROG
    'S/he's returning (not quite home yet but just approaching).'

(35a) *nee'eebaayh* (n momentaneous, imperfective)
    nee # *ne* + ∅   + *baayh*
    DS   # M   + CL + swim + MOM
    'She's swimming there (and is going to stay there).'

(35b) *neeghebaał* (progressive)
    nee # *ghe* + ∅   + *baał*
    DS   # M   + CL + swim + PROG
    'She's approaching there (describing the actual course of the movement).'

(36a) *tlee'eehoyh* (n momentaneous, imperfective)
    tlee # *ne* + ∅   + *hoyh*
    DS   # M   + CL + SG go + MOM
    'S/he's going outside (but will be back); s/he's going to the outhouse.'

(36b) *tleeghehoł* (progressive)
    tlee # *ghe* + ∅   + *hoł*
    DS   # M   + CL + SG go + PROG
    'She's just going out the door right now.'

With nonmotion verbs, the progressive carries the meaning of movement over time, which, in these cases, does not overlap with the meaning of the imperfective:

(37a) *ełkonh* (durative, imperfective)
    ∅ + *ł*   + *konh*
    M + CL + rain + DUR
    'It is raining.'

(37b) *ghełkeeł* (progressive)
    ghe + *ł*   + *keeł*
    M   + CL + rain + PROG
    'The rain is coming, moving.'

    With classificatory verbs,[8] the progressive can refer to ongoing movement of a subject with the classified object, but movement is not necessarily specified. In these cases, the progressive can also express the static holding of the object over a time span:

(38a) *tsaay daaneenokk* *(n* momentaneous)
    tsaay   *de* + *ne* + ∅   + *nokk*
    tea   G   + M   + CL   + CLASSIF: granular + MOM
    'S/he brought a little tea, some loose tea.'

(38b) *tsaay donuhtl*
    tsaay   *de* + *ghe* + ∅   + *nuhtl*
    tea   G   + M   + CL   + CLASSIF: granular + PROG
    'She is holding some tea in her hand; she is bringing some loose tea.'

(39a) *ts'eh nes'onh* *(n* momentaneous)
    ts'eh   *ne* + *s*   + ∅   + *'onh*
    hat   M   + 1SG S + CL   + CLASSIF: compact + MOM
    'I arrived with a hat.'

(39b) *ts'eh ghes'oł* (progressive)
    ts'eh   *ghe* + *s*   + ∅   + *'oł*
    hat   M   + 1SG S + CL   + CLASSIF: compact + PROG
    'I'm holding a hat, carrying a hat along.'

    This static interpretation of the progressive can also have idiomatic uses, as in the following:

(40) *bekkaakenh te yonehtl*
    bekkaakenh *te*   *ye*   + *ghe* + ∅   + *nehtl*
    her boots   PP   3SG O + M   + CL   + flexible moves + PROG
    'It (skirt) falls down around her boots, hangs down to her ankles.'
      Lit. 'It is progressively falling down around her boots.'

    The progressive may appear with derivational strings to further

---

8. Classificatory verbs refer to the existence or handling of objects. Different roots are used according to the shape, texture, and composition of the object.

specify the time span or process involved in the activity or state referred to.

(41a) *yeetlts'etl* (conclusive)
ye + *le* + *ł* + *ts'etl*
3SG O + M + CL + toast + CNCL
'S/he scorched it, made it shrivel from heat.'

(41b) *neleyołts'ełtl* (with *nele#* PROG 'in batches')
nele # *ye* + *ghe* + *ł* + *ts'ełtl*
DS # 3SG O + M + CL + toast + PROG
'S/he is toasting them (fish skins) one after the other, in batches; she is scorching more and more.'

Finally, the progressive can also be used with an inchoative sense, as in the following:

(42a) *sek'edeneełnenh* (∅ momentaneous)
se + *e* # *k'e* + *de* + *ne* + ∅ + *ł* + *nenh*
1SG P + PP # T + T + T + M + CL + compact moves + MOM
'It caught sight of me.'

(42b) *sek'edeneeghłleyhtl dehoon yuh oonso* (progressive)
se + *e* # *k'e* + *de* + *ne* + *ghe* + *ł* + *leyhtl*
1SG P + PP # T + T + T + M + CL + compact moves + PROG
'I rushed at it just as it was catching sight of me.'

(43a) *belo' dlenuts* (*l* neuter)
be + *lo'* *le* + *le* + *nuts*
3SG + hand M + CL + swell + NEU
'Her hand is swollen, remains swollen.'

(43b) *eelnoots* (transitional)
∅ + *le* + *noots*
M + CL + swell + TRNS
'Her foot swelled up.'

(43c) *eeghelnustl* (progressive)
ghe + *le* + *nustl*
M + CL + swell + PROG
'It is swelling up.'

4.3. Postaspectual derivations

I am using the term *postaspectual derivation* to refer to four

specific derivation types: conative, inceptive, errative, and negative.
This group of derivation types has characteristics in common both
with superaspect and with aspect-dependent derivational strings.
Like aspect-dependent derivational strings, the postaspectual derivations always choose or trigger the use of specific mode prefixes and
may require a specified combination of other prefixes as well. They
are unlike the aspect-dependent derivational strings, however, and
more like superaspect in their productivity and range. Like the superaspects, postaspectual derivations can, in general, be added onto
any regular aspectual derivation. Remember that aspect-dependent
derivational strings are mutually exclusive (i.e., they may not co-
occur with one another); the postaspectual derivations may occur
with an aspect-dependent derivational string and are thus, by definition, not a member of that class.[9] In contrast with the superaspects, however, they do not have a regular stem variation pattern
associated with them, though they may produce some stem changes
in some cases.

Like the superaspects, the postaspectual derivations form a
cohesive group on semantic grounds as well: all four have irrealis
interpretations. The conative conveys the notion of trying to do
something (but not actually doing it); the inceptive expresses the
beginning of a state or activity (but not its accomplishment); the
errative denotes the incorrect accomplishment of a state or activity;
and the negative negates the proposition of a state or activity.

4.3.1. Conative

The conative has the meaning 'trying, attempting to V'. The
derivation involves the addition of oo- and ne- conjunct prefixes
plus $\emptyset$- imperfective and ne- perfective prefixes. The conative stem
set may be identical to that of the underlying aspect, or may differ
from it in unpredictable ways. The following examples show the
conative overlaid on several regular aspectual derivations.

(44a) *k'edeetl'onh* ($\emptyset$ momentaneous)
       k'e   + *de* + $\emptyset$ + $\emptyset$ + *tl'onh*
       INDF O + T   + M + CL + hear + MOM
       'S/he heard something.'

9. Postaspectual strings may also occur with one another and so truly
constitute a different class, rather than a different set of the same class,
from the aspect-dependent derivational strings.

(44b) *k'oodeneetl'on'* (conative)

k'e	+ *oo*	+ *de*	+ *ne*	+ ∅	+ ∅	+ *tl'on'*
INDF O	+ CONA	+ T	+ CONA	+ M	+ CL	+ hear + CONA

'S/he is trying to hear something; s/he's listening for something.'

(45a) *noyegheełkooł* (with *no# gh* MOM 'down')

no	# *ye*	+ *ghe*	+ *ł*	+ *kooł*
DS	# 3SG O	+ M	+ CL	+ CLASSIF: flexible + MOM

'S/he took it (flag) down.'

(45b) *noyoonaaneełkooł* (conative)

no	# *ye*	+ *oo+ne*	+ *ne*	+ *ł*	+ *kooł*
DS	# 3SG O	+ CONA	+ M	+ CL	+ CLASSIF: flexible + CONA

'S/he was trying to take it (flag) down.'

(46a) *deyeetlkeł* (conclusive)

de	+ *e*	# *ye*	+ *le*	+ *ł*	+ *keł*
REFL P	+ PP	# 3SG O	+ M	+ CL	+ tie + CNCL

'S/he tied a knot in it.'

(46b) *deyooneełkaał* (conative)

de	+ *e*	# *ye*	+ *oo+ne*	+ ∅	+ *ł*	+ *kaał*
REFL P	+ PP	# 3SG O	+ CONA	+ M	+ CL	+ tie + CONA

'S/he is trying to tie a knot in it.'

(47a) *yedegheełlaatl* (durative)

ye	+ *de*	+ *ghe*	+ *ł*	+ *tlaatl*
3SG O	+ G	+ M	+ CL	+ chop + DUR

'S/he was splitting it (wood).'

(47b) *yoodeneełtlaał* (conative)

ye	+ *oo*	+ *de*	+ *ne*	+ ∅	+ *ł*	+ *tlaał*
3SG O	+ CONA	+ G	+ CONA	+ M	+ CL	+ chop + CONA

'S/he's trying to split it (wood).'

The 'trying to' meaning of the conative may, with verbs with nonanimate or abstract subjects, have an inchoative sense:

(48) *oonaaneełkon'*

oo+ne	+ *ne*	+ *ł*	+ *kon'*
CONA	+ M	+ CL	+ rain + DUR CONA

'It is trying to rain; it looks like rain and a few drops have fallen but the storm has not begun.'

The conative is possible, though, with the inceptive postaspectual derivation in agentive derivatives. Notice in the following example that the combination of inceptive plus conative appears with the *le-*perfective prefix and stem required by the inceptive:

(49) *k'ootenaalhonh*
      k'e   + *oo*   + *te*   + *ne*   + *le* + ∅   + *onh*
      INDF O + CONA + INCP + CONA + M   + CL + eat + INCP
      'S/he started to try to eat.'

The conative can never co-occur with the optative, progressive, errative, consecutive, or semelfactive. Its occurrence with other aspects and superaspects varies according to theme and root. The conative sometimes has a separate stem set from that of the aspect it supplements and sometimes takes the same stems as that aspect. Its stems, however, are rarely, if ever, a distinct set in the way that superaspects have a completely different and unique stem set.

4.3.2. Inceptive

The inceptive is used to refer to the inception of an activity, event, or state. Derivatives always require an *le-* perfective mode prefix and perfective stem, but they may have a perfective or imperfective sense.

(50a) *gheełkon'* (durative)
      ghe + *ł*   + *kon'*
      M   + CL   + rain + DUR
      'It was raining.'

(50b) *taatlkon'* (inceptive)
      te   + *le* + *ł*   + *kon'*
      INCP + M   + CL   + rain + DUR
      'It started to rain.'

(51a) *ledo* (neuter)
      le + ∅   + *do*
      M   + CL   + SG, DU sit + NEU IMPF
      'S/he sits, stays.'

(51b) *taaldo'* (inceptive)
      te   + *le* + ∅   + *do'*
      INCP + M   + CL   + SG, DU sit + NEU PERF
      'S/he is starting to stay, sit.'

(51c) *naaldo* (*l* momentaneous)
      ne + *le* + ∅   + *do*
      T   + M   + CL   + SG, DU sit + MOM
      'S/he sat down.'

(52a) *no'eedeyo* (*n* momentaneous)

    no   # *ne* + *de* + *yo*

    ITER # M   + CL + SG go + MOM

    'S/he went home; s/he walked back.'

(52b) *notaałeyo* (inceptive)

    no   # *te*   + *le* + *de* + *yo*

    ITER # INCP + M + CL + SG go + MOM

    'S/he started back home.'

(53a) *nek'edlukk* (durative)

    ne # *k'e* + ∅   + ∅   + *dlukk*

    T   # T   + M + CL + laugh + DUR

    'S/he is laughing.'

(53b) *nek'etaaldlukk* (inceptive)

    ne # *k'e* + *te*   + *le* + ∅   + *dlukk*

    T   # T   + INCP + M + CL + laugh + DUR

    'S/he started laughing.'

Because the transitional is also used to refer to entrance into a state, there is some overlap in meaning between the inceptive and the transitional in neuter verb themes. In general, though, the inceptive refers to the gradual, beginning stages of the state, while the transitional is used to express the sudden transition into the state. Compare the following examples:

(54a) *lekk'tł* (∅ neuter)

    ∅ + *le*   + *kk'tł*

    M + CL + white + NEU

    'It is white.'

(54b) *taadlekk'tł* (inceptive)

    te   + *le* + *le*   + *kk'tł*

    INCP + M + CL + white + NEU

    'It is starting to be white; it is somewhat white.'

(54c) *eedekk'otl* (transitional)

    ∅ + *de* + *kk'otl*

    M + CL + white + TRNS

    'It became white, faded.'

(55a) *yaadedneyh* (∅ neuter)

    ye   + *aa* # *de* + ∅ + *de* + *neyh*

    3SG P + PP # T   + M + CL + feel + NEU

    'It is hurting him.'

(55b) *yaanodetaałeneyh* (inceptive)

ye	+ aa	# no	# de	+ te		+ le	+ de	+ neyh
3SG P	+ PP	# ITER	# T	+ INCP		+ M	+ CL	+ feel + NEU

'It starts hurting him again (i.e., it's been hurting on and off and now it's starting to hurt again).'

(55c) *yaanodaałeneek* (*l* transitional)

ye	+ aa	# no	# de	+ le	+ de	+ neek
3SG P	+ PP	# ITER	# T	+ M	+ CL	+ feel + TRNS

'It starts hurting him again (i.e., the pain was gone and now, all of a sudden, it's really hurting again).'

4.3.3. Errative

Although there are several aspect-dependent derivational prefix strings with semantic and formal characteristics in common with the errative, the errative itself, like the other postaspectual derivations, is not tied to any particular mode prefix or aspect. The errative has the meaning of doing the activity referred to by the verb excessively or incorrectly and being unable to stop or escape from the consequences. It introduces a *ne-* conjunct prefix plus ∅ - imperfective and *le-* perfective prefixes plus the classifier voicing phenomenon called D-effect. Most of the aspect-dependent derivational strings that share with the errative the meaning of doing something wrong or overdoing something also trigger D-effect. The errative, however, may occur along with aspect-dependent derivational strings. Compare the following examples with the aspect-dependent derivational prefix string *taa#* plus *n* momentaneous, 'submerged':

(56a) *taak'eneełkooł* (with *taa#* *n* MOM 'submerged')

taa	# k'e	+ ne	+ ł	+ kooł
DS	# INDF O	+ M	+ CL	+ CLASSIF: flexible + MOM

'S/he set something (fishnet) in the water.'

(56b) *taak'enaadlekooł* (errative)

taa	# k'e	+ ne	+ le	+ le	+ kooł
DS	# INDF O	+ ERR	+ M	+ CL	+ CLASSIF: flexible + MOM

'S/he set something (fishnet) in the water at the wrong time or place (thereby causing it to have bad luck).'

The following examples illustrate the errative with other aspects:

(57a) *k'egheehonh* (durative)

k'e	+ ghe	+ ∅	+ honh
INDF O	+ M	+ CL	+ eat + DUR

'S/he ate something.'

(57b) *k'enaałdon'* (errative)
    k'e   *+ ne*   *+ le* *+ de* *+ on'*
    INDF O + ERR + M + CL + eat + ERR
    'S/he overate.'

(58a) *gheetsaah* (durative)
    ghe *+ ∅* *+ tsaah*
    M   + CL + cry + DUR
    'S/he cried.'

(58b) *naałetsaah* (errative)
    ne *+ le* *+ de* *+ tsaah*
    ERR + M + CL + cry + DUR
    'S/he cried really hard.'

(59a) *gheedo'* (neuter)
    ghe *+ ∅* *+ do'*
    M   + CL + SG, DU sit + NEU
    'S/he was sitting, staying.'

(59b) *naaledo'* (errative)
    ne *+ le* *+ de* *+ do'*
    ERR + M + CL + SG, DU sit + NEU
    'S/he started staying and couldn't make her/himself leave.'

As illustrated by example (57), the errative occasionally has a separate stem set from that of the aspect with which it is occurring.

4.3.4. Negative

Although the negative is not, strictly speaking, an aspectual derivation, it does require the use of a distinct set of stem alternates and so requires some discussion. The prefix morphology associated with the negative in Koyukon is particularly varied. In perfective verbs the prefix *ee-* is used in place of the affirmative perfective prefixes. In imperfective verbs, an *ł-* prefix is used in third person singular and plural and in the first person plural; *le-* is used elsewhere. I will leave a complete description of the variation for later researchers and will concentrate here on the stem variation involved in negative derivations.

The negative in Koyukon has the meaning typically associated with the negative in most languages (i.e., a negation of the affirmative assertion). It is marked by the negative *-aa* suffix with concomitant voicing of final consonant(s) or insertion of glottal stop after open stems. In the optative, the suffix is deleted (after producing the voicing) and the verb is followed by the prohibitive enclitic *yu*.

It is only in the perfective, however, that the stem set varies substantially from that of its corresponding affirmative. The durative and momentaneous perfective negative stems are most often identical to the progressive stem (i.e., with vowel ablaut or shortening and -*ł* suffix). Compare the following stem sets from the verbs -*kon* 'rain' and -*yotl* 'snow', and the subsequent examples:

-kon 'rain'

	IMPF	PERF	FUT	OPT
DUR	konh	kon'	kon'	kon'
DUR NEG	konaa	keelaa	konaa	kon yu
PROG	keeł			

-yotl 'snow'

	IMPF	PERF	FUT	OPT
DUR	yoł	yotl	yoł	yoł
DUR NEG	yolaa	yułdlaa	yolaa	yol yu
PROG	yułtl			

(60a) *ełkonh*
    ø + ł   + konh
    M + CL + rain + DUR IMPF
    'It's raining.'

(60b) *etlkonaa*
    le + ł   + konaa
    M + CL + rain + DUR NEG IMPF
    'It isn't raining.'

(61a) *gheełkon'*
    ghe + ł   + kon'
    M   + CL + rain + DUR PERF
    'It rained.'

(61b) *eełkeelaa*
    ee + ł   + keelaa
    M + CL + rain + DUR NEG PERF
    'It didn't rain.'

(62a) *gheełyotl*
    ghe + ł   + yotl
    M   + CL + snow + DUR PERF
    'It snowed.'

(62b) *eełyułdlaa*
  ee + ł + yułdlaa
  M + CL + snow + DUR NEG PERF
  'It didn't snow.'

4.4. Determining Koyukon aspect

Determining the aspect of a particular verb form in Koyukon is not always a trivial matter. As the preceding discussion makes clear, a single morpheme or a discrete and distinct unit of meaning corresponding to each separate aspect cannot be isolated. There is instead a multiplicity of morphological patterns and semantic characterizations associated with each aspect. Some homophony also acts to conflate the morphological correlates of separate aspects, and there can be compounding of aspects with superaspects, which obscures the derivational history of a particular form. Deciding what aspectual label is appropriate for a given form, then, is always a more complicated task than simply finding a form with affix X and labeling it, therefore, aspect X.

As demonstrated in chapter 3 (section 3.2), it is often possible to determine what aspect a particular verb form reflects by looking at any one of the four criteria already discussed: (1) stem set variation (i.e., the stem shape used for each of the four modes in each of the fifteen aspects and four superaspects), (2) prefix morphology (i.e., mode and other derivational prefixes), (3) distributional potential, and (4) aspectual meaning. For most verbs, taking suffixal and prefixal morphology, semantics, and distribution as a four-part measure allows the analyst to determine the aspect of a particular form. Because of the homophony and the semantic and distributional overlap inevitable in such a complicated aspectual system, however, there are a certain number of cases in which aspect is more difficult to determine. In those cases, each of the four criteria outlined above must be measured not by pluses and minuses, but rather as a match to an established central member of the category in question.

Category membership in morphosyntax and semantics is generally determined by one of two methods: (1) an objective test based on the presence or absence of certain criterial attributes requisite for membership, or (2) a prototype approach (e.g., Rosch 1977; Lakoff 1987) in which a token is assigned to a category based on how closely it matches a central member or another member similarly linked to the core token of that category. Although these two methods have been considered mutually exclusive, determination of the aspectual category of many Koyukon verbs actually requires a combination of the two. It is important to note that one of the four criteria outlined above is more critical to the determination than another; morphology and semantics are, in fact, inseparable in the description of aspect. This section is intended as an illustration of the process of determining aspectual category using the examples of the continuative, persistive, and repetitive aspects along with the distributive superaspect, categories whose formal and semantic domains are often indistinct.

Before proceding to these examples, it may be helpful to re-examine some simpler instances of identifying Koyukon aspectual category. We begin, then, by looking again at the momentaneous.

4.4.1. The momentaneous

Remember that verbs are considered to be of a particular aspect if they have the stem set variation (i.e., the pattern of stem shapes for each mode) associated with that aspect. As detailed in chapter 3 (section 3.2.3), the momentaneous aspect in Koyukon is associated with the following stem sets:

A. Most open and sonorant-final roots have an imperfective stem with -*yh* suffix, a perfective stem with -*nh* suffix, a future stem with -*ł* suffix, and optative stem also with -*ł* or -*'* suffix. The following momentaneous verbs with the root -*baa* 'swim' illustrate the stem set pattern:

(63a) *eebaayh*
     ne + ∅   + *baayh*
     M + CL + swim + IMPF
     'S/he arrives swimming.'

(63b) *neebaanh*
     ne + **ŋ* + ∅   + *baanh*
     M + M + CL + swim + PERF
     'S/he arrived swimming.'

(63c) *tobaał*
     te + *ghe* + ∅   + *baał*
     M + M   + CL + swim + FUT
     'S/he will arrive swimming.'

(63d) *ghubaał*
     ghe + *oo* + ∅   + *baał*
     M   + M + CL + swim + OPT
     'S/he should arrive swimming.'

B. Closed roots have spirantized final consonants in the imperfective and optative. The perfective stem is unspirantized. Roots with reduced vowels show vowel lengthening in those stems. The future stem has a *-l* suffix; this future suffix produces vowel reduction in roots with full vowels. The following examples illustrate typical momentaneous stems sets from closed roots:

ts'oots 'dry up'
  ts'oos   ts'oots   ts'ustl   ts'oos

bets 'be wide'
  bees   bets   bestl   bees

These stem set patterns are diagnostic for the momentaneous.

Prefixal components (i.e., the set of mode prefixes—and often, adverbial disjunct prefixes as well) associated with each aspect, constitute the second morphological criterion for determining aspect. For example, the *ne-* perfective and imperfective mode prefixes in (63a) and (63b) are diagnostic of the momentaneous. Although momentaneous stem sets may appear with other mode prefixes, no other aspect appears with *ne-* as the mode prefix in both the imperfective and perfective.

The semantic criterion also establishes the examples in (63) as momentaneous: no other aspect has the meaning of 'arriving'. The distribution criterion is perhaps the weakest of the four in this particular instance. The momentaneous is generally found in verbs that can permit other aspectual derivations used to describe the deliberate physical activity of a human or animal involving movement from one locus to another. The distribution of the momentaneous, however, is by far the broadest and most free of any aspect.

Momentaneous forms, like those in (63) above, then, can be confused with no other aspect because of their unique combination of stem set, prefix morphology, and meaning.

4.4.2. Aspects with overlapping form and meaning

Most Koyukon verbs, like the momentaneous ones just illustrated, can be labeled as being of a given aspect by going through this checklist of morphological, semantic, and distributional characteristics. However, in some cases, like those in examples (64) and (65), one finds oneself engaged in a more complex process. Describing that process may provide some insight into the organization of the semantics of the Koyukon aspectual system.

(64) *huntlaadeltleyh*
    hʉ + *e*   + *ne* # *tlaa* # *de* + Ø + *le* + *tleyh*
    P   + PP + DS # head # T + M + CL + place sticklike
    'S/he is peeking at the place; s/he is spying on them.' Lit. 'S/he is
    repeatedly putting her/his head here and there, or back and forth.'

(65) *netleekelts'eh*
    ne # *tleeke*   # Ø + *le* + *ts'eh*
    DS # top of head # M + CL + wobble
    'It (button, nut, screw) is attached, tied, sewed, bolted loosely and
    wobbles, dangles.'

Examples (64) and (65) each have a form and meaning consistent
with any of three aspects—the persistive, repetitive, and continuative—and with one superaspect, the distributive.

4.4.3. The persistive

As detailed in chapter 3 (section 3.2.6), the persistive aspect is
used to describe repeated back and forth movement, usually movement performed against some restraint so that one portion of the
subject remains fixed in position. The persistive requires a Ø imperfective or *ghe-* perfective mode prefix. The following examples are
typical:

(66a) *dek'endebes*
    de   + *e* # *k'e* + *ne* + Ø + *de* + *bes*
    INDT + PP # T   + M   + CL + flutter + PERS
    'It (small bird, butterfly) is trying to fly but is caught, restrained.'

(66b) *he'etaah*
    hʉ   + *e* # Ø + Ø + *taah*
    AREA + PP # M   + CL   + SG, DU lies down + PERS
    'S/he is thrashing around in her/his sleep.'

(66c) *nedegetuts*
    ne# *de* + Ø + *s*   + *le* + *tuts*
    DS# T   + M   + 1SG S + CL + poke + PERS
    'I am poking around with a pole.'

Distributionally, persistive verbs are most often found as derivatives of motion themes, and such derivatives frequently have the
aspect-dependent derivational prefix string (132):

(67)   *ne* # D + PERS
       'back and forth repeatedly'

The persistive shows the following stem set variation: Open roots
have an *-h* suffix and retain their full vowel. Sonorant-closed roots
have a lengthened vowel and *-h* suffix. Closed roots have a reduced
vowel and spirantized final in all modes.

ken 'force' (persistive)
   keeh   *keeh*   *keeh*   *keeh*

daatl 'PL go' (persistive)
   deł   *deł*   *deł*   *deł*

daakk 'PL experience events' (persistive)
   deh   *deh*   *deh*   *deh*

4.4.4. The repetitive

Examples (64) and (65) are compatible with the description of
the persistive, but they are also much like the repetitive derivations
described in chapter 3 (section 3.2.10). The repetitive also requires
∅- imperfective or *ghe-* perfective mode prefixes. As with the persistive, repetitive verbs are found as derivatives of motion themes
and refer to repeated movement:

(68a) *deets'eh*
       de + ∅ + ∅ + *ts'eh*
       T + M + CL + open mouth + REP
       'S/he opens her/his mouth repeatedly (as a person trying to catch
       her/his breath or a fish out of water).'

(68b) *tl'eeyh ehʉnłtoyh*
       tl'eeyh *e* # *hʉ* + *ne* + ∅ + *ł* + *toyh*
       mosquito PP # T + T + M + CL + bother + REP
       'S/he is being annoyed by mosquitoes.'

Repetitive stem sets are as follows: open and sonorant-closed
roots have stems with *-yh* suffix in the imperfective and *-k* suffix in
the perfective, optative, and future. Closed roots have unvaried
stem sets with reduced vowel and a suffix that appears as *-yh* before root-final *-tl*, and as spirantization with other root-final consonants. Root-final *-t* may be replaced by *-k*. The following sets exem-
plify this pattern.

lo/laa 'CLASSIF: plural objects' (repetitive)
   laayh   *laak*   *laak*   *laak*

daatl 'PL go' (repetitive)
  deyhtl   *deyhtl*   *deyhtl*   *deyhtl*

daakk 'PL experience events' (repetitive)
  deh   *deh*   *deh*   *deh*

tset 'move hands quickly' (repetitive)
  tsek   *tsek*   *tsek*   *tsek*

Note that repetitive stems drawn from roots closed with a nonalveolar final are identical to persistive stems. It is with open roots that the distinction can be most clearly seen, as in the derivatives of *-'o* 'classificatory compact object' shown in the following examples.

(69) *yets'e neloghet'oh*
      ye   + ts'e ne + lo   # ghe + de   + 'oh
      3SG P + PP   DS + hand # M   + CL   + CLASSIF: compact + PERS
      'S/he had been waving at him/her.'

(70) *yeyeghee'ok*
      ye # ye   + ghe + ∅   + 'ok
      DS # 3SG O + M   + CL + CLASSIF. compact + REP
      'S/he raised it repeatedly, lifted it up and down.'

4.4.5. The continuative and distributive

Examples (64) and (65) are derivatives of reduced-vowel (nonalveolar-) closed roots. They also both have ∅ - imperfective mode prefixes and refer to a repeated back and forth movement. They are therefore, possible examples of either the repetitive or the persistive aspect. Continuative derivatives, however, and distributive derivatives also match this description. Compare examples of the continuative in (71) with the distributive in (72).

(71a) *hutugh k'edaaltset*
       he   + tugh k'e   + de   + le   + ∅   + tset
       3PL P + PP   INDF + T   + M   + CL + move hands quickly +
       CONT
       'S/he distributed or served something to them quickly.'

(71b) *neyenaatltset*
       ne # ye   + ne   + le   + l   + tset
       DS # 3SG O + DS   + M   + CL + move hands quickly + CONT
       'S/he gestured, signaled to her/him, made the sign of the cross over her/him.'

(71c) *hute nedledzets*
  he + te　　*ne # le + le + dzets*
  3PL P + PP　DS # M　+ CL　+ punch + CONT
  'S/he was taking punches among them; s/he swung at them.'

(72a) *yeghun'etltsot*
  ye 　+ ghu + ne # le + l 　+ tsot
  3SG P + PP　　+ DS # M + CL + cut + DIST
  'S/he cut holes here and there in it (hide—while skinning it hastily).'

(72b) *haanhetltset*
  hu 　+ aa + ne # he　　+ le + l 　+ tset
  AREA + PP + DS # 3PL S + M + CL + move hands quickly + DIST
  'They braced themselves quickly with their hands.'

(72c) *hu'unyeldaah*
  hu 　+ e + ne # ye　　+ ∅ + l 　+ daah
  AREA + PP + DS # 3SG O + M + CL + PL experience events +
  DIST
  'It (chunks of ice) comes up in many places.'

Distributionally, the continuative and distributive, like the persistive and repetitive, are found as derivatives of motion themes,
though the distributive, as a superaspect, is also commonly found in
derivatives of neuter themes and elsewhere.

Continuative and distributive stem sets are identical in closed
roots. In both, closed roots with full vowels retain the full vowel in
all modes and have spirantized finals in the imperfective, future,
and optative. Closed roots with reduced vowels have unsuffixed,
unvaried stem sets. The examples below show typical stem sets for
both the continuative and the distributive.

> *daatl* 'PL go' (continuative and distributive)
> 　*daal*　　*daatl*　　*daal*　　*daal*

> *t'ukk* 'SG flies' (continuative and distributive)
> 　*t'ukk*　　*t'ukk*　　*t'ukk*　　*t'ukk*

Continuative stems derived from nasal-final roots are usually unsuffixed and unvaried. Distributive stems from nasal-final roots are
more irregular, with variation between unsuffixed, unvaried stem
sets as in the continuative, and sets with lengthening, ablaut, or
glottal suffix. It is only in open roots that a clear distinction can be
seen between the two aspects. In these cases, both aspects usually

have perfective stems with an *-nh* suffix, but the continuative has
an unsuffixed imperfective stem and future and optative stems with
-l suffix. The distributive, on the other hand, always has a glottal
suffix on the imperfective stem. Future and optative stems have
either a glottal or an *-l* suffix. Compare the continuative stem set
and example in (73) with the distributive set and example in (74).

(73a) *baa* 'swim' (continuative)
     baa   *baanh*   *baal*   *baal*

(73b) *netobaal*
   ne # te + ghe + ∅ + baal
   DS # M   + M   + CL + swim + CONT
   'S/he will swim to there and back.'

(74a) *baa* 'swim' (distributive)
     baa'   *baanh*   *baa'*   *baa'*

(74b) *nu'untobaa'*
   no # ne + te + ghe + ∅ + baa'
   DS # DS + M + M   + CL + swim + DIST
   'S/he will swim across here and there.'

The distributive always occurs with a disjunct prefix *ne#*, and
the continuative frequently occurs with aspect-dependent derivational prefix strings, as in (75):

(75) *ne#* continuative 'go and come back, make a round trip'

Note that examples (64) and (65) both have the disjunct prefix *ne#*.
  Continuative derivatives, then, can be identical with distributive derivatives. Compare the forms of examples (76) and (77):

(76) *nehootltseenh* (distributive)
   ne # hu   + le + l + tseenh
   DS # AREA + M + CL + make + DIST
   'S/he built tunnels this way and that.'

(77) *nehootl-'enh* (continuative)
   ne # hu   + le + l + 'enh
   DS # AREA + M + CL + see + CONT
   'S/he saw something unexplained happen; s/he saw a sudden
   apparition.'

In form, the prefix complex and stem suffixation of (76) and (77) are

identical. Only by knowing the full stem sets can we determine that
(76) is distributive and (77) is continuative. Although both are used
to refer to a 'back and forth', 'here and there' movement, examining
many derivatives of the two aspects allows us to distinguish a semantic difference. A smoothness and continuity of zigzag motion is
found to be decisive for thinking of verbs as continuative. In those
cases where the distributive can be seen as a superaspectual derivation on morphological grounds (i.e., where we can be certain that
the form is distributive rather than anything else), this smoothness
is absent. Note that native-speaker intuition about the primacy of
smooth zigzag motion over the fact of the activity moving from one
locale to another is critical here. It is sometimes a subtle distinction,
though; continuative and distributive forms can be quite similar.

The form and semantic character of continuative and persistive
derivatives may also be extremely similar. Recall that the persistive
also often occurs with the *ne#* disjunct prefix in forms with the derivational string cited in (67). Compare example (78) to example
(77).

(78)   *bets'e neholtsee'* (persistive)
       be   + ts'e   ne   # hu   + ghe   + le   + tsee'
       3SG P + PP   DS   # AREA   + M   + CL   + poltergeist acts + PERS
       'Unexplained things were appearing to her/him.'

As examples (77) and (78) suggest, the continuative and distributive differ from the persistive and repetitive in that they take an
le- perfective mode prefix while persistive and repetitive take *ghe-*
perfective prefixes.

4.4.6. Determining the aspect of problem cases

Returning to examples (64) and (65), we can see that they could
conceivably be examples of any of the four aspects discussed
here.[10] In order to narrow it down to a choice between the *ghe-*

10. A fifth aspect, the consecutive, also refers to repeated activity.
Compare the following consecutive example in (i) with the repetitive example in (ii):

(i)   *nelaan ghee'utl*
       nelaan   ghe   + ∅   + 'utl
       meat   M   + CL   + chew + CONS
       'S/he bit the meat repeatedly.'

perfective repetitive or persistive and the *le-* perfective distributive
or continuative, we examine the perfective forms in (64a) and (65a)
to discover that both have a *ghe-* perfective mode prefix.

(64a) *huntlaadoltleyh*

hu	+ *e*	+ *ne*	# *tlaa*	# *de*	+ *ghe*	+ *le*	+ *tleyh*
P	+ PP	+ DS	# head	# T	+ M	+ CL	+ place sticklike

'S/he was peeking at the place; s/he was spying on them.'

(65a) *netleekghelts'eh*

ne	+ *tleeke*	# *ghe*	+ *le*	+ *ts'eh*
DS	+ top of head	# M	+ CL	+ wobble

'It (button, nut, screw) was attached, tied, sewed, bolted loosely and
wobbled, dangled.'

Our choices are thus reduced to the persistive or the repetitive.
In order to decide between the two, we must examine as many examples as possible of each aspect to determine a pattern of form and
meaning particular to each. The process becomes, at this point, a
pattern-matching exercise. Because examples (64) and (65) both
have a *ne#* disjunct prefix, we look for other examples with that
prefix and find the following in (79):

(79a) *nedelggaat*

ne	# *de*	+ ∅	+ *le*	+ *ggaat*
DS	# DS	+ M	+ CL	+ poke

'It (mosquito) is poking around.'

(79b) *nededeghel*

ne	# *de*	+ ∅	+ *de*	+ *ghel*
DS	# DS	+ M	+ CL	+ flat object moves

'It (canoe) is tippy.'

(ii) *dzaah gheekk'usk*

dzaah	*ghe*	+ ∅	+ *kk'usk*
gum	M	+ CL	+ chew + REP

'S/he was chewing gum.'

These two aspects are, however, rarely, if ever, used in derived forms of the
same theme. The consecutive is usually found with verb themes that refer
to punctual activities like cutting, which are primarily expressed with the
semelfactive aspect, indicating a single abrupt action. Distributionally,
then, the consecutive is disqualified as a possible aspectual label for examples (64) and (65).

(79c) *nededeghʉł*
ne # de + ∅ + de + ghʉł
DS # G + M + CL + sticklike object moves
'It (piece of wood) moves back and forth (because it is loosely attached to the sawhorse).'

(79d) *nedeltset*
ne # de + ∅ + le + tset
DS # DS + M + CL + move hands
'S/he is quickly moving her/his hands here and there, feeling around.'

(79e) *nedelleyh*
ne # de + le + leyh
DS # DS + CL + compact object moves
'It (loose tooth) is wobbling.'

(79f) *nedetluh*
ne # ∅ + de + tluh
DS # M + CL + CLASSIF: mushy object
'It (jello) is wobbling.'

The semantic and morphological similarity between (64), (65), and the examples in (79) persuades us that all must be derivatives of the same aspect. The semantic congruence of examples (79c) and (79e) and example (65), in particular, suggests that the notion of wobbling, of moving back and forth with one end attached, is the salient semantic principle here, and that these forms should all be labeled persistive.

Example (79d) is the critical example: it is the only one that derives from a root of the shape that provides morphological evidence. Recall that repetitive stems from the root *-tset* have a final *-k*, as shown above, while persistive stems from roots of that shape are unvaried and unsuffixed. Example (79d) has such an unsuffixed shape and thus must be persistive rather than repetitive. We can feel confident, therefore, in calling all the forms in (79) and the examples in (64) and (65) persistive as well.

4.4.7. Summary

In the course of making a final determination of the aspects of examples (64) and (65), checking morphology and semantics of the two forms was combined with a procedure of matching them to morphologically and semantically similar examples that could potentially provide the critical evidence for their being derivatives of one aspect or another.

The analyst begins by examining stem sets and prefixes. Especially in those cases where the suffixal and prefixal morphology of two aspects are homophonous, as in distributive and continuative stems from closed roots, one must then look to some semantic characterization defined for each aspect. Because the semantic characterizations may also overlap somewhat, other possible aspectual derivations for the stem must be checked. When those distributional characteristics overlap as well (or when themes are unproductive), one must adopt the more complicated process described above, a process that involves finding a pattern of form and meaning correlates that matches the verb in question until a case is found that does have clear motivation for assigning to it an aspectual label.

Although this combination of a checklist approach with a pattern matching, or prototype construction, procedure is a system I have developed for language analysis—and specifically for lexicographic work—I believe it sheds considerable light on the semantic principles underlying the extremely complex aspectual system of Koyukon. Further, it demonstrates the importance of both morphophonological cues and semantic prototypes in comprehension and suggests the possibility that some combination of criterial attributes and semantic prototype structures are involved in the cognitive organization of language and in language production as well.

5
Verb Theme Categories

According to Carlota Smith, "speakers associate an actual situation with an idealized situation type, by using the linguistic forms associated with a given situation type" (1983:496). In Koyukon, speakers seem to associate a particular situation with a certain *set* of aspects. Of that set of aspects, one aspect or the contrast between two or more aspects appears to be primary. For example, 'walking', a motion verb, is associated with the set of aspects of which the momentaneous is primary. The set also includes the continuative, perambulative, and others listed in table 3.5. 'Striking', on the other hand, is generally associated with a set of aspects in which a contrast between doing that action once, abruptly (semelfactive) is contrasted with doing it repeatedly (consecutive) or at length (durative). These groupings of aspects recur as fixed sets with different verb themes; the sets are called aspectual verb theme categories.

Athabaskan verb theme categories have been described in Kari (1979), where the details of this framework were discussed for Ahtna, another Alaskan Athabaskan language. Kari demonstrated how verb themes, composed of root, classifier, a marker for transitivity, and thematic prefixes, can be grouped into categories on the basis of shared formal and semantic characteristics. Recall from the introductory sketch of Koyukon in chapter 1 that the verb theme is an "abstract" lexical unit composed of the verb root and prefixes occurring in all actual derivatives. I call the theme abstract because it never occurs as a spoken form without further derivational or inflectional modification. I call it a lexical unit because it is associated with a unique meaning not predictable from its constituents and not attributable to the later derivational and inflectional modification. According to Kari, "Most Ahtna verb themes can be assigned to broad but definable semantic categories." Those verb theme categories are "predictive of many of the derivations that can apply to a theme to form verb bases" (1979:31).

The situation in Koyukon is quite similar to that of Ahtna. There are three neuter theme categories and four major active theme categories: a motion category and three activity categories.

As outlined in chapter 1, the criteria for deciding the category membership of a given theme in Koyukon are based on aspectual derivational potential. If a verb theme has derivatives that are of a particular set of aspects, we say it is of a particular category. For example, the three activity theme categories are: (1) operative, (2) conversive, and (3) successive. The diagnostic aspects for the three activity categories are: (1) durative, used to describe processes, (2) conclusive, used to describe telic activities; and (3) semelfactive, used to describe abrupt single instances of an activity, paired with the consecutive, which refers to repeated single instances of an activity.

If a theme has durative derivatives but none of the other activity aspects, we say it belongs to the operative category. If a theme has conclusive and durative derivatives, but not semelfactive or consecutive ones, we say it belongs to the conversive theme category. Finally, if a theme has semelfactive and consecutive derivatives, we assign it to the successive category. Table 5.1 illustrates the aspectual derivations possible for each category.

The table also shows that all three activity categories permit durative and momentaneous derivatives. If a theme has momentaneous derivatives and derivatives of other motion aspects (as outlined in table 3.5), but none of the activity aspects, we say it is a member of the motion category.

Operative themes, then, generally refer to activities that take place over a period of time or to activities done as a means of employment (e.g., 'to pick berries', 'to pluck feathers', 'to cry', 'to rain'). Conversive verb themes generally describe actions that result in the creation of a single discrete end product—but which, of course, may be done over a period of time without the goal being achieved, as well (e.g., 'to make a single object', 'to cook', 'to kill a single person or animal', 'to freeze'). Successive themes generally refer to punctual activities such as 'to chop', 'to stab', 'to bite', all of which can be done once (semelfactive), or a series of times (consecu-

Table 5.1. Aspectual Derivations in Each Theme Category

ASPECT	MOTION	OPERATIVE	CONVERSIVE	SUCCESSIVE
		THEME CATEGORY		
SEMELFACTIVE				x
CONSECUTIVE				x
CONCLUSIVE			x	x
DURATIVE		x	x	x
MOMENTANEOUS	x	x	x	x

tive), or toward a goal (conclusive), or as a habitual activity or process (durative).

Although Kari (1979) characterizes Ahtna verb theme categories on the basis of the perfective mode prefix found in the "primary aspectual string" of each theme category, for Koyukon it seems more illuminating to look at the categories in terms of aspectual oppositions. For instance, rather than seeing the successive as a category with a *ghe-* perfective primary derived form (i.e., its durative bases) as Kari does for Ahtna, the Koyukon successive is more revealingly described as that class of verb themes whose derived forms refer to activities occurring as a single abrupt instance (semelfactive) versus a series of discrete instances (consecutive) versus a duration of those instances from a viewpoint in which they are no longer distinct or discrete (durative). Conclusive themes pair reference to activities focusing on their end products (conclusive) with reference to the process toward that end product (durative). Operative can be seen as a category of themes whose derived verb forms refer to a process (durative) or to a punctual or terminative view of that process (momentaneous). Operative, conversive, and successive, then, represent different categories of activity.

In addition to the four major active theme categories, there are three major neuter theme categories: stative, descriptive, and extension. Each of the three has primary derivatives of the neuter aspect. The distinction between them, therefore, is based not on a diagnostic aspect, but rather on a diagnostic mode plus aspect combination. Themes of the stative category describe the position or existence of an object; its primary, and often its sole, derivatives are of the neuter aspect with an *le-* imperfective or *ghe-* perfective prefix. The descriptive category is comprised of themes whose primary, or sole, derivatives are neuter verbs with ∅ imperfective or *ghe-* perfective prefixes. Descriptive verbs express an object's attributes or qualities—its size, shape, texture, or affective disposition. Extension verbs usually describe an object's linear extension in space; they may have any of the imperfective mode prefixes, including *ne-*.

Verb theme categories, then, are a means of abbreviating or symbolizing the morphological and semantic similarities shared by a group of verb themes.

5.1. Neuter theme categories

In his analysis of Ahtna verb theme categories, Kari (1979) distinguishes five neuter theme categories. Those categories can also be distinguished for Koyukon and, in fact, are used to label theme entries in the *Koyukon Athabaskan Dictionary*, now in progress. On semantic and formal grounds, however, it is better to collapse these five categories into three: (1) stative, which includes what has been previously described as the stative and positional categories; (2) descriptive, which includes what has been termed the descriptive and the dimensional categories; and (3) extension. Each of these three larger categories is distinguished from the others by important semantic and morphological characteristics. Although there are clear subgroups within each, the larger categories do form coherent wholes. To expand on the summary provided at the beginning of the chapter, the stative category is characterized by themes with primary *l* neuter derivatives. Those themes refer to position, existence, or achieved condition (e.g., 'be present', 'be upright', 'be black'). The descriptive category encompasses those themes with primary ∅ neuter derivatives, which refer to attributive, descriptive notions (e.g., 'be chilly', 'be dry', 'be big'). The last neuter theme category, the extension category, is characterized by themes with primary *n* neuter derivatives, but this category most resembles a neuter version of the motion category, permitting derivatives with a wide range of mode-choosing aspect-dependent derivational strings referring to the direction and manner in which an object is positioned in space (as motion themes refer to direction and manner in both time and space). Typical extension themes are '(trail) extends', '(land) slopes', and '(water) flows'.

The *Koyukon Athabaskan Dictionary* contains some 1,621 verb themes,[1] of which 512 are neuter themes.[2] Thirty-eight of the neuter themes are unproductive and uncategorized.[3] I have closely

---

1. The total number of themes was calculated from a computer search of the *Koyukon Athabaskan Dictionary* corpus in the fall of 1989. As work on the dictionary proceeds, new themes are isolated and previously identified themes are occasionally collapsed with other themes. A similar search was made of the corpus some six months earlier, however. A comparison of the two searches reveals that the number of themes in each category has changed only slightly over the months and that the relative proportion has remained constant. The figures presented here, then, must be understood as approximations which represent a fairly accurate picture of the size of each theme category.

2. A complete list of all 1,621 themes arranged according to aspectual theme category is provided in Axelrod (1990).

3. Twenty-three of the uncategorized themes have only transitional derivatives and the remaining fifteen have neuter derivatives. In addition,

examined the remaining 474 in preparing the descriptions of the
neuter theme categories that follow.

5.1.1. Stative themes

I have determined 189 themes in the corpus to be of the stative
category. These are mostly intransitive themes (only twenty-four
are transitive), all of which have primary derivatives that are *l* neuter in aspect. Of the 189 stative themes, only thirty-two can be said
to be of the smaller positional and classificatory stative subcategories distinguished by Kari (1979). Fifteen are of the positional subcategory. Positional themes refer to physical position: sitting, standing, lying down. Those themes always pair with intransitive motion
themes meaning 'assume _____ position', which no other neuter
category theme does. Positional themes include, $\emptyset$ +*do* 'SG, DU (animate) sits, stays, dwells', $\emptyset$ +*(h)aa* 'SG, DU (animate) stands', and
$\emptyset$ +*taa* 'SG, DU (animate) reclines, lies down (prone or supine)'. Examples from the first of these themes are as follows:

(1a)   *kkunkk'aa ledo*
       kkunkk'aa   le + $\emptyset$ + do
       house   M   + CL   + SG, DU sit + NEU
       'S/he is staying home; s/he is house-sitting, baby-sitting.'

(1b)   *yeetldo* (causative)
       ye   + le + ł   + do
       3SG O   + M   + CL   + SG, DU sit + NEU
       'S/he is causing her/him to sit, stay; s/he is keeping her/him.'

(1c)   *dzaanh ledo*
       dzaanh   le + $\emptyset$ + do
       day   M   + CL   + SG, DU sit + NEU
       'It is the day of the solstice (when the day neither lengthens or
       shortens).' Lit. 'The day sits.'

Seventeen of the 189 stative themes are drawn from classificatory verbs (verbs that describe the existence, location, or handling of
objects according to their shape, size, and composition). Classifica-
tory-stative themes refer to such objects in position. For example,
from the classificatory verb *kooł* 'classificatory: flat, flexible object',

---

fifteen themes of the root *yoh/nee/loh/lee* 'happen' have only transitional
derivatives. Those themes, the only ones of this type in the corpus, are
productive enough to warrant being categorized as transitional themes.

we find the following stative theme: $G+l+kool$ 'flat, flexible object is in position'. Derivatives of this theme include:

(2a) *etlkool*
      le + *l*   + *kool*
      M + CL + CLASSIF: flexible + NEU
      'It (flat, flexible object) is there; she (small child, thin person) is there.'

(2b) *yegge hu etlkool*
      yegge hu le + *l*   + *kool*
      down   M + CL + CLASSIF: flexible + NEU
      'It (flag) is at half-mast.' Lit 'It is down low.'

(2c) *taak'etlkool* (with *taa*# *l* NEU 'completely submerged')
      taa # *k'e*   + *le* + *l*   + *kool*
      DS # INDF + M + CL + CLASSIF: flexible + NEU
      'Something (fishnet) is in the water; s/he has something (fishnet) in the water.'

Both positional and classificatory stative themes allow neuter derivatives with aspect-dependent derivational strings requiring other modes. The 157 themes that represent the majority of stative themes, however, admit only transitional and, occasionally, $\emptyset$ neuter derivatives in addition to the primary l neuter derivatives.

It is possible to isolate a semantic core of each of the seven verb theme categories. The stative category themes have a fairly coherent semantic range. Like the positional and classificatory stative themes described above, they describe an animate object, a body part, or an inanimate object maintaining a particular position or location. By extension from that meaning, perhaps, stative themes can also refer to something or someone remaining still, calm, unmoving, or confined. Sixty-five of the 157 themes under discussion refer to possessing or maintaining a certain position or to remaining motionless. Perhaps extending from the meaning of confinement, stative themes can also refer to animates or inanimates being tied, bound, or dressed.[4] Finally, the meaning of being curved, bent, circular, or round—also associated with stative themes—is probably extended from their use in expressing the idea of being bound or

4. Being bare (of foliage or clothing) is also expressed by stative verb themes.

wrapped around. Forty stative themes refer to objects being tied or curved.

The themes *k'e+G+ł+gets* 'be bent', and *de+le+tlookk* '(chinking material) is in position; (human) nestles, settles inconspicuously, unnoticed; (bird) broods, nestles' can be taken as representative of stative themes. Examples include:

(3)   *ten k'ehootlgets*
      ten   k'e   + hu   + le   + ł   + gets
      trail INDF + AREA + M   + CL   + be bent + NEU
      'The trail curves, bends.'

(4)   *daadletlookk*
      de   + le   + le   + tlookk
      T   + M   + CL   + nestle + NEU
      'S/he, it nestled.'

The *l* neuter-primary stative themes are used to imply the achievement of a particular position or condition. Compare that use to descriptive themes, which refer more often to an inherent characteristic or quality of an object or situation. Notice, for example, that stative themes are used to describe dark colors—black, red, and ochre:[5] *de+de+tl'ets* 'be black, dark', *de+de+zen* 'be dark in color, be blackish', *de+G+de+t'aas* 'be black', *de+G+de+kk'es* 'be red, reddish, orange, rust-colored', *hu+de+(ne)+de+tseek* '(area) is ochre-colored; (area) has black marks', *O+de+∅+tseek* 'O is ochre-colored'.

(5)   *daałetl'ets*
      de   + le   + de   + tl'ets
      T   + M   + CL   + be black + NEU
      'It is black, dark in color.'

It is interesting that the colors expressed by stative themes are the ones traditionally used to dye or ornament the skin and hair. Two other colorlike expressions conveyed with stative themes are *de+de+tsetl* 'be bruised, be black and blue from bruising' and *de+de+ggoyh* 'become white-haired, gray-haired', both of which clearly refer to entering a particular state. All stative color themes have a *de-* qualifier prefix and (except for the one transitive theme, 'O is

5. These particular themes allow many neuter derivational strings choosing a variety of mode prefixes.

ochre-colored') a *de-* classifier prefix. Introduced derivationally, the
de- classifier is associated with agentless passive constructions,
among others. That situation is suggestive, though of course by no
means conclusive, of the possibility that these themes once implied
a 'taking on' of the referenced color. Compare the two descriptive
themes referring to red and to ochre: *de+ne+le+deł* 'be red, be blood-
red', which is derived from the noun *deł* 'blood' and *G+∅+tseek* 'be
the color of ochre', the simplest verb theme derived from the noun
root *tseek* 'ochre'. The other descriptive color themes are *G+le+kk'uł*
'be white, off-white, pale, faded', *G+le+baa* 'be off-white, gray', *G+
le+gheen* 'be silver', *G+le+zen* 'be shiny black', and *G+le+tluh* 'be
yellow, tan, brown, olive green, be the color of a smoke-tanned skin'.

5.1.2. Descriptive themes

Of the 506 neuter verb themes, 218 belong to the descriptive
category. Only thirty of the descriptive themes are transitive.

Of the 218 descriptive themes, twenty-five are members of the
dimensional subcategory. Dimensional themes are always marked
for gender and always allow derivatives with one of seven comparative derivational strings—aspect-dependent derivational strings
that require the *gh* neuter. No other neuter theme permits comparative derivatives. The dimensional themes express adjectival qualities such as 'good' and 'bad', 'big' and 'small', 'heavy' and 'light',
'long' and 'short', 'thick' and 'thin', 'strong' and 'weak', and so on.
Fifteen of the twenty-five dimensional themes have a ∅ classifier.[6]
Examples (6) and (7) represent dimensional theme derivatives.

(6a)   *nenaał*
       ne + ∅ + ∅ + naał
       PF + M + CL + be long + NEU
       'It is long; s/he is tall.'

(6b)   *yegholnaał* (with *P+e#ghe+le gh* NEU 'be as V as P')
       ye   + e   # ghe + ghe + le   + naał
       3SG P   + PP # DS   + M   + CL   + be long + NEU
       'It is as long as it; s/he is as tall as s/he is.'

6. With the ∅ imperfective mode prefix, ∅ classifier, and no other
conjunct prefixes, all descriptive verbs have a *ne-* prefix, reflecting the
Proto-Athabaskan palatal nasal sonorant perfective prefix best described in
Krauss and Leer (1981).

(7a) *nedoł*
   ne + ∅ + ∅   + *doł*
   PF + M + CL + be heavy + NEU
   'S/he, it is heavy.'

(7b) *nenonłe degholdoł* (with *P+nonłe##de+ghe+le- gh* NEU 'more than P')
   ne   + *nonłe de* + *ghe* + *ghe* + *le* + *doł*
   2SG P + more DS + DS   + M   + CL + be heavy + NEU
   'S/he is heavier than you are.'

The color terms introduced in the previous section comprise a small subgroup within the dimensional subcategory. These themes all require gender marking and have a *le-* classifier. They differ from other dimensional themes in being able to occur with a wide range of aspect-dependent derivational prefix strings and/or super-aspects that allow derivatives referring to patterns of color. Examples are:

(8a) *lekk'uł*
   ∅ + *le* + *kk'uł*
   M + CL + be white + NEU
   'It is white.'

(8b) *bedone nodlekk'uł* (with *no# l* NEU 'in a circle')
   be   + *done*   *no* # *le* + *le*   + *kk'uł*
   3SG P + mouth DS # M   + CL + be white + NEU
   'It is white around her/his mouth (as with a child who has been
      drinking milk).'

(9a) *letluh*
   ∅ + *le* + *tluh*
   M + CL + be yellow + NEU
   'It is yellow, tan.'

(9b) *no'eeltluh* (with *no# n* NEU 'across')
   no # *ne* + *le*   + *tluh*
   DS # M   + CL + be yellow + NEU
   'There is a line of yellow going across.'

(9c) *nu'undletluh* (with *no# n* NEU 'across' and DIST superaspect)
   no # *ne*   # *le* + *le*   + *tluh*
   DS # DIST # M   + CL + be yellow + NEU DIST
   'There are lines of yellow going across here and there.'

Most of the nondimensional descriptive themes have little derivational potential beyond ∅ neuter and, often, transitional derivatives. According to Kari, the semantic range of the Ahtna descriptive theme category "is not very coherent; it is a catch-all ∅ -neuter
grouping" (1979:174). In Koyukon, however, 140 of the 193 nondimensional descriptive themes are adjectival, describing some physical
or psychological characteristic of the subject.[7] Typical adjectival
descriptive themes include: *ne+le+get* 'be afraid, scared, frightened'
(which allows *l* transitional derivatives), *ne+le+k'uh* 'be warm, hot'
(which allows ∅ transitional derivatives), and *G+de+k'et* 'be tough,
durable, hard to chew or tear, sinewy' (which allows no transitional
derivatives).

(10)   *nelget*
       ne + ∅ + le + get
       T   + M + CL + be afraid + NEU
       'S/he is afraid.'

(11a) *nelk'uh* (C)
       ne + ∅ + le + k'uh
       T   + M + CL + be warm + NEU
       'S/he, it is warm, hot.'

(12)   *nelaan dek'et*
       nelaan ∅ + de + k'et
       meat   M + CL + be tough + NEU
       'The meat is tough.'

Example (11a) is a form used only in the Central dialect of
Koyukon. In the Lower dialect, this theme has derivatives with an
aa- imperfective mode prefix rather than the usual descriptive ∅
imperfective mode prefix.

(11b) *naalk'uh* (L)
       ne + aa + le + k'uh
       T   + M   + CL + be warm + NEU
       'S/he, it is warm, hot.'

The few themes with a primary *gh* neuter derivative are also
classed as descriptive themes. An example of such a theme is *ghe+*
∅ +no 'be alive, moving; (body part) is twitching; (earthquake) occurs':

---

7. All but thirty of the descriptive themes are intransitive.

(13) *ts'eghono*
 ts'e   + *ghe* + *ghe* + ∅   + *no*
 1PL S + T   + M   + CL + be alive + NEU
 'We are alive; someone, s/he is alive.'

The existential verb, 'to be', is also expressed via descriptive themes. Jetté (1905) says of derivatives of the theme *de#∅+t'aa* 'be thus, be in such circumstances':

> This is the circumstance verb, and its meaning is properly 'I am in such a circumstance', 'I am so circumstanced'. It can be compared to some uses of the Greek. We generally render it by our verb 'to be', because, in English, this verb is very elastic in its signification, but *t'aa* covers only a part of the meanings of to be. We use 'to be': (1) as a copulative verb, 'I am his son', 'he is a native', and this is expressed in Ten'a[8] by *eslaanh: bedenaa' eslaanh, tl'eeyegge hut'aan nelaanh.* (2) as a substantive verb: 'God is', 'I exist', rendered by the *hu-* form of *-laanh: Denaahuto' hoolaanh.* (3) as a locative verb, 'I am at Nulato', 'he is in the house', rendered by *lesdo: Noolaaghedoh lesdo, yeh ledo,* and by various forms of *ledlo* ['classificatory: pl. objects'], categorical. (4) as circumstantial verb, expressing other circumstances of the subject: 'I am hungry', 'I am sleepy', rendered by *dest'aa: k'etlekk'aa dest'aa, bel aahaa dest'aa.*

Of derivatives of the theme *comp.##G+∅+laa* 'exist, be in state denoted by comp.', Jetté reiterates,

> In the copulative construction its use is limited to predicates expressing a state which intimately affects the subject. Accidental circumstances (such as 'to be hungry', 'to be sleepy') are not predicated through *laanh* but by means of *t'aa* 'be thus'; much less circumstances of location and position, to express which the language has a variety of roots such as *dol* 'sit, stay', *'o* 'classificatory: compact object', *taa* 'sg. du. animate lies', etc.

Note that *l* transitional derivatives of the theme *comp.##G+∅+laa* 'exist, be in state denoted by *complementizer*' have *P+e#* rather than '*complementizer*' and have the meaning 'become P'. Transitional derivatives of the theme *de#∅+t'aa* 'be thus, be in such circumstances' have the meaning 'circumstances change'.

The remaining fifty or so descriptive themes express such verbal notions as: 'have, own, possess', 'think, desire, want', 'know, be

---

8. Ten'a was Jetté's designation for the Koyukon language. Koyukon forms in this and other Jetté quotations have been retranscribed into the modern orthography.

familiar with', 'consider', 'exaggerate', 'dislike', 'like', 'hear noise', and 'see poorly'.

5.1.3. Extension themes

The extension verb theme category is the smallest of the neuter categories, with only about sixty-five verb themes. Extension themes usually pair with motion themes and refer to something extended in a linear fashion (e.g., streams, trails, rays of sunshine, gusts of wind). All but two of the themes are intransitive. The simplest derivatives of extension themes are of the n neuter mode-aspect combination, but derivatives are possible with most of the aspect-dependent derivational strings discussed in chapter 4 (section 4.1). Consider the following derivatives of the theme $G+\emptyset+k$'et 'be stretched, taut; extend in a line', which applies to linear, extensible, flexible objects such as rope, fabric, or the body, and also to linearly arranged objects or geographical features such as a ridge line.

(14a) *neek'et* (*n* neuter)
       ne + *ø*   + *k'et*
       M   + CL   + be stretched + NEU
       'It is stretched out; he (tall person) is lying at full length.'

(14b) *betlool ts'aaneek'et* (with *ts'aa#* *n* NEU 'out into the open')
       be   + *tlool*   *ts'aa* # *ne* + *ø* + *k'et*
       3SG P + tongue DS   # M   + CL + be stretched + NEU
       'Its tongue is hanging out.'

(14c) *nogheek'et* (with *no#* *gh* NEU 'down')
       no # *ghe* + *ø*   + *k'et*
       DS # M   + CL   + be stretched + NEU
       'It (cloth) is hanging down.'

(14d) *bek'engheek'et* (with *P+e#ne-* *gh* MOM 'attaching to P')
       be   + *e*   # *k'e*   + *ne* + *ghe* + *ø*   + *k'et*
       3SG P + PP # INDF + DS + M   + CL + be stretched + NEU
       'Something (string, rope) is attached to it.'

(14e) *neetloy hodek'et* (with *P+loy##* *gh* NEU 'to the end of P')
       neet + *loy hʉ*   + *ghe* + *de* + *k'et*
       RECP + PP AREA + M   + CL + be stretched + NEU
       'They (houses) are connected end to end.'

(14f) *k'eetenaalk'et* (with *ee+te+ne– l* NEU 'becoming taut')
    k'e   + *ee* + *te* + *ne* + *le* + ∅   + *k'et*
    INDF + DS   + M + CL + be stretched + NEU
    'Something (clothesline, rope) is stretched out taut.'

(14g) *yeleneek'et* (with *ye#* ∅ NEU 'up vertically' and S incorporated)
    ye # *le*   # *ne* + ∅ + ∅   + *k'et*
    DS # smoke # G   + M + CL + be stretched + NEU
    'Smoke *(le#)* is extending up in the air; a line of smoke is going up.'

5.2. Active theme categories

Of the 1,621 themes that have been identified, 948 are active.[9] This section begins with an examination of motion themes and then proceeds to discuss each of the three activity theme categories. Although motion and activity themes are all included in the category of active themes, note that the three activity theme categories form a group separate from the single category of motion themes.

5.2.1. Motion themes

Kari describes Ahtna motion themes as "the most conspicuous and derivationally elaborate of the theme categories. Motion themes characterize movement . . . [they] can be transitive or intransitive. Most transitive motion themes can take gender prefixes. . . . there are many lexically paired motion themes for singular and plural subjects or objects.[10] . . . In addition, many motion themes are lexically paired for slow vs. rapid movement" (1979:77–78).

In Koyukon, too, the motion theme category is by far the largest. Of the 948 categorized active themes, 375 (roughly 40 percent) are motion themes. Those themes generally refer to movement over space and time and are characterized by having momentaneous derivatives as their simplest derivational products. Perhaps the most prototypical motion themes are the singular, dual, and plural themes meaning 'walk, go by foot' and the themes 'swim, go by swimming' and 'go by boat'. The following examples are derived from ∅+*yo* 'SG walk, go by foot' and illustrate some of the aspect-dependent derivational prefix strings that are possible with this

9. There are also 146 unproductive and uncategorized themes with active derivatives.
10. Koyukon also has a separate root for the dual of 'walk, go by foot'.

very productive theme:

(15a) *neeyo* (*n* momentaneous)
    ne + ∅ + *yo*
    M + CL + SG go + MOM
    'S/he arrived on foot.'

(15b) *noneeyo* (with *no*# *n* MOM 'across')
    no # *ne* + ∅ + *yo*
    DS # M + CL + SG go + MOM
    'S/he walked across.'

(15c) *ts'aaneeyo* (with *ts'aa*# *n* MOM 'out into the open')
    ts'aa # *ne* + ∅ + *yo*
    DS # M + CL + SG go + MOM
    'S/he walked out into the open.'

(15d) *dolyo* (with *do*# *ll* MOM 'elevated')
    do # *le* + ∅ + *yo*
    DS # M + CL + SG go + MOM
    'S/he went to the top, onto an elevation.'

(15e) *dodeeyo* (with *do*#*de-* ∅ MOM 'down an incline')
    do#*de* + *ee* + ∅ + *yo*
    DS + M + CL + SG go + MOM
    'S/he went down the bank, slope.'

(15f) *hogheeyo* (with *ho*# *gh* MOM 'up and out')
    ho # *ghe* + ∅ + *yo*
    DS # M + CL + SG go + MOM
    'S/he came up and out.'

Motion themes also allow a range of superaspectual and postaspectual derivations and commonly have the aspectual derivations listed in table 3.5 as the motion aspects: perambulative, continuative, persistive, and reversative. The examples in (16) illustrate only a few of these derivations in derivatives of the theme ∅ +*baa* 'swim, go by swimming':

(16a) *neebaanh* (*n* momentaneous)
       ne + ∅   + baanh
       M   + CL + swim + MOM
       'S/he arrived swimming.'

(16b) *ghebaał* (progressive)
       ghe + ∅   + baał
       M   + CL + swim + PROG
       'S/he is swimming along.'

(16c) *kk'o'eedebaayh* (perambulative)
       kk'o # ne + de + baayh
       DS   # M   + CL + swim + PRMB
       'S/he is swimming around.'

(16d) *eeyet nelbaanh* (continuative)
       eeyet ne # le + ∅   + baanh
       there DS # M   + CL + swim + CONT
       'S/he swam there and back.'

Pairing with the seventeen classificatory stative themes discussed in section 5.1.1 are twelve classificatory motion themes. This
subgroup of themes has derivatives that express the handling, holding, throwing, or dropping of an object with reference to that object's shape, size, and composition. Compare the following examples
of the classificatory motion theme *O+G+ł+kooł* with the classificatory stative examples in (2):

(17a) *ts'ede neełkooł* (*n* momentaneous)
       ts'ede   ne + ł   + kooł
       blanket   M   + CL + CLASSIF: flexible + MOM
       'S/he arrived with the blanket.'

(17b) *taak'eneełkooł* (with *taa#* *n* MOM 'submerged')
       taa # k'e   + ne + ł   + kooł
       DS   # INDF + M   + CL + CLASSIF: flexible + MOM
       'S/he set something (fishnet) in the water.'

(17c) *kk'oyeełkooł* (perambulative)
       kk'o # ye   + ne + ł   + kooł
       DS   # 3SG O + M + CL + CLASSIF: flexible + PRMB
       'S/he is handling it; s/he is carrying it around.'

(17d) *eeyet neyeetlkooł* (continuative)

  eeyet   *ne* # *ye*   + *le* + *ł*   + *kooł*

  there   DS # 3SG O + M + CL + CLASSIF: flexible + CONT

  'S/he took it there and back.'

(17e) *k'ets'e noyedaatlkooł* (reversative)

  k'ets'e *no* # *ye*   + *de* + *le* + *ł*   + *kooł*

  over   DS # 3SG O + G   + M + CL + CLASSIF: flexible + REV

  'S/he turned it (paper) over; s/he turned it (pelt) inside out.'

5.2.2. Operative themes

The operative theme category is the second largest of the active categories; 182 of the 948 categorized active themes are operative. Operative themes describe activities that take place over a period of time. Derived forms focus on the ongoing process of the activity as a whole rather than on its completion (as with conversive themes), or on smaller units that may be repeated to make up the whole activity (as with successive themes). Prototypical examples of operative themes include those with the meanings: 'to see', 'to buy', 'to sell', 'to sing', 'to eat', and 'to drink'. Those themes are characterized by having derived forms that are durative. They may also allow derivatives of any of the motion aspects—in particular the momentaneous —but the durative forms are the simplest and are therefore considered primary. Typical durative derivatives of operative themes are provided in the following examples.

(18) *k'edeslee* (durative)

    k'e   + *e*   # *de* + ∅ + *s*   + ∅   + *lee*

    INDF + PP # T   + M + 1SG S + CL + sing + DUR

    'I'm singing a song.'

(19) *yeneeł'aanh* (durative)

    ye   + *ne* + ∅ + *ł*   + *'aanh*

    3SG O + T   + M + CL + see + DUR

    'S/he's looking at her/him.'

(20) *hʉtl ek'ooghelkkaat* (durative)

    hʉtl *e* # *k'e* + *oo* + *ghe* + *le*   + *kkaat*

    sled PP # T   + T   + M   + CL + sell + DUR

    'S/he sold a sled; s/he was selling sleds.'

Three small groups of themes have a semantic range similar to that of the operative themes, but do not have durative derivatives.

The largest of this group contains twenty-four themes with primary repetitive derivatives. Another group has seven themes with primary reversative derivatives and a third contains three themes with primary persistive derivatives. In all thirty-four of these themes, the sense of a repeated or prolonged activity and the primacy of a *ghe-* perfective mode prefix is motivation for their inclusion as operative subcategory themes. The operative-persistive themes are *O+de +ne+∅+kk'o* 'grind O (snuff, coffee)', *nel+e#hoo#k'e+l+kk'oh* 'grind one's teeth', and *O+oo+de+l+kkaat* 'question O, ask O (question)'. The operative-reversative themes include *P+e#hu+le+'aan* 'learn P', *P+e#ghe+de+ee+∅+no* 'touch P', and *O+de+l+lon* 'tan O (skin)'. The operative-repetitive themes include *P+e#hu+ne+l+to* 'be bothered, annoyed by P', *de+yeek* 'breathe', and *he+(ne)+∅+(y)o* 'SG DU talks, speaks, utters'.

5.2.3. Conversive themes

The 136 conversive themes are distinguished by primary, or sole, derivatives of the conclusive aspect. Conversive themes, in general, describe actions that result in the creation of a single discrete end product. Examples (21) and (22) illustrate typical derived forms of an operative theme and a conversive theme, respectively. The theme in (21) is *G+∅+ghon* 'make plural objects', and the theme in (22) is *G+le+tsee* 'make singular object'.

(21) *hutl gheeghonh* (durative)
  hutl ghe + ∅ + ghonh
  sled M + CL + make PL O + DUR
  'S/he made (a series or number of) sleds; s/he was a sled-maker.'

(22) *hutl etltseenh* (conclusive)
  hutl le + l + tseenh
  sled M + CL + make SG O + CNCL
  'S/he made a (single) sled.'

The contrast between conversive and motion themes can be seen in examples (23) and (24). Example (23) is derived from the theme *O+ne+∅+tutl* (conversive) 'spin O (thread), ply O (rope)', and example (24) is derived from the theme O+G+l+totl (motion) 'turn, twist O':

(23) *yenaaltutl* (conclusive)
  ye + ne + le + ∅ + tutl
  3SG O + T + M + CL + spin + CNCL
  'S/he plied it (rope).'

(24) *neeyeneeltotl* (momentaneous)
      (with *nee# n* MOM 'up to a point')
      nee # *ye*   + *ne* + *l*   + *totl*
      DS   # 3SG O   + M   + CL   + turn + MOM
      'S/he turned it up to a point.'

The conversive theme in (23) has derived forms that focus on the article being produced, while the theme in (24) focuses on the the the motion of turning. Other typical conversive themes include those with the meanings 'to kill a single person or animal', 'to cook', 'to seal', and 'to freeze'.

Conversive themes occasionally have a second kind of basic perfective derivation as well—a durative that emphasizes process rather than completed goal. Compare the following conclusive and durative perfective forms derived from three conversive verb themes. The conclusive (a) forms all imply the achievement of the activity's goal, while the durative (b) forms make no reference to an endpoint.

(25a) *yeetltseenh* (conclusive)
       ye   + *le* + *l*   + *tseenh*
       3SG O   + M   + CL   + make SG + CNCL
       'S/he made it.'

(25b) *yegheeltsee'* (durative)
       ye   + *ghe* + *l*   + *tsee'*
       3SG O   + M   + CL   + make SG + DUR
       'S/he whittled it.'

(26a) *yelaatlghaanh* (conclusive)
       ye   + *le* + *le* + *l*   + *ghaanh*
       3SG O   + T   + M   + CL   + kill SG + CNCL
       'S/he killed it; s/he beat her/him up.'

(26b) *yelgheelghaa'* (durative)
       ye   + *le* + *ghe* + *l*   + *ghaa'*
       3SG O   + T   + M   + CL   + kill SG + DUR
       'S/he used to beat her/him up.'

(27a) *yeetlbaats* (conclusive)
       ye   + *le* + *l*   + *baats*
       3SG O   + M   + CL   + cook + CNCL
       'S/he cooked it by boiling, scalded it.'

(27b) *yegheełbaats* (durative)
    ye   *+ ghe* *+ ł*   *+ baats*
    3SG O + M   + CL   + cook + DUR
    'S/he had been boiling it (but didn't necessarily finish); s/he had been soaking it (her/his hand).'

In addition to the typical conversive themes with conclusive derivatives, there are twenty-nine themes whose primary derivatives are reversative and two themes whose primary derivatives are repetitive. Those themes do not have conclusive derivatives but, following Kari, are considered conversive subthemes because of some perceived semantic kinship and because all of them have primary derivatives with *le-* perfective mode prefixes. Kari says, "While these conversive-reversatives seem to conform to the general semantic character of the conversive theme category, there is no clear semantic contrast between conversive-reversatives and conversive-conclusives" (1979:154). It is unclear whether this is the best way to treat them, but pending further research, I assign these thirty-one themes to the conversive category. The conversive-repetitive themes are *P+aa#no#ɸ+loł* 'dream about P, foretell P by dreaming' and *O+ne+ɸ+'een* 'steal O'. The conversive-reversative themes include those with the following meanings: 'become established, acquire a habit', 'P is born', 'count P', 'exercise O', 'grow', 'catch, kill P', 'set O (snare)', 'rob O', and 'punish P'.[11]

5.2.4. Successive themes

There are 99 successive themes in the corpus. Successive themes have two aspectual derivations that require *ghe-* perfective and *ɸ-* imperfective mode prefixes. One is the consecutive, which pairs with the semelfactive and is unique to successive themes; the other is the durative, which also occurs with operative and conversive themes. The consecutive refers to repeated single instances of an activity while the durative refers to activities that are sustained over a period of time. Compare examples (28a) and (28b):

(28a) *ghest'utl* (consecutive)
    ghe *+ s*   *+ ɸ*   *+ t'utl*
    M   + 1SG S + CL + cut + CONS
    'I made repeated cuts in it.'

---

11. Recall from the discussion in chapter 2 that P represents a postpositional object while O represents a direct object.

(28b) *ghest'otl* (durative)

　　 ghe 　+ *s* 　　　+ ∅ 　+ *t'otl*
　　 M 　　+ 1SG S 　+ CL 　+ cut + DUR
　　 'I was cutting it.'

Along with the consecutive, the aspect whose presence marks a theme as successive is the semelfactive. The semelfactive means 'to perform the activity (indicated by the root) once'. Example (28c) illustrates the semelfactive derivative of the successive theme illustrated in (28a) and (28b):

(28c) *lest'uł* (semelfactive)

　　 le 　+ *s* 　　+ ∅ 　+ *t'uł*
　　 M 　+ 1SG S 　+ CL 　+ cut + SML
　　 'I cut it once.'

In addition to the semelfactive, consecutive, and durative, the full range of motion aspects is also found in derivatives of successive themes. Examples (29) through (31) illustrate derivatives of some prototypical successive themes.

(29a) *yeeltleł* (semelfactive)

　　 ye 　　+ *le* + ∅ 　　+ *tleł*
　　 3SG O 　+ M 　+ CL 　+ chop + SML

　　 'S/he chopped it once, struck it once with an axe.'

(29b) *yegheetletl* (consecutive)

　　 ye 　　+ *ghe* + ∅ 　+ *tletl*
　　 3SG O 　+ M 　　+ CL 　+ chop + CONS
　　 'S/he chopped it repeatedly, struck again and again with an axe.'

(29c) *yegheetlaatl* (durative)

　　 ye 　　+ *ghe* + ∅ 　+ *tlaatl*
　　 3SG O 　+ M 　　+ CL 　+ chop + DUR
　　 'S/he chopped it; s/he was chopping it for a while.'

(29d) *hohdegheetlaatl* (momentaneous)
　　 (with *ho# gh* MOM 'clearing out')

　　 ho 　# *hu* 　　+ *de* 　+ *ghe* 　+ ∅ 　+ *tlaatl*
　　 DS 　# AREA 　+ G 　　+ M 　　+ CL 　+ chop + MOM
　　 'S/he cleared an area, chopped it out.'

(30a) *yeel'ʉł* (semelfactive)
       ye   + le   + ∅   + 'ʉł
       3SG O + M   + CL   + bite + SML
       'S/he bit it, bit down on it.'

(30b) *yeghee'ʉtl* (consecutive)
       ye   + ghe + ∅   + 'ʉtl
       3SG O + M   + CL   + bite + CONS
       'S/he bit it repeatedly.'

(30c) *yeghee'otl* (durative)
       ye   + ghe + ∅ + 'otl
       3SG O + M   + CL + bite + DUR
       'S/he chewed it.'

(30d) *neeyeenee'otl* (momentaneous)
       (with *nee# n* MOM 'up to a point')
       nee # ye   + ne + ∅   + 'otl
       DS   # 3SG O + M   + CL   + bite + MOM

       'S/he chewed it up, chewed it to pieces.'

(31a) *yeelt'eh* (semelfactive)
       ye   + le   + ∅   + t'eh
       3SG O + M   + CL   + hit + SML
       'S/he hit it once with a stick.'

(31b) *yegheet'ekk* (consecutive)
       ye   + ghe + ∅   + t'ekk
       3SG O + M   + CL   + hit + CONS
       'S/he hit it several times in succession.'

(31c) *yegheet'ekk* (durative)
       ye   + ghe + ∅   + t'ekk
       3SG O + M   + CL   + hit + DUR
       'S/he was beating it (rug).'

The successive, like the other activity theme categories, has a subcategory of successive themes: in this case, the successive-ono-matopoetic category. Its ninety-one themes refer to sounds generated by an object or animal. Derivatives take the quasi aspect, ono-matopoetic (discussed in chapter 3, section 3.2.15). Because these themes have derivatives with *le-* perfective mode prefix (expressing a single instance of the sound) paired with derivatives with *ghe-* perfective mode prefix (expressing a repetition of the sound over time), they resemble the typical successive theme and so are given the hyphenated label. The themes allow many of the superaspectual derivations described in chapter 4 (section 4.2), in addition to the two onomatopoetic derivations.

The ninety-one successive-onomatopoetic themes can be divided into two general types. Themes of the first type, comprising about 30 percent of the total, describe a sound, such as ripping or crunching, produced by a particular inanimate object. This object is expressed by a postpositional object and *aa-* postposition. Most of these themes can express both the impersonal concept 'sound of X comes from P' or the personal 'S makes P produce sound of X', though a few can express only one or the other. Examples include *P+aa#de+le+kket* 'snapping, cracking sound comes from P (joint)' and *P+aa#de+le+ggutl* 'ripping sound comes from P (cloth, paper)'.

Themes of the second type refer to animal calls or to sounds like an echo, a bang, or the sound of choking. Examples include *de+le+ggukk* '(gull) cries' and *de+le+ts'oots* 'make squeaking sound (as of muskrat, mouse, weasel)'. A few of these themes have a second paired successive-onomatopoetic theme with direct object and *l-* classifier. A typical example is the theme *O+de+l+ts'oots* 'call O (muskrat, mouse) by imitating its squeak; (muskrat, mouse) calls O (another muskrat, mouse) during mating season'.

5.3. The organization of verb theme categories

Much has been written regarding the organizational principles involved in noun classification systems. As Lakoff points out, this type of linguistic classification constitutes one of the "richest sources of data that we have concerning the structure of conceptual categories as they are revealed through language" (1987:92).

According to what Fillmore (1975) has termed "checklist theories," the meaning of a semantically complex word is composed of a set of features or semantic components. Coleman and Kay, among others, point out that "semantic categories frequently have blurry edges and allow degrees of membership" (1981:27). These facts are more appropriately accounted for by a prototype theory of word meaning. The work of Rosch (1973, 1977, 1978), Fillmore (1975), Croft (1984), Lakoff (1987), and numerous others, argues that human categorization is a nonarbitrary process. Prototypes represent groupings based on conceptual similarities. Categories have a complicated internal structure with central, or prototypical, exemplars forming a core and less central, or less salient, instances filling out the periphery. Categories also have an external structure, with some items perceived as nonprototypical with respect to more than one category.

Although much of the literature on prototype analysis focuses on perceptual phenomena or on the nominal component of language, Coleman and Kay show that "the prototype phenomenon is also to be found in the semantics of words referring to less concrete things—in this case a type of speech act, namely lies" (1981:27). Their prototype scheme contains a "finite list of properties," though those properties are gradient ones and their importance in constituting the category may vary. In general, however, explorations of the verbal component of languages have proposed categories based on syntactic and semantic features that have little explicit connection to a prototype approach.

Koyukon's complex system of categorizing verb themes according to aspectual derivational potential provides a uniquely rich opportunity to examine the conceptual categorization of activities and events, rather than of objects. Lakoff reminds us "that speakers do not learn category members one by one, but operate in terms of some general principles" (1987:93). His research on noun classification suggests several such general principles underlying conceptual categorization. Of those, the notion of prototype structure is the one most clearly suited to description of Koyukon verb categorization and the one employed as the operating principle in preparing the preceding discussions of the seven verb theme categories.

The previous sections of this chapter described prototypical examples of Koyukon verb theme categories. This section compares those examples with more peripheral theme groupings, groups that seem, in fact, to straddle category boundaries. This crossing of categories is different from what is generally encountered in noun classification systems, and this type of phenomenon constitutes an important difference between verb categorization and noun classification.

The overlapping of verb categories in Koyukon is closely tied to the interaction of lexical and derivational aspect in Koyukon. Many scholars have noted that verb roots themselves generally carry some inherent aspectual meaning. As Talmy points out, "it is doubtful that any verb root can have a meaning wholly neutral to aspect— even in languages where the root is always surrounded by aspect-specifying inflections" (1985:77–78). The verb root's inherent aspectual character determines what aspectual derivations it can participate in and what nuances of meaning that derivational aspect will

then convey. The distinction between lexical and derivational aspect
serves as a useful explanatory principle in understanding why, for
example, some Koyukon verbs can accept an aspectual derivation
expressing single, abrupt, punctual activity—and further, why with
some verbs such activity is expressed by the semelfactive aspect,
and with others by a momentaneous aspectual derivation with
variously ∅ - and *le-* perfective prefix. This particular issue is
discussed further in section 5.3.2.

Several factors are involved in the semantic content of a particular form.[12] One can isolate a particular meaning contributed by
derivational aspect, and one can also discern meaning attached to
the lexical form itself. Two components contribute to lexical meaning: the meaning inherent to the verb root, and the meaning conveyed by the entire verb theme. The inherent lexical aspectual character of the verb theme (and root) constitutes the covert category
that determines what overt derivational aspect themes can allow,
and thus to what theme category the theme belongs.

As noted in chapter 1, many scholars have explored the possibility of categorizing verbs according to their inherent meaning or
situation type. A brief discussion of Smith's (1989b) work on such a
categorization schema for Navajo is appropriate here.

Smith's research is based on the four classes of verbs described
by Vendler (1967) (see chap. 1, section 1.2). Vendler's proposed four
classes of verbs are considered covert, or morphologically unmarked,
categories that require the application of syntactic tests to affirm
the position of a particular verb in one covert category or another.
For Smith, this notion of situation type as a covert category is
critical: "the distinction between situation types in Navajo is overt
to the extent that it patterns with formal grammatical categories; it
is covert if it depends on co-occurrence possibilities and semantic
entailments" (1989:1). For Smith, then, the formal aspectual
categories of that Athabaskan language are not necessarily cotermi-
nous with the situation type categories. She claims instead that
certain Navajo verb bases and sentences can be identified as belonging to a particular one of the four situation types on the basis of
their meaning and adverbial co-occurrence possibilities rather than

12. I am reluctant to refer to these factors as levels because the notion
of levels may carry the implication of sequential application, and there is no
evidence that the production or comprehension of the semantics of a Koyukon verb form is not an indissoluble process.

according to their aspectual category. "Thus," she concludes, "the situation types do not pattern with particular aspect categories. They have natural rather than grammatical situation type"(4).[13]

Because of the close relationship between Navajo and Koyukon, Smith's work is relevant to any discussion of Koyukon aspectual categorization. It has been amply demonstrated (Hardy 1979; Young and Morgan 1987; Midgette 1987) that the terminology and framework used to discuss the aspectual systems of Alaskan Athabaskan languages like Koyukon is appropriate also for Navajo. The proliferation of overt morphological marking for aspect is a distinguishing trait for that family in general. Although the details of the distribution and scope of each element within the aspectual system may vary somewhat from language to language, the semantic primitives expressed within that system remain constant.

As Bybee (1985) demonstrates, meaning is responsible for determining at least certain aspects of form. To underestimate the elaborate formal categorization of verbal aspectual categories in Athabaskan in the interests of maintaining a classification based on covert semantic categories in English, or other languages, is a serious mistake.

For example, using Vendler's categories as a framework, Smith classes both the conclusive and the durative aspects of Navajo as "durative events," or "accomplishments." Remember that accomplishments include those events that refer to an endpoint, while activities have duration but do not include reference to a goal or boundary. Looking at the meanings of the conclusive and durative aspects in Koyukon yields quite a different conclusion. As described in chapter 3, the conclusive aspect (section 3.2.14) refers to telic activities (those that focus on a particular goal), while forms derived in the durative aspect (section 3.2.8) refer to activities carried out over an extended period without any reference to their endpoint or goal. According to the situation type schema then, while it is appropriate to consider conclusive verbs as within the category of accomplishments, durative verbs are more properly considered as expressing activities.

Co-occurrence with certain adverbials is taken as the clearest test of category membership in Smith's framework. The use of Koyukon adverbs, however, does not coincide with the posited situation

---

13. Smith does, however, allow that in some cases "situation type and aspect category coincide" (5).

types. To be sure, the co-occurrence of adverbial complements with
Koyukon verbs is not determined solely by a verb's aspectual category either. This fact must be interpreted, though, as a function of
the wider semantic scope of Koyukon adverbs rather than as an
indication that the formal aspectual categories are not drawn
according to basic semantic principles. Indeed, one would expect
that a verbal system that allows so much precision in specifying
temporal adverbial notions within the morphology of the verb itself
would hardly need adverbs to accomplish the same task.[14]

Recall that achievements are said to include one-stage activities
such as tapping, clapping, or dying. In Koyukon, these events are
usually expressed by the semelfactive aspect. As suggested above,
we might think of accomplishments as including the telic Koyukon
conclusive verbs and activities as being the situation type to which
Koyukon durative verbs would belong. The following examples show
that while a Koyukon semelfactive verb is impossible with the adverb *neełlots'e* 'for a long time', both the conclusive and durative
verbs occur freely with this adverb. It is clear, however, that the
conclusive example in (32b) indicates the achievement of an endpoint or goal while the durative example in (32c) does not.

(32a)   *neełlots'e kkun' letleł* (semelfactive)
        neełlots'e   kkun' le + ∅   + tleł
        for long time wood   M   + CL   + chop + SML
        * 'S/he gave the wood a chop for a long time.'

(32b)   *neełlots'e yeetlbaats* (conclusive)
        neełlots'e   ye   + le   + ł   + baats
                     3SG O   + M   + CL   + boil + CNCL
        'S/he boiled it for a long time.'

(32c)   *neełlots'e yegheełbaats* (durative)
        neełlots'e   ye   + ghe + ł   + baats
                     3SG O   + M   + CL   + boil + DUR
        'S/he boiled it for a long time without necessarily finishing.'

Further, notice that with the adverb *hot* 'carefully, slowly, gently',
both the semelfactive and durative verbs are acceptable; the conclusive verb, on the other hand, is only marginally so.

---

14. I am grateful to David Rood for pointing this out to me.

(33a) *hot yeeltleł* (semelfactive)
       hot   ye   + le   + ∅   + tleł
       3SG O + M   + CL   + chop + SML
       'S/he gave it a gentle chop, a slow swing from start to finish.'

(33b) *hot yegheetlaatl* (durative)
       hot   ye   + ghe + ∅   + tlaatl
       3SG O + M   + CL   + chop + DUR
       'S/he chopped it gently.'

(33c) *? hot yeetlbaats* (conclusive)
       hot   ye   + le   + ł   + baats
       3SG O + M   + CL   + boil + CNCL
       ? 'S/he boiled it slowly, gently.'

The first fourteen aspects described in chapter 3 are based on *both* semantic and morphological characteristics. These aspects can be classed into three large groups (outlined in table 3.5) according to semantic and distributional criteria: state, motion, and activity. These groups can be further subdivided, also according to semantic and distributional characteristics. The resulting categories, the aspectual verb theme categories, do not correspond with the four situation type categories identified by Vendler and discussed further by Smith. The categorization schema illustrated by the Koyukon data is simply different. Membership in a particular category is overtly marked. The categories form cohesive semantic groups, and the formal aspectual categories are usually identical to the semantic ones. Where variations occur—that is, where verbs seem to be more peripheral members of a category either on formal or semantic grounds—the variations are not related to the Vendler categories but rather to lexical variation that calls for a mixture of two or more of the Koyukon categories. This phenomenon will be discussed in greater detail in the following sections.

5.3.1. Cross-cutting and overlapping of categories

At the beginning of this chapter I claimed that verb theme categories may be best described in terms of aspectual oppositions. We will see, though, that there is not a one-to-one mapping between the set of semantic aspectual oppositions that the language encodes and the set of morphological aspectual strategies for encoding such oppositions. Although the categories described above provide a useful general framework for classifying verb themes, there is a great deal of semantic overlap across categories.

Within each category one can discern smaller subcategories or groupings of themes. Some, like the five motion verb themes that describe the independent movement of objects specific to the shape, texture, and quantity of those objects,[15] form a group on the basis of their shared semantic character but still remain clear examples of the motion category. Other themes form groups on semantic grounds that are tied to shared aspectual features that distinguish them from other themes of the category. These cases represent themes less central to the category and illustrate the kind of formal and semantic overlapping that occurs within and across categories.

5.3.2. The successive semantic pattern in other categories

One case of a theme grouping that has formal or semantic features of more than one category is the group of four verb roots in Koyukon that express the production of oral sound associated with strong emotion. All four have primary themes we call operative because their derivatives are morphologically marked as durative and momentaneous.

(34a) $\emptyset$ +tsaah   'cry'

(34b) $\emptyset$ +zeel   'shout, yell'

(34c) $\emptyset$ +kk'ok   'cry loudly, wail, howl'

(34d) $\emptyset$ +ts'ookk   'scream, squeal'

Like themes of the successive category, however, these four themes are distinguished by a semantic aspectual opposition between prolonged action and a sudden, single instance of the action. Where in successive themes that opposition is expressed by consecutive and semelfactive derivations respectively, in the operative themes of crying and crying out, it is expressed respectively by durative derivatives[16] and by what I have called the $\emptyset$ momentaneous—momen-

15. The five themes are: de+G+le+nen/leyh 'compact or animate object moves independently, falls', G+$\emptyset$ +ghel 'rigid, flat object moves independently, falls', G+$\emptyset$ +ghUl 'sticklike object moves independently, falls', G+l+ kkaatl 'bag, knife, enclosed object moves independently, falls', and G+$\emptyset$ + nekk 'flat, flexible, or clothlike object moves independently, falls'.
16. The durative stem sets for -tsaah and -zeel have a reduced vowel in the nonperfective modes (i.e., -tseh and -zel) and a full vowel in the perfective (i.e., -tsaah and -zeel). Such an arrangement is not the typical

taneous derivatives with *ee-* perfective mode prefix (suggestive of the semelfactive *ee-* prefix). Compare the durative and momentaneous examples in (35a–c) with the consecutive and semelfactive examples in (28)–(31).

(35a) *ezeł* (durative, imperfective)
    ∅   + ∅   + *zeł*
    M   + CL   + shout + DUR
    'S/he is shouting.'

(35b) *gheezeeł* (durative, perfective)
    ghe   + ∅   + *zeeł*
    M   + CL   + shout + DUR
    'S/he was shouting.'

(35c) *eezeeł* (∅ momentaneous, *ee-* perfective)
    ee   + ∅   + *zeeł*
    M   + CL   + shout + MOM
    'S/he gave a shout, shouted once.'

This group of operative themes, then, is very reminiscent of successive themes, both semantically and formally, with forms that have prefix complexes and a semantic thrust that approximates those of consecutive and semelfactive derivatives but with stem sets of durative and momentaneous aspect.

The semantic and morphological pattern described for successive verbs—that is, with derivatives contrasting repeated action with single instances of the action (along with secondary motion and bisective derivatives)—is occasionally observed, then, in operative themes as well. In some cases these themes refer to an activity that is inherently semantically incompatible with the notion of "repeated single instances"—that temporal concept expressed by the consecutive aspect. Instead, they refer to an activity most naturally seen as occurring over an extended period of time, that is, dura-

---

durative stem but looks, rather, like a consecutive stem set with a suppletive perfective (with full vowel) drawn from the momentaneous set. Further, the perfective momentaneous paradigms have an *ee-* prefix in the second and third person singular and the first and third person plural, as in the following:

1SG	*estsaah*	1PL	*ts'eetsaah*
2SG	*eentsaah*	2PL	*uhtsaah*
3SG	*eetsaah*	3PL	*heetsaah*

tively. Viewed from the perspective of their ultimate result, however, this activity can also be seen as a single outcome. These
themes then, express single versus extended action with ∅ momentaneous and durative aspects, respectively. The examples in
(36)—from the classificatory verb root referring to wet, mushy,
doughy objects, -*tlaakk*—illustrates this contrast and shows further
similarity to the successive pattern in having the typical secondary
derivatives in motion and bisective aspects. The operative theme
underlying all these verbs is *G+∅+tlaakk* 'dissolve, disintegrate, fall
apart; tattered or rotten object falls'.

(36a) *etlaah* (durative)
    ∅ + ∅ + *tlaah*
    M + CL + CLASSIF: mushy + DUR
    'It (fabric) is falling apart, disintegrating.'

(36b) *hegheetlaah* (durative)
    hʉ + *ghe* + ∅ + *tlaah*
    AREA + M + CL + CLASSIF: mushy + DUR
    'It (riverbank) was caving in.'

(36c) *hootlaakk* (∅ momentaneous)
    hʉ + *ee* + ∅ + *tlaakk*
    AREA + M + CL + CLASSIF: mushy + MOM
    'It (riverbank) caved in once.'

(36d) *bebaade haadeneetlaakk* (∅ momentaneous)
    (with *P+aa#de+ne-* ∅ MOM 'detaching from P')
    be + *baade* *hʉ* + *aa* # *de* + *ne* + *ee* + ∅
    3SG P + sleeve AREA + PP # DS + M + CL
    + *tlaakk*
    + CLASSIF: mushy + MOM
    'Its sleeve rotted off it.'

(36e) *deenaaltlaakk* (*l* momentaneous)
    (with *de+ee+ne-* *l* MOM 'toppling over')
    de + *ee* + *ne* + *le* + ∅ + *tlaakk*
    DS + M + CL + CLASSIF: mushy + MOM
    'It (rotten tree) fell.'
    (cf. *deenaalghaats* 'It (healthy tree) fell.')

(36f) *taa'etlaah* (*n* momentaneous)
    (with *taa#* *n* MOM 'into the water')
    taa # ∅ + ∅ + *tlaah*
    DS # M + CL + CLASSIF: mushy + MOM
    'It (overcooked fish) is falling apart in the water.'

(36g) *bede'aage neeneetlaakk* (*n* momentaneous)
(with *nee# n* MOM 'to a point)
be   + *de'aage* nee # *ne* + ∅   + *tlaakk*
3SG P + dress   DS   # M   + CL + CLASSIF: mushy + MOM
'Her dress got all tattered, torn up, ragged.'

(36h) *naaltluh* (bisective)
ne + *le* + ∅   + *tluh*
DS   + M   + CL + CLASSIF: mushy + BIS
'It (string, rotten boat) broke in two, fell apart in two.'

In the above examples, (36a) and (36b) present the semantically
primary derivatives of the theme, the aspectual derivation most
consonant with the meaning of the theme. Examples (36b) and (36c)
illustrate the contrast between extended action and a single instance of that action. Following the terminology of Smith (1983),
example (36b) can be said to present an interior view of the activity,
while (36c) presents an exterior view of it, even though both are
perfective forms. Examples (36d) through (36g) are motion derivatives and (36h) is a bisective derivative.

In another set of examples from a theme with the same verb
root, we can see another case of the successive semantic pattern of
repeated versus single activity expressed via a different theme category. As in the previous case, where the lexical character of the verb
theme itself was most appropriately expressed by the durative and
not suited to the consecutive, here again we have a verb theme that
has an inherent semantic character somewhat different from the
typical successive verb. In the present case the primary semantic
focus of the theme *P+aa#O+de+ł+tlukk* 'flip animate O over onto P'
is on the completion of a change of state rather than on the unitary
character of the activity alone. Hence, the primary aspectual derivation is conclusive.

(37a) *haayedaatltlukk* (conclusive)
hʉ + *aa* # *ye*   + *de* + *le* + *ł*   + *tlukk*
P   + PP # 3SG O   + T   + M   + CL + CLASSIF: mushy + CNCL
'S/he flipped her/him over on her/his back.'

(37b) *haayedełtlukk* (consecutive)
hʉ + *aa* # *ye*   + *de* + ∅ + *ł* + *tlukk*
P   + PP # 3SG O + T   + M   + CL + CLASSIF: mushy + CONS
'S/he flips her/him repeatedly onto her/his back.'

Here, then, we have a semantic and formal amalgam of the conversive and successive theme categories, an amalgam motivated by lexical meaning.

5.3.3. Overlapping of conversive and motion categories

Another group of themes that has characteristics of more than one category is the set of five conversive verb themes that describe sewing. Each has the form *kk'o#O+de+ł+stem* and means 'sew O (with stitches of a particular length or tightness)'. The most frequent and semantically neutral of these themes is *kk'o#O+de+ł+ kkon'* (C, U) 'sew O'.[17]

(38a) *kk'oyedaatlkkon'* (conclusive)

    kk'o   # *ye*   + *de*   + *le*   + *ł*   + *kkon'*

    T   # 3SG O + T   + M   + CL   + sew + CNCL

    'S/he sewed it; s/he sewed for her/him, kept her/him in clothes.'

(38b) *kk'ok'edegheełkkon'* (durative)

    kk'o   # *k'e*   + *de*   + *ghe*   + *ł*   + *kkon'*

    T   # INDF   + T   + M   + CL   + sew + DUR

    'S/he was sewing it.'

The other themes of sewing are:

(39a) *kk'o#O+de+ł+ghuts*   'sew O with short, close stitches'

(39b) *kk'o#O+de+ł+luyhtl*   (U) 'baste, sew O with long, loose stitches'

(39c) *kk'o#O+de+ł+tsuł*   'sew O with coarse stitches'

(39d) *kk'o#O+de+ł+beeł*   'sew O with loose stitches'

Note that the disjunct prefix *kk'o-* in each theme of this group is one that is otherwise exclusively associated with the perambulative aspect. The perambulative is commonly found in derivatives of motion themes and carries the meaning 'to go around in various directions, cover an area (doing the activity), go here and there'.[18]

---

17. In the Lower dialect, the theme has an additional disjunct prefix, *no-: kk'o + no # O + de + ł + kkon'* 'sew O'.

18. Recall that the perambulative stem set has a *-nh* suffix in the perfective and a *-k* suffix in the future and optative; open roots have a *-yh* suffix in the imperfective and closed roots have no suffix but instead a lengthened vowel in the imperfective. It requires the *kk'o-* disjunct prefix and takes *ne-* imperfective and *le-* perfective prefixes.

(40a) *yeeneetonh (n* momentaneous)
  ye   *+ ne + ∅   + tonh*
  3SG O + M   + CL   + CLASSIF: elongated + MOM
  'S/he arrived with it.'

(40b) *kk'oyeeltonh* (perambulative perfective)
  kk'o # ye   + le + ∅   + tonh
  DS   # 3SG O + M   + CL   + CLASSIF: elongated + PRMB
  'S/he carried it around.'

The verbs of sewing seem to be referenced for both conversive and motion categories, taking conclusive and durative stem sets with a motion perambulative prefix string. The verbs refer to activity that clearly has two salient characteristics for Koyukon speakers: it is goal oriented and is accomplished by a back-and-forth motion.

5.3.4. Summary of verb theme organization

Many of the principles previously described for noun categorization also operate in the organization of the major verb theme categories of Koyukon. In noun classification systems, each category has a set of qualities that define it (e.g., male animate, heavy objects, dangerous things, round objects). Each of the Koyukon verb theme categories also has a defining characteristic, as illustrated in table 5.2:

Table 5.2. Semantic Characteristics of Koyukon Aspectual Verb Theme Categories

CATEGORY	DEFINING CHARACTERISTIC
NEUTER	
Stative	achievement of state
Descriptive	characteristic or quality
Extension	position extending over space
ACTIVE	
Motion	movement extending over space or time
Activity	
Operative	process
Conversive	goal
Successive	punctuality

Each noun category, as Lakoff and others have shown, can be seen as a complex with some members more central than others. Similarly, we can think of some themes as prototypical members of theme categories, that is, themes that are more semantically and formally regular: 'dancing' or 'singing' as operative verbs, 'killing' or 'making a single object' as conversive verbs, 'chopping' as a successive verb. A major difference between the two types of classification, however, lies in the fact that verb theme categories contain subgroups that have the defining characteristic of some other category (e.g., the set of successivelike themes within the operative and conversive categories, the set of motionlike themes within the conversive category) Where in noun classification objects have one salient characteristic which takes precedence in determining its class membership, Koyukon verb classification is far more fluid with cross-referencing between categories accomplished by the interplay of aspect-dependent prefix strings and aspectual stem suffixation.

5.4. Summary

This chapter presented an overview of the three neuter and four active verb theme categories. The seven large categories fall into three main groups: state, motion, and activity. Verb themes in the state group generally refer to static conditions; verb themes in the motion group refer to the path, direction, or manner of movement over time and space; verb themes in the activity group tend to refer to actions or events viewed according to whether that action or event is a single one or a repeated or prolonged one.

An important issue raised in this chapter was the flexibility provided within the organization of aspectual verb theme categories by the interaction of prefixal verb constituents with stem variation. Recall that in chapter 4 (section 4.4) it was shown that both prefixal morphology and stem shape are used as cues to understanding the meaning of a form by providing reminders of other, clearer (or more prototypical) exemplars of various elements of that meaning. Similarly, in section 5.3 we saw that by bringing to memory central members of more clear-cut categories, prefixal elements and stem shape serve to provide meanings that combine the characteristic semantic features of separate verb theme categories. I offer one more small example of this semantic interplay between prefix complex and verb stem—a frequently used verb form derived from the conversive verb theme *O+G+l+tsee* 'make SG, DU O':

(41)   *ggaayee hebeedletseenh* (conclusive, passive)
       ggaayee hebe + le + le + tseenh
       win   3PL O + M + CL + make SG + CNCL
       'They got beaten in a game.'

The constituents of this verb derivative have also been attested with
a different root: *doots* 'excrement'. It is by analogy with *ggaayee
hebeedletseenh,* that *ggaayee hebedaadledoots* is understood to
mean 'they really got beaten, trashed, thrashed, creamed, clobbered
in a game'.

    In section 5.3 the point was also made that lexical semantic
properties are crucial in determining the distributional range and
function of derivational aspect. Lexical meaning, carried both by the
root itself and by the verb theme, delimit to a great extent what
aspectual derivations will be possible for a given verb form. This
fact is central to an understanding of how the Koyukon aspectual
system functions in discourse, the topic of chapter 6.

6
The Role of Aspect and Theme Category
in Discourse

The preceding three chapters describe a particularly rich and complex aspectual system and its organization into formal and semantic categories. This chapter is an introduction to how that system is used in narrative discourse.

Hopper suggests that aspect is "an essentially discourse-level, rather than a semantic, sentence-level phenomenon. . . . a more profitable direction of research," he proposes, "is to study the types of aspectual functions which are central to discourse as a universal phenomenon and then to examine the typical extensions of these functions as they become grammaticized" (1982:16). The topic of the discourse function of aspect has received considerable attention in recent years. Most of the work has addressed the use of perfective versus imperfective (e.g., Hopper 1982; Wallace 1982; Kalmar 1982; Smith 1983; Silva-Corvalán 1985) or of various past tense constructions (e.g, Schriffrin 1981; Waugh and Monville-Burston 1986) to organize narratives in terms of sequencing and foregrounding of events. To my knowledge, however, no previous study has considered a language with as elaborate a system of morphologically marked aspects as Koyukon.

In the traditional Koyukon story *Tobaan Etseh*, I found that while the aspectual system of that language does indeed structure and organize information in discourse, that function seems secondary. The area in which the aspectual system functions in its fullest is the more local domain of sentence and verb semantics.

6.1. The aspectual system in narrative: *Tobaan Etseh*

This following discussion concentrates on an examination of one of the structurally simplest of the Koyukon *kk'edonts'ednee*, or traditional stories: *Tobaan Etseh* 'She's Crying on the Beach'. The Koyukon *kk'edonts'ednee* are stories of the time long ago, recounting the creation of the earth and its inhabitants and outlining rules of behavior. Structurally, *Tobaan Etseh* is one of the simplest of those stories: it is short, it has a relatively uncomplicated plotline and considerable repetition, and it focuses on a single character. It is said that if a Koyukon speaker can tell any one story, it will be this one. For our purposes, the story is a useful beginning because it contains a rather limited inventory of aspectual derivations.

The version of *Tobaan Etseh* used here was told by Catherine Attla on tape in 1976. Eliza Jones and I translated it, with the storyteller's assistance, in 1982. The translation was divided into lines and paragraphs to reflect the pauses and dramatic breaks of the original oral version. In general, a paragraph break represents a longer pause in the oral version than does a line break, but speaker intuition about the logical places for breaks (where these differed from the structure of pauses in the original) also played a part in determining the paragraphing and line arrangement.

The semantic structure of the story is shown in table 6.1.[1] In the following pages, I present the entire story, separated into the divisions given in the table. A brief summary of the aspectual inventory is provided at the beginning of each section. Verbs in the Koyukon text appear in bold type.[2] Their English glosses below are followed by a parenthetical abbreviation noting their theme category, mode, and aspect. Notice how the sections distinguished by means of their semantic content, as presented in the table, can be seen to be distinguished as well by the aspectual character of their content.[3]

I. PARAGRAPHS 1–2: INTRODUCTION AND BACKGROUND

In the introduction to the story all verbs are of the neuter (including stative and descriptive) or operative theme categories. Of the eight verbs in this section, all but one are neuter or durative imperfective derivatives.

1   *Yegge gheel* **ts'uhut'aanh**
   'In the time very long ago (DESC: NEU PERF)'

---

1. I have divided the story into sections according to my own intuition (and with the assistance of Jones) regarding what constitutes the coherent semantic chunks of the story's plot. It would, however, be possible to divide and outline the story in slightly different ways.

2. I have selected and analyzed only those verbs within the storyline, excluding those verbs of saying that are used with evidential force (e.g., 'they say' or 'it is said'), whose aspect rarely changes and seems not to be involved in the larger use of aspect in discourse.

3. This claim makes apparent the possibility of a certain circularity inherent in the distinguishing of sections. See section 6.3 for discussion of the relationship between lexical semantics and derivational aspect within the sections of the story.

Table 6.1. Plot and Structure of *Tobaan Etseh*

I. Paragraphs 1–2
    Introduction and background: The story is set on the bank of a river;
    the protagonist is introduced: a porcupine woman who wants to cross
    the river to more desirable territory.

II. A. Paragraphs 3–8
        Episode 1: A muskrat comes along and offers to carry the porcu-
        pine woman across the river, but she refuses his offer.
    B. Paragraphs 9–13
        Episode 2: An otter comes along and offers to carry her across the
        river, but she again refuses the offer.
    C. Paragraphs 14–17
        Episode 3: A baby beaver offers to carry her across the river, and
        again she refuses.
    D. Paragraph 18
        Demiepisode 4: A big blanket beaver comes and offers his
        services; this time she accepts.

III. A. Paragraphs 19–23
         Dramatic sequence: The porcupine woman gets on the blanket
         beaver's tail and he starts swimming across the river with her.
         Meanwhile she builds a fire on his tail in order to heat water for
         tea. He shrieks in pain and flips her into the river.
     B. Paragraphs 24–26
         Transition sequence: She falls in the river and walks ashore. The
         blanket beaver asks if she is all right and then swims off. The
         porcupine woman sits herself down on a bear trail. The bear
         appears and orders her off but she refuses to go.
     C. Paragraphs 27–30
         Climax: The bear attacks her and she slaps him with her tail,
         killing him.
     D. Paragraphs 31–32
         Resolution-conclusion: She realizes that she's killed her own rela-
         tive and laments his death by climbing a tree and singing a
         memorial song.

---

*degheel yoogh tsook'aal **ledo**.*
'there lived (STAT: *l* NEU IMPF) an old woman.'

*Degheel go **ledo** degheel **edaak'uhdeedon**'.*
'Around there where she was living (STAT: *l* NEU IMPF), she had
    eaten (OPER: *n* MOM PERF) everything there was to eat.'

*Et'eeyło dekenh kkotsel yeen' **ehonh.***
'Apparently she ate (OPER: DUR IMPF) only tree bark.'

2   *Hʉyeł yoonaan **hʉneeł'aanh.***
'And so she was looking (OPER: DUR IMPF) across (the river).'

*Hʉyeł gheel yoonaan yoodo' hʉkk'aa **dent'aa** gheelhee,*
'Then, all of a sudden, she must have wanted (DESC: NEU IMPF) to cross downriver,'

*yoonts'e nots'en dekenh **hoolaanh** hu.*
'across there on the other side where there were (DESC: NEU IMPF) trees.'

Et'eeyło dekehone, dekenh ehone.
'Apparently she was a porcupine, a wood eater.'

II. A. PARAGRAPHS 3–8: EPISODE 1

The episode begins with a momentaneous perfective. In the last line of the first paragraph, an inceptive perfective derivative signals the true beginning of this first narrative episode. There are seventeen verbs in the seventeen lines of this section. Of these, only four are of the neuter category. Thus, the section contrasts sharply with the preceding one. There are six motion theme derivatives, six operative theme derivatives, and one conversive-reversative theme derivative. Only four verbs in this beginning episode, however, are perfective.

3   *Kk'ʉdaa notlen **nʉkk'ʉzee'ots.***
'Now she went down (MOT: ∅ MOM PERF) the bank.'

*Ts'ʉh tobaan **ts'eldo.***
'And she was sitting (STAT: *l* NEU IMPF) on the beach.'

*Dehoon gheel **saaltsaah saaltsaah.***
'And meanwhile she started to cry and cry (OPER: *l* MOM INCP PERF).'

4   *Hʉyeł nedaagh doneets'e hʉn bekenaal **ghebaał***
'Then to her surprise, a muskrat came swimming (MOT: PROG) downriver close by.'

*Dotlee bʉgh **neeyeeneebaanh.***
'It swam (MOT: *n* MOM PERF) up to her, down there on the beach.'

5   *"Tsook'aał,* **dodeenee?**
     '"Grandma, what are you saying (OPER: DUR IMPF)?"'

Dodeenee ts'e go **netseh?***" gheel Tsook'aał ełnee gheelhee.*
'Why are you you crying (OPER: DUR IMPF)?" he asked Grandma.'

"Koyaa', yoonts'e yoodo ts'ebaa yeł kk'eeyh yeł neełte
     k'eghenaadeyonh *de*
'"Grandchild, across and downriver, where there are spruce trees
     and birch trees all grown together (CONV-REV: REV PERF),'

hʉkk'aa ees go **dedesnee.***"*
'that is the place I'm crying (OPER: DUR IMPF) for."'

6   *"Haa! Tsook'aał donee senee* **neeneehoyh,***" beeznee.*
     '"Haa! Grandmother, go (MOT: *n* MOM IMPF) back there behind
     me," he told her.'

"Sekaal tleekk'e **doleehoyh,***" yełnee.*
'"Climb up (MOT: *l* MOM IMPF) on my tail," he told her.'

7   **Yeneeł'aanh.**
     'She looked at him (OPER: DUR IMPF).'

Hʉyeł, "Aa, nʉgh nekaa' hołdedle **kk'aant'aa,***" yełnee.*
'Then she said to him, "Aa, your tail is like (DESC: NEU IMPF)
     rope."'

Et'eeyło, "Nʉgh nekaa' tl'aah naałdedle **kk'aant'aa,***" beesnee
     yełnee denh.*
Literally, she was saying to him, "Your tail is like (OPER: DUR
     IMPF) spun sinew."'

8   *"Hʉ! Neketl toseyookk* **dodnee** *ehaa?"*
     '"Hʉ! The big old tunnel nose, why is she crying (OPER: DUR IMPF)
     then?"'

Go heł benketl **hʉdeneekoh** *gheelhee.*
'She must have had big (DESC: NEU IMPF) nostrils.'

Kk'ʉdaa nodo' t'aanh **ghebaał.**
'And so the last time she saw him, he was swimming (MOT: PROG)
     downriver.'

B. PARAGRAPHS 9–13: EPISODE 2

The episode begins with durative imperfective and progressive verbs. It then immediately backtracks with an explanatory aside—with all the verbs in the neuter or durative imperfective. The remaining four paragraphs contain only two motion verbs: a *gh* momentaneous progressive, and an *ll* momentaneous imperfective.

9   *Yoogh tobaan **etseh etseh.***
'She was crying and crying (OPER: DUR IMPF) on the beach.'

*Nedaagh doogh doneets'e hun belaazon **needzeghebaal.***
'And then an otter came swimming down river (MOT: *gh* MOM, PROG)⁴ close to her.'

Bezeye,
'Bezeye'

*go heł yoogh don heł sołt'en kkaa belaazon **deeneelaa.***
'a long time ago, women never used (OPER: DUR IMPF) the word *belaazon.*'

*Bezeye **hednee** ts'uhuyaan'.*
'They only said (OPER: DUR IMPF) *bezeye.*'

*Go heł **ts'ohoołtlaagge***
'They (otters) are messy (DESC: NEU IMPF) when they defecate'

*dehoon koon **denletsut***
'and they also snort (OPER: DUR IMPF)'

***dendeneenh** kk'aat'aanh gheelhee.*
'and their heads twitch (OPER: DUR IMPF).'

10   *"Tsook'aał, **dodeenee** ts'e go **netseh?"** yełnee.*
'"Grandma, why are you crying (OPER: DUR IMPF) this way (OPER: DUR IMPF)?" he asked her.'

---

4. Note that this verb has a *gh* momentaneous aspect-dependent derivational string *(needze# gh* MOM 'going downstream') and so can be analyzed as underlyingly *gh* momentaneous with the progressive superaspect. Where there is no justification for identifying an underlying mode and aspect, progressive forms are marked simply as progressive.

11   *"He! Koyaa', nonts'e nodo ts'ebaa yeł kk'eeyh yeł neełte*
     k'eghenaadeyonh *denh*
     '"Oh! Grandchild, across and downriver, where there are spruce
     and birch trees all grown (CONV-REV: REV PERF) together,'

     ees go hukk'aa **dedesnee,***" nee.*
     'that's the place I'm crying (OPER: DUR IMPF) for," she said.'

12   *"O! Donee sekaal tleekk'e* **doleehoyh***," yełnee.*
     '"Oh! Climb (MOT: *ll* MOM IMPF) back there on my tail," he said to
     her.'

13   **Yeneeł'aanh.**
     'She looked (OPER: DUR IMPF) at him.'

     Huyeł hun, "Aaa! Nugh nekaa' kkun' ggestl **kk'aant'aa***," yełnee.*
     'Then she said to him, "Oh! Your tail is too much like (DESC: NEU
     IMPF) a stove poker."'

     "Hu! Neketl toseyookk **dodnee** *ehaa?" yełnee.*
     '"Hmh! The old tunnel nose, what is she crying (OPER: DUR IMPF)
     for then?" he asked her."'

C. PARAGRAPHS 14–17: EPISODE 3

Much like the previous two episodes, this one contains mostly
imperfective derivatives of the operative and neuter categories. Just
as in episode 2, there are two motion verbs, one an *n* momentaneous
perfective and the other an *ll* momentaneous imperfective.

14   *Ts'uh nodo' t'aanh.*
     'And downriver he went.'

     Ts'e yoogh tl'ee eet **etseh.**
     'And so, by and by, she was still crying (OPER: DUR IMPF).'

     Huyeł tobaan **etseh** *tobaan* **etseh.**
     'She was crying and crying (OPER: DUR IMPF) on the beach.'

     Huyeł hun aatleets'e aaneets'e hun k'enohusloon **ghebaał.**
     'Suddenly, coming close by the beach, a baby beaver was swim-
     ming (MOT: PROG).'

     Bugh **neeghoyeeneebaanh.**
     'It swam ashore (MOT: *n* MOM PERF) to her.'

15 *"Tsook'aał, dodnee ts'e go **netseh?**"*

'"Grandma, what are you crying (OPER: DUR IMPF) for?" he asked her.'

*"Koyh, nonts'e nodo kk'eeyh yeł ts'ebaa yeł neełte **k'eghenaadeyonh** de hʉkk'aat," yełnee.*

'"Grandchild, across and downriver, where there are spruce and birch trees all grown (CONV-REV: REV PERF) together, that's what I'm crying for," she told him.'

*"Eeydaa' donee sekaal tleekk'e **doleehoyh**," yełnee.*

'"Then climb (MOT: *ll* MOM IMPF) back there on my tail," he told her.'

16 ***Yeneeł'aanh.***

'She looked at him (OPER: DUR IMPF).'

*Hʉyeł, "K'edeeteey hełten' **kk'aant'aa**," yełnee.*

'Then she said to him, "It's too much like (DESC: NEU IMPF) a ladle."'

Et'eeyło koon sekkoł, dekenh sekkoł.

'Apparently she meant a spoon, a wooden spoon.'

17 *"Neketl toseyookk **dodnee** ehaa?" yełnee.*

'"The big old tunnel nose, what is she crying (OPER: DUR IMPF) for then?" he asked her.'

Kk'ʉdaa nodo' t'aanh.

'Now he went downriver.'

D. Paragraph 18: demiepisode 4

This episode is smaller than the previous three and contains only one neuter verb. Notice that there are three motion verbs: a *gh* momentaneous progressive and an *ll* momentaneous perfective (exactly as in episode 2), and an *n* momentaneous perfective (as in episode 3).

18 *Dehoon tl'ee eet **ledo** dehoon **etseh** tobaan **etseh**.*

'Meanwhile, still staying (STAT: *l* NEU IMPF) there, she was crying and crying (OPER: DUR IMPF) on the beach.'

*Hʉyeł hʉn dotloogh doneets'e hʉn ggaagge teey kuh **needzeghebaał***

'Suddenly a big blanket beaver came swimming (MOT: *gh* MOM, PROG) downstream right there by the beach.'

Go bugh **neeyeeneebaanh.**
'He swam (MOT: *n* MOM PERF) right up to her.'

Kk'udaa eeydee koon, "Tsook'aał **dodeenee?***" yełnee.*
'Now this one too asked her, "Grandma, why are you crying
   (OPER: DUR IMPF)?"'

"Donts'e dodo ts'ebaa yeł kk'eeyh neełte **k'eghenaadeyonh** *de
   hukk'aat," yełnee.*
'"Across and downriver, where there are spruce and birch trees
   all grown (CONV-REV: REV PERF) together, that's what I'm
   crying for," she said to him.'

"Tsook'aał nonee sekaal kk'e **doleehoyh,***" yełnee.*
'"Grandma, climb (MOT: *ll* MOM PERF) back there on my tail," he
   told her.'

"Oho', haatlaa."
'"Okay, wait."'

III. A. PARAGRAPHS 19–23: DRAMATIC SEQUENCE

As in episode 1, this narrative sequence also begins with an
inceptive derivative. Of twenty verbs in this sequence, eighteen are
perfective—in striking contrast to the previous story sequences. Of
the eighteen perfectives, fifteen are momentaneous derivatives, one
is a durative derivative, one transitional, and one semelfactive.

19 *Nodegge* **tonohodetaadleghel.**
'She started shuffling (MOT: *ll* MOM PERF INCP) up the bank.'

Kk'udaa dek'ebets'eedaakkoge yeł łaats oołok yeł kk'udaa **k'egheeł-
   zook.**
'Now she went and got (OPER: DUR PERF) her sewing bag and clay
   pot.'

Ts'uh noduhts'en'.
'And she came rushing back down.'

Kk'udaa yekaal tleekk'e **dolyo.**
'Now she climbed (MOT: *ll* MOM PERF) on his tail.'

Kk'udaa nonaan beyeł **noyetaalbaanh.**
'And he started swimming (MOT: *n* MOM PERF INCP) across with
   her.'

20 *Kk'ʉdaa nonaanee* **ghebaał**
'He was swimming (MOT: PROG) way across now.'

Dehoon yekaal tleekk'e **hʉdeełkk'onh.**
'Meanwhile she built (MOT: ∅ MOM PERF) a fire on his tail.'

Go kkun' kkon yekaal tleekk'e **dodaaldlo.**
'She had also put (CL MOT: *ll* MOM PERF) some wood on his tail.'

Kk'ʉdaa łaats oołok kkunaaghe **needaanee'onh.**
'Now she put (CL MOT: *n* MOM PERF) the clay pot at the edge of the fire.'

Kk'ʉdaa nonłe **eenaadlek'ooh**
'And it was just coming to a boil (DESC: *l* TRNS PERF) out there,'

dehoon, "Etlebaa'! Sekaa'!" daadeyoh.
'when he shrieked, "Ouch! My tail!"'

Dehoon **kełet'eh.**
'And slapped (SUCC: SML PERF) his tail.'

21 *Tsook'aał* **todolnenh.**
'Grandma bounced into the water (MOT: *gh* MOM PERF).'

Taadaalggots *eenh go tobaan hʉts'uhu.*
'She sank (MOT: *n* MOM PERF) but it was close to the beach.'

Ts'ʉh taah kkaatl'ogh **neeghoneeyo.**
'And she walked ashore (MOT: *n* MOM PERF) on the bottom of the river.'

22 *Ts'ʉh daangge* **tolyo.**
'And so she went back up (MOT: *ll* MOM PERF) the bank.'

Tobaan **ledo** *dehoon donługh* **kkʉnodobaał** *go bekaa' let'aayee.*
'While she was sitting (STAT: *l* NEU IMPF) on the beach, the one whose tail was burnt was swimming around (MOT: *l* MOM PROG) out there.'

"Tsook'aał, nelo too **gheebenee?"** *yełnee.*
'"Grandma, did water go (MOT: *gh* MOM PERF) in your mouth?" he asked her.'

"Nedeenh," nee.
'"No," she said.'

23   *"Tsook'aał nedzey too **negheebenee'**?" yełnee.*
'"Grandma, did water go (MOT: *gh* MOM PERF) in your ear?" he
asked her.'

"Nedeenh," nee.
'"No," she said.'

*"Tsook'aał, nʉnkk'ʉ too **negheelodee'**? yełnee.*
'"Grandma, did water go (MOT: *gh* MOM PERF) in your eyes?" he
asked her.'

"Nedeenh," nee.
'"No," she said.'

*"Nentseyh too **negheelodee'**?" yełnee.*
'"Did water go (MOT: *gh* MOM PERF) in your nose?" he asked her.'

"Nedeenh," nee.
'"No," she said.'

B. PARAGRAPHS **24–26**: TRANSITION SEQUENCE

This section provides both a break from the dramatic tension of
the preceding sequence and an introduction and background to the
climax that follows. There are three progressive derivatives in this
section, more than in any other. The section also contains the only
irrealis derivatives—two future verbs. There are six neuter imperfective derivatives out of thirteen verbs; the preceding sequence had
only one neuter imperfective out of twenty verbs.

24   *Kk'ʉdaa, "Tsook'aał **do'eeneel** łonh," yeneelenh.*
'So he thought, "I guess nothing happened (OPER: PROG) to
Grandma."'

*Kk'ʉdaa nodo' gheel **ghebaalee**.*
'And then I guess he kept on swimming (MOT: PROG) downriver.'

*Dehoon kk'ʉdaa dodegge **holyo**.*
'Meanwhile she went up (MOT: *ll* MOM PERF) the bank.'

*Ts'ʉh dodeggu gheel **doledo**.*
'And apparently she was sitting up (STAT: *l* NEU IMPF) there on
the bank.'

*Huyeł hun **hudodeggul** eetl'ekk.*
'When she heard a thumping noise coming (SUCC-ONO: ONO, PROG) toward her.'

*Doogh k'etok'eten **ledo**.*
'She was sitting (STAT: *l* NEU IMPF) on an animal trail.'

25 *"Nugh setene," beeznee eehoo.*
'"Off my trail," he said to her, but to no avail.'

26 *Kk'udaa eet **ledo**.*
'Now she was sitting (STAT: *l* NEU IMPF) there.'

*Onts'aa yuh legedze **ledo**.*
'She was sitting (STAT: *l* NEU IMPF) just like a porcupine.'

"Nugh setene
'"Off my trail'

*nugh netl'ets **eetaaghstuł**," beeznee.*
'or I will stamp (SUCC: SML FUT) on your gall bladder," he told her.'

*"Heehaa! Setl'ets **hoolaanee**?" nee.*
'"Heehaa! Do I have (DESC: Ø NEU IMPF) a gall bladder?" she asked.'

"Nugh setene
'"Off my trail'

*nugh nekole'one **eetaaghstuł**," yełnee.*
'or I will stamp (SUCC: SML FUT) on your liver." he told her.'

*(Et'eeyło daałetl'edze go **dedneeyee**.)*
'(Apparently it was a black bear who spoke (OPER: DUR IMPF) to her.)'

*"Heehaa! Sekole'one **hoolaanee**?" nee.*
'"Heehaa! Do I have (DESC: Ø NEU IMPF) a liver?" she asked.'

C. PARAGRAPHS 27–30: CLIMAX

This climax sequence is bounded by transitional derivatives. This section is by far the most aspectually diverse of any in the story. Of fifteen verbs, there are three transitional forms, four successive theme derivatives, three motion, two conversive, and one operative derivative. Ten of the fifteen verbs are perfective.

27 *Kk'ʉdaa tl'ogho **beyeehʉtaaldlet.***
   'Now he really got angry (DESC: TRNS PERF).'

   *No'o yʉh yʉgh **nee'eeltluh,***
   'He rushed (MOT: *n* MOM PERF) over to her,'

   *ts'ʉh yetl'ets **eetaaltuł***
   'and he began to stamp (SUCC: SML PERF INCP) on her gall
   bladder.'

   *Hʉyeł **bekaayeedleghuł,***
   'Then she slapped him with her tail (SUCC: SML PERF),'

   *yekole'on **eetaaltuł** hʉyeł.*
   'just as he was going to stamp (SUCC: SML PERF INCP) on her
   liver.'

   *Kk'ʉdaa tl'ogho yʉh bekkaatl'oh yʉh k'uh yaan' **ehooldlaat.***
   'Now the bottom of his foot became (DESC: *l* TRNS PERF)
   completely covered with quills.'

   *"Ts'aa'! Ts'aa'! **baakk'aanlees**," yełnee.*
   '"Cousin, Cousin, urinate on it (CONV: MOM IMPF) (into the
   wound)," she told him.'

28 *Deheghe'en koon yoogh don*
   'It was for that reason that,'

   *yoogh k'ʉh łeekkaa k'ʉh **needehoyh** te*
   'long ago when quills got (MOT: ∅ MOM IMPF) into dogs,'

   *heł koon łets **henohedeneyhtl.***
   'they used to pour (MOT: PROG) urine on them.'

   *Ʉhte heł koon **hodedeyhtl** beeznee.*
   'It is said that they (quills) fall out (MOT: CUST) then.'

   *Koon **heyedegheenee'.***
   'That's what they used to say (OPER: DUR PERF) about it.'

29 *Kk'ʉdaa **yelaatlghaanh.***
   'Now she had killed him (CONV: CNCL PERF).'

No'o etltaanh,
'He was lying (STAT: *l* NEU IMPF) over there,'

yekaaghelghutl ts'uh.
'because she had hit him again and again with her tail (SUCC: CONS PERF).'

30 *Kk'udaa*
'Now,'

"Yeee'!"
'"Oh dear!"'

Et'eeyło doogh go deyeeloghee.
'Apparently it was her older brother whom she killed (TRNS: TRNS PERF).'

D. PARAGRAPHS 31–32: RESOLUTION-CONCLUSION

This conclusion to the story provides us with two momentaneous perfective derivatives followed by a song. The last paragraph contains the formulaic Koyukon story-ending line.

31 *Kk'udaa daadegge deghaaghedeeyo.*
'Now she climbed up (MOT: Ø MOM PERF) the tree, up this way.'

Ts'uh doogh kk'aa taaltsaah.
'And she began crying (OPER: *l* MOM PERF INCP) for her older brother (with a song).'

"Doogheggu soogh neełtughun tseetsel."
'"Right down here are my older brother's soft feces on the trail."'

"Doogheggu soogh neełtughun tseetseł,"
'"Right down here are my older brother's soft feces on the trail,"'

detaalnee'.
'she began singing.'

32 *Kk'udaa et'eghł huydo hutaaldlet yeenslenh de huyh ghon' naaltl-gus.*
'I thought that the winter had just begun (MOT: *l* MOM PERF INCP) and now I've chewed (CONV: BIS PERF) off part of it.'

The text contains ten of the fifteen Koyukon aspects: neuter, transitional, momentaneous, reversative (one derivative, repeated three times), durative, conclusive, semelfactive, consecutive, bisective, and onomatopoetic. It also contains two of the Koyukon superaspects: progressive and customary. Examining the occurrence of these ten aspects and two superaspects and their interaction with the three modes found in the story (imperfective, perfective, and future), we find at least two clear functions:

- Aspect and mode are used as a sequencing device: to mark episode shifts and shifts of attention or focus, and to sequence events within a single sentence or pair of sentences.

- Aspect is used to indicate the manner or temporal contour of the activity or state referred to by the verb. This second function involves the relationship of aspect to the lexical character of the verb.

6.2. Mode and aspect used as a sequencing device

Mode and aspect are used to signal shifts from one episode or sequence to another. The first three episodes (each of which begins with our protagonist sitting on the beach, crying) begin with durative and neuter imperfectives. The major narrative sequences in II and III are signaled by momentaneous inceptive perfective derivatives. The final climax (IIIC) is bounded by transitional derivatives.

Shifts in focus or attention within each sequence are also marked by the use of particular combinations of mode and aspect. In general, background information tends to be found in neuter or durative imperfective derivations;[5] compare paragraphs 1 and 2 and 9, which provide background and explanatory information, with paragraphs 19 through 23, in which the porcupine woman finally makes the trip across the river.

Both the shifts in focus and the bounding of units of discourse seem to rely on the distribution of perfective versus nonperfective derivatives. (Section 6.2.2 discusses this phenomenon in greater detail.)

6.2.1. The use of aspect in sequencing events

The use of aspect to sequence events within a single sentence is less frequent (at least in this story) than are the other two uses

---

5. Conversation within the narrative, as in paragraphs 5 and 6, also tends to be in the neuter and durative imperfective.

referred to above. One example is the following:

(1)   *degheel go* **ledo** *degheel* **edaak'uhdeedon'**
       'Around there where she was living (NEU IMPF), she had eaten every-
       thing there was to eat (MOM PERF).'

While the sentence above uses momentaneous perfective to
place the activity referred to by that verb as prior to the activity
referred to by the neuter imperfective derivation, the following sentence uses two imperfective forms, a neuter and a durative, to indicate simultaneous activities:

(2)   *Dehoon tł'ee eet* **ledo** *dehoon* **etseh** *tobaan* **etseh**
       'Meanwhile, still staying (NEU IMPF) there, she was crying (DUR IMPF)
       and crying (DUR IMPF) on the beach.'

Here the neuter is used to indicate an ongoing state; the durative
refers to an activity whose end points are within that state. Notice
that within the class of activity verbs, the durative aspect carries a
charge of unboundedness in the sense of Dahl: "A class of situations
or a characterization of a situation is bounded if and only if it is an
essential condition on the members of the class or an essential part
of the characterization that a certain limit or end-state is attained"
(1985:29). Duratives usually refer to processual or habitual activities in which end points are not involved. Only by examining their
use in discourse, however, can we see that, in relation to neuter
derivatives, the durative does imply a more bounded state.
    Like the durative, the progressive refers to ongoing activities. It
is often used to contrast the processual nature of an action with the
more delimited nature of active perfective events. Again in this text,
however, it is used in juxtaposition with the neuter to imply an ongoing activity with end points. The following example demonstrates
this use:

(3)   *Tobaan* **ledo** *dehoon donługh* **kkunodobaał** *go bekaa' kent'aayee.*
       'While she was sitting (NEU IMPF) on the beach, the one whose tail
       was burnt was swimming (*l* MOM, PROG) around out there.'

Mode, aspect, and superaspect, then, are used to indicate the
succession or simultaneity of events within individual sentences. It
is only the neuter imperfective, durative imperfective, and progres-

sive that come into play in this use, however. Similarly, in sequencing larger units of the discourse it is again largely the distribution of perfectives and neuter or durative imperfectives that carries the functional load.

6.2.2. The use of perfective to highlight discourse

The major factor in the use of mode and aspect as a focusing or sequencing device in larger units of the discourse is the arrangement of perfective versus nonperfective derivatives. In order to determine whether or not the perfective is used as a discourse-foregrounding strategy, it is crucial to have a clear picture of that arrangement.

Table 6.2. Verbs According to Mode, Aspect, and Theme Category

THEME CATEGORY	PERFECTIVE	NONPERFECTIVE[6]
DESCRIPTIVE AND STATIVE		
Neuter	1	19
Transitional	4	0
MOTION		
Momentaneous	24	5
Progressive	-	9
Customary	-	1
OPERATIVE		
Durative	2	24
Momentaneous	2	0
Progressive	-	1
CONVERSIVE		
Conclusive	1	0
Reversative	3	0
Momentaneous	0	1
SUCCESSIVE		
Semelfactive	4	2
Consecutive	1	0
Bisective	1	0
Ono.-Prog.	-	1
TOTALS	43	63

6. The non-perfective category includes imperfective, future, progressive, and customary. The text of *Tobaan Etseh* contains no optative forms and no other superaspectual derivations.

Forty-three verbs in the text (40 percent of the total) are perfective. Table 6.2 illustrates the number of verbs in the text according to mode, aspect, and theme category.

Almost two-thirds of all perfectives (32 of 43, or 74 percent) occur in the final fourteen of the thirty-two paragraphs (i.e., in sections IIIA-C). Only one of those perfectives is in section IIIB, the transition sequence; five are in section IIID, the conclusion. Thus, the two most dramatic sequences of the story (sections IIIA and IIIC, accounting for only nine of the story's thirty-two paragraphs) contain 60 percent of the story's total perfective derivatives. Fully 74 percent of the thirty-five verbs in sections IIIA and IIIC are perfective. By contrast, those two sections contain only seven nonperfective derivatives, or only 11 percent of the story's total.

We must consider whether the high percentage of perfective derivatives in sections (IIIA) and (IIIC) of the text represents foregrounding as it is generally understood. Hopper defines foreground as "the parts of the narrative which relate events belonging to the skeletal structure of the discourse" (1979:213). Kalmar adopts a similar approach and points out that the Inuktitut modes "make it possible to single out essential as opposed to background information, to distinguish events that develop rather than elaborate the speaker's message" (1982:46).

In the present Koyukon story too, it seems that picking out only those sentences with perfective derivatives will bring into focus the more dramatic sequences of the text. The following presents just those lines in *Tobaan Etseh* that contain perfective derivatives:

'In the time very long ago (DESC: NEU PERF)'
'Around there where she was living (STAT: *l* NEU IMPF), she had eaten (OPER: N MOM PERF) everything there was to eat.'
'Now she went down (MOT: ∅ MOM PERF) the bank.'
'And meanwhile she started to cry and cry (OP: *l* MOM INCP PERF).'
'It swam (MOT: *n* MOM PERF) up to her, down there on the beach.'
'"Grandchild, across and downriver, where there are spruce trees and birch trees all grown together (CONV-REV: REV PERF),'
'"Oh! Grandchild, across and downriver, where there are spruce and birch trees all grown (CONV-REV: REV PERF) together,'
'It swam ashore (MOT: *n* MOM PERF) to her.'
'"Grandchild, across and downriver, where there are spruce and birch trees all grown (CONV-REV: REV PERF) together, that's what I'm crying for," she told him.'
'He swam (MOT: *n* MOM PERF) right up to her.'
'"Across and downriver, where there are spruce and birch trees all grown (CONV-REV: REV PERF) together, that's what I'm

crying for," she said to him.'

'"Grandma, climb (MOT: *ll* MOM PERF) back there on my tail," he told her.'

'She started shuffling (MOT: *ll* MOM PERF INCP) up the bank.'

'Now she went and got (OPER: DUR PERF) her sewing bag and clay pot.'

'Now she climbed (MOT: *ll* MOM PERF) on his tail.'

'And he started swimming (MOT: *n* MOM PERF INCP) across with her.'

'Meanwhile she built (MOT: ∅ MOM PERF) a fire on his tail.'

'She had also put (CL MOT: *ll* MOM PERF) some wood on his tail.'

'Now she put (CL MOT: *n* MOM PERF) the clay pot at the edge of the fire.'

'And it was just coming to a boil (DESC: *l* TRNS PERF) out there,'

'And slapped (SUCC: SML PERF) his tail.'

'Grandma bounced into the water (MOT: *gh* MOM PERF).'

'She sank (MOT: *n* MOM PERF) but it was close to the beach.'

'And she walked ashore (MOT: *n* MOM PERF) on the bottom of the river.'

'And so she went back up (MOT: *ll* MOM PERF) the bank.'

'"Grandma, did water go (MOT: *gh* MOM PERF) in your mouth?" he asked her.'

'"Grandma, did water go (MOT: *gh* MOM PERF) in your ear?" he asked her.'

'"Grandma, did water go (MOT: *gh* MOM PERF) in your eyes?" he asked her.'

'"Did water go (MOT: *gh* MOM PERF) in your nose?" he asked her.'

'Meanwhile she went up (MOT: *ll* MOM PERF) the bank.'

'Now he really got angry (DESC: TRNS PERF).'

'He rushed (MOT: *n* MOM PERF) over to her,'

'and he began to stamp (SUCC: ƷML PERF INCP) on her gall bladder.'

'Then she slapped him with her tail (SUCC: SML PERF),'

'just as he was going to stamp (SUCC: SML PERF INCP) on her liver.'

'Now the bottom of his foot became (DESC: *l* TRNS PERF) completely covered with quills.'

'That's what they used to say (OPER: DUR PERF) about it.'

'Now she had killed him (CONV: CNCL PERF).'

'because she had hit him again and again with her tail (SUCC: CONS PERF).'

'Apparently it was her older brother whom she killed (TRNS: TRNS PERF).'

'Now she climbed up (MOT: ∅ MOM PERF) the tree, up this way.'

'And she began crying (OPER: *l* MOM PERF INCP) for her older brother (with a song).'

'I thought that the winter had just begun (MOT: *l* MOM PERF INCP) and now I've chewed (CONV: BIS PERF) off part of it.'

Notice that reading just the lines given above provides only a sketchy synopsis of the story's plot. *Tobaan Etseh* does not show a consistent shifting back and forth between perfective and imperfective corresponding to Kalmar's description of "development" and "elaboration," with the perfective clauses relaying the "gist of the story," a connected plotline. What we find instead is a *clustering* of perfectives in the two dramatic sequences of section III. Those sequences do seem to be delimited by the change in frequency of perfective versus imperfective derivatives. It may be somewhat post hoc, however, to label those sequences as foregrounded or even as "the most dramatic" of the story's related events simply because they contain more perfectives. Further, it would be hard to defend the position that the preceding paragraphs, which are made up largely of imperfective derivatives, all convey only backgrounded information.

In the paragraphs of section II, our porcupine heroine is approached by three different creatures in succession, each offering to transport her across the river to more wooded territory. Each in turn is refused. The fourth offer, in paragraph 18 (section IID), is accepted and thereafter begins the first clustering of perfective derivatives. This clustering corresponds to the description of more movement and activity for our heroine in the sequence related in paragraphs 19 through 23 (section IIIA). Perhaps a more appropriate characterization of the use of perfective, in this text at least, is to say that it highlights or accentuates those episodes in which the protagonist is engaged in more vigorous activity.[7]

It is important to reiterate that the first of the functions of aspect in discourse that I have singled out is performed by a limited set of the mode and aspect possibilities, i.e., by the use of neuter or durative imperfective to relay background or "low focus" material, and by the use of perfective forms to convey dramatic or "high focus" activity. The significant distinction here is between perfective and imperfective.

7. In this regard, it would be interesting to examine conversation to see if the use and distribution of the perfective there varies from that found in narrative. The one conversation I was able to examine was transcribed by Eliza Jones from a tape made by Catherine Attla of her discussion with Bessie Henry of Koyukuk. Jones and I translated the transcription in 1983. The conversation has significantly more repetition and, of course, a far less episodic structure than do typical narrative texts. However, my preliminary study revealed that, as in narrative, the perfective was more frequently used in those portions of the exchange that recounted more vigorous activity.

6.3. Aspect and lexical semantics in discourse

While the distinction between perfective and imperfective is involved in the bounding and highlighting of discourse sequences, the three-way distinction within activity-event verbs of process (durative) versus goal (conclusive) versus punctuality (semelfactive) seems to have a far less direct relationship with global discourse phenomena. Rather, this distinction appears to have much more to do with the lexical or semantic properties of individual verbs. It is interesting in this regard to recall Jakobson's (1957) reference to aspect as a "designator" since it characterizes only the narrated event, while calling mood a "connector" since it relates "one narrated variable to another" (Friedrich 1974:35). The imperfective, perfective, future, optative set does, then, function more like mood (or mode), while the clearest function of the Koyukon aspects fit Jakobson's definition of aspect in being tied to a narrower domain of the discourse. According to Smith's (1983:480) formulation, mode functions in the manner of "viewpoint aspect" while the Koyukon aspects function as "situation aspect."

The Koyukon aspects are used to indicate the manner or temporal contour of the activity or state referred to by the verb. In chapter 5, I said that derivational aspect is constrained to a great extent by the semantic character of the verb root and theme. In fact, many scholars (e.g., Friedrich 1974, Comrie 1976, Dahl 1985) have discussed the constraints that inherent aspectual meaning puts on a verb's derivational potential (although few, if any, have examined the consequences of those constraints in discourse). As Friedrich points out, "in all languages, there exist many sets of verbs with features of inception, completion, and the like as part of their inherent meaning. . . . Such aspectual meanings are secondary in that they are the derived consequences or implications of the activity referred to by the verbal root" (1974:4). In Koyukon, these "secondary aspectual meanings" are grammaticized in the aspectual morphology. For example, because 'chopping' is inherently a punctual, nonstate activity, it can be expressed with the semelfactive aspect but not with the stative neuter aspect. 'Walking' can be expressed with neither punctual nor stative aspectual derivatives, and 'standing' can be expressed with stative aspectual derivatives only.

Mode is also linked to the inherent aspectual character of the verb. As pointed out in chapter 3 (sections 3.2.12 and 3.2.14), the semelfactive and conclusive aspects most often occur in the perfective mode. Because the semelfactive refers to abrupt single actions and the conclusive to the attainment of an activity's goal, we would expect that both aspects would be less compatible semantically with notions of imperfectivity and would appear in narrative discourse more often in the perfective mode. Similarly, we would expect to see a correlation between durative verbs and imperfectivity. Studying the distribution of perfective derivatives according to aspect in *Tobaan Etseh* shows that this is, in fact, the case.

Table 6.3 illustrates the percent of perfectives among the total number of verbs in the text, according to aspect. It is clear that semelfactive and conclusive verbs are most often, if not always, perfective (the two nonperfective semelfactive verbs are not imperfective, but rather, future). That situation is a natural consequence of the inherent meaning of boundedness carried by those aspects, their semantic perfectivity. Momentaneous derivatives, too, tend to carry a terminative meaning and are more often found in the perfective. Duratives, on the other hand, are most often morphologically marked as imperfective, in accord with their semantic imperfectivity in indicating ongoing activity. Koyukon neuter derivatives too, are rarely found in any mode other than imperfective.

Table 6.3. Percentage of Perfectives for Verbs in Each Aspect

	Neu	Dur	Mom	Cncl	Sml
Total	20	26	32	1	6
Perfectives	1	2	26	1	4
% of Total	5%	8%	81%	100%	66%

Note that the first and second functions of aspect outlined above must overlap here. As a "consequence" of the activity referred to by the verbal root meaning 'kill', for example, the primary aspectual derivation is necessarily completive (i.e., conclusive). Conclusive verbs most often occur in the perfective mode. 'Killing' then, is, by virtue of its inherent semantics, associated with completion and with perfectivity, and, consequently, derivationally conclusive and perfective. One would expect a sentence referring to killing to consist of "high focus," dramatic, foregrounded information, but the use of perfective in this case is as much a product of its inherent semantic character as of its "foregroundedness." It seems that relative "focus" is very much constrained by the particular information being conveyed—not just anything can be either foregrounded or backgrounded. The distribution of mode and aspect in the text of *Tobaan Etseh* suggests that both derivational aspect—and the foregrounding and backgrounding of narrative material associated with it—are driven by lexical choice.

We must then ask, what motivates the narrator's lexical choice. For recounting the death of one individual at the hands of another, for example, any language provides a range of lexical, morphological, or syntactic forms. In Koyukon, where different verbs are associated with different clusters of aspectual derivation types and only perfectivity seems to have a direct relationship with highlighted or foregrounded material, the choice of verb (and concomitantly, of derivational aspect) can serve to produce a particular narrative effect. Which perfective verb will a speaker choose to relate a particular event and to what effect? How is this narrative effect related to foregrounding? It is useful in this regard to examine different storytellers' renditions of the same tale to see the narrative consequences of aspectual choice.

To that end, I looked at another available version of *Tobaan Etseh*, one told by Jenny Huntington of Koyukuk. Each village has its own version of this story and, though the basic structure and plot remains the same, there are interesting variations. For example, in the version of Catherine Attla of Huslia, the story's heroine is a single porcupine. In the version told in the village of Ruby (Eliza Jones, p.c.), the heroine is a married porcupine who is left alone to care for her young children when her husband goes off to hunt and never returns. This is her motivation for wanting to cross the river. The Koyukuk version is different in perhaps a more interesting respect. Instead of killing the bear in a deliberate, agentive fashion as we find in the Huslia version *(huyeł bekaayeedleghuł* (SUCC: SML PERF) 'then she slapped him with her tail'. . . *kk'udaa yelaatlghaanh* (CONV: CNCL PERF) 'now she had killed him'), the porcupine protagonist in the Koyukuk version merely slaps him repeatedly (consecutively) with her tail. Some time later, as the quills work their way into his heart, he dies.

The variation between agentive and nonagentive description is also present in two versions of the story *Kaazene* 'Lynx'—a story of a woman who is told by a seagull that her husband, supposedly off hunting for the winter, is actually living with two young women downriver. After going to investigate, she discovers the seagull was correct. She drowns the two women by holding their heads down in a pot of soup and then turns her faithless husband into a lynx.

The first version of *Kaazene* that I looked at was told by Catherine Attla of Huslia; the second version was told by Chief Henry of Koyukuk. In some details, the two stories are remarkably similar, with identical verbs used to express certain things. There is a difference though, in the way the death of the two women is expressed. In Attla's version, the killing is reported as, *"doo', hugheeghonh"* 'well (what do you know), she killed them'. The verb here is a durative perfective.[8] In Chief Henry's version of *Kaazene*, the killing of the two women is conveyed by the words, *"ts'uh, neeheneelet"* 'and then, they died'. In this case the verb is a momentaneous perfective with the aspect-dependent derivational string, *nee# n* MOM 'up to a point'. Although both renditions express the deaths with a perfective verb, the Attla version carries a much more active, agentive sense. (This intuition was confirmed by Jones, p.c.) Notice that this variation is equivalent to the variation noted between the Huslia and Koyukuk versions of *Tobaan Etseh.*

Perhaps it is more useful to consider the phenomenon of foregrounding not as an all-or-nothing affair, but rather as a continuum from narrative material that is greatly emphasized or accentuated, to material that can be considered a background aside, relatively inessential to the development and elaboration of the story. Aspect may be employed by Koyukon storytellers to add to or detract from the highlighting of material associated with the use of perfective mode. In the story pairs discussed above, aspect was used to convey a greater or lesser degree of agentivity. This relationship between aspect and agency has been noted elsewhere, as Chung and Timberlake point out:

> A commonly invoked criterion for distinguishing processes from states involves agency: if an event has an agent (a conscious, willful, responsible instigator), then it is a process rather than a state. . . . A number of operational tests for stativity are based on agency: states do not occur in the imperative . . . or subordinated to certain governing verbs . . . because both of these modal contexts require an agent who is responsible for the event. . . . The criterion of agency is useful, but provides only a one-way implication: an event with an agent is dynamic, but there are events without agents that

8. Recall that the verb used to express the porcupine's killing of the bear in *Tobaan Etseh* was a conclusive perfective. The conclusive verb, however, refers only to killing singular animates. To kill more than one, as is the case in *Kaazene*, takes a longer period of time and so must be expressed with a durative verb.

are not stative. [1985:215]

The relationship between agency and foregrounding is less clear, however; perhaps the use of a durative perfective—when the more semantically natural mode for a durative verb is imperfective, for instance—conveys a more agentive, and "more foregrounded," sense in general than does a momentaneous. On the other hand, it could be argued that the less agentive tone of the Koyukuk versions of the two stories does not imply less foregrounding but instead highlights the event by using understatement.

Foregrounding is undoubtedly a more complicated issue than just the highlighting of "essential" information. It may be associated not only with perfectivity and agentivity, but also with transitivity. Note, for example, the role of transitivity in producing the differences between the story pairs discussed above. Recall that Attla in both cases chose a transitive verb, while Huntington and Chief Henry chose intransitive verbs. The interaction between transitivity and the morphosyntax of aspect has also often been addressed in the literature, as has a relationship between aspect and case marking. A clear statement of the relationship of those morphosyntactic strategies with both aspect and foregrounding requires further study.

6.4. Summary

The aspectual system of Koyukon provides support for previous work that cites a relationship between aspect and narrative structure. However, it also raises questions about the explanatory adequacy of the posited correlation of foregroundedness and perfectivity. Mode, the component of the Koyukon aspectual system that has functional significance in a more global discourse domain, is both separate from and inextricably bound to aspect, a component more closely aligned with a narrower domain of propositional semantics. As Hopper (p.c.) points out, the sentence and larger discourse units cannot be considered separate, discrete, and contrasting levels between which some directional semantic process may be posited. Further, a sharp division between global and local semantics is difficult to draw. Global issues of narrative style and of story structure and theme are linked in complex ways with local issues of lexical choice; the use of derivational aspect is motivated and constrained by this complex combination of factors.

7
Conclusions

I have presented an account of the aspectual system of a language rich with derivational means for expressing temporal distinctions. The primary temporal distinctions in Koyukon may be diagrammed as a hierarchy of oppositions in order of significance as follows:

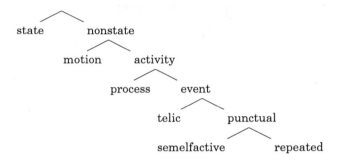

Figure 7.1. Aspectual distinctions in Koyukon.

In describing this aspectual system, I have raised three related issues concerning aspect and conceptual categorization. The first issue pertains to the structure of aspectual categories. I suggested that both the fifteen aspect categories and the seven aspectual verb theme categories could be described along two parameters. The first parameter is based on the observation that aspectual categories have central members, or semantically prototypical exemplars. The second parameter has to do with the use of morphophonological cues in the perception of aspectual meaning. The use of aspect types suggests that morphophonological cues and the existence of semantic prototype structures both play a crucial role in the production and comprehension of temporal information.

A second issue was the flexibility provided within the categorization of aspects and of theme categories by the interaction of prefixal and suffixal morphology—that is, by the semantic interplay of prefix complex and verb stem. That interplay allows speakers the possibility of using these morphological chunks as separate sets of phonological and semantic cues in cross-referencing prototype categories.

The third issue I addressed was the relationship of lexical and derivational means of expressing temporal semantics. I showed that lexical meaning determines category membership and the concomitant distribution of morphological aspect. The interaction of lexical and derivational elements allows an extremely wide range of temporal expression, but inherent aspectual meaning both constrains and motivates the use of aspect in discourse.

7.1. Areas for future research

In addition to its relevance to the broader study of aspect and of linguistic categorization, the discussion of the Koyukon aspectual system touches on general issues of theoretical morphology, such as: (1) the distinction between morphological rules and representations; (2) the division of morphological phenomena into the categories of lexicon, inflection, and derivation; and (3) the interaction between morphology and the phonological, syntactic, and semantic components of language.

Regarding this last issue, I have suggested some of the ways in which the analysis of aspectual morphology in Koyukon is tied to phonological and semantic expression. However, as suggested within the discussion at the close of chapter 6 regarding discourse foregrounding, the interaction of aspectual morphology with morphosyntactic strategies for expressing agentivity and transitivity is an area that requires more study. According to Chung and Timberlake, "The morphosyntactic interaction between event categories and participant categories—notably aspect and case—is well-known. It is often the case that ergative case marking (or agreement) occurs in the perfective or perfect aspect, while nominative case marking occurs in the imperfective or non-perfect aspect" (1985:257). DeLancey also discusses the relationship of transitivity, case, and perfective marking. He argues that there is "a semantic parallel between the structure of aspectual and voice distinctions, involving a category which I call viewpoint" (1979:168). He considers cases of aspectual split ergativity, showing that imperfective in those languages is associated with agent-oriented nominative-accusative marking, while perfective is associated with patient-oriented ergative-absolutive marking. In this regard, recall that the Koyukon neuter verbs, which are most often intransitive patient-oriented verbs, have perfective morphology even in their imperfective variants.

The interaction of aspect and detransitivizing operations bears investigation under this heading as well. Some aspects, such as the perambulative and the persistive, require the D-effect voicing of the classifier prefix, which is otherwise most often found in such valency-altering constructions as passive and reflexive. Additionally, many of the aspect-dependent derivational prefix strings allow, or require, the deletion of a direct object. These detransitivizing uses of aspect are generally restricted to the motion aspects. (Cf. Talmy 1985 for a definition of "motion" as a separate semantic-grammatical category.)

Another area within the morphology of Koyukon aspect that could profit from further analysis is the distinction between inflection and derivation—the subject of much discussion in the literature on morphology in recent years. While some researchers, such as Bybee (1985), propose a continuum from inflectional to derivational processes, most linguists have traditionally assumed a fairly sharp division between those two word formation categories. It is this boundary that can be most fruitfully examined within the Koyukon aspectual system. In chapter 3, I implied that it was not useful to posit any structural difference between mode and aspect, and throughout the book I have treated both as derivational categories. It could be argued, however, that while aspectual distinctions are indeed derivational, mode can be considered inflectional.

Mithun, in her discussion of derivational number marking, reminds us (per Bybee 1985) that "inflectional distinctions are obligatorily specified on all members of a lexical class or subclass. . . . Inflectional categories must therefore be sufficiently general in meaning to be applicable to all members of a lexical class or subclass" (1988:231). In other words, while some distinctions may be equally applicable to all members of a category, other distinctions may be pertinent only to certain subgroups of the category. Aspect in Koyukon is much like verbal number distinctions, which, Mithun says, "rarely become inflectional [in languages of the world], because the pertinence of number varies so greatly from one type of event to another"(1988:232). It has been demonstrated that the meanings expressed by the Koyukon aspects, too, are central only to certain subcategories of verb. Unlike those distinctions that "vary widely in their importance and applicability to events" (1988:233), however, all four of the Koyukon mode distinctions do seem to be relevant and applicable to all verbs, and thus can be classed as inflectional.

Anderson, arguing for a separation of the categories of inflection and derivation in the grammar, summarizes Perlmutter's discus-

sion of portmanteau morphemes and points out that "there never
seem to be elements which combine inflectional and derivational
categories in the same portmanteau. If the two sorts of operation
[inflection and derivation] are performed in the same component,
why should they display this unwillingness to combine with one
another?" (1988:29). If one considers Koyukon mode and aspect to
be representatives of the two separate categories, then that language does provide an example of portmanteaux that carry both
(i.e., inflectional mode and derivational aspect), suggesting that
there is indeed a single component in which those operations are
performed.

    The constituency of the category 'mode' in Koyukon and its rela-
tionship with aspect is clearly in need of further research, as Chung
and Timberlake point out:

    As a consequence of the similarity between tense-aspect and
    mood, these categories interact morphosyntactically in some con-
    crete ways. Perhaps the most obvious restrictions have to do with
    the morphosyntactic elaboration of categories: for example, realis
    mood makes more tense distinctions than irrealis; imperfective
    aspect makes more tense distinctions than perfective, and neutral
    aspect makes more tense distinctions than perfect or progressive;
    past tense makes more aspectual distinctions than present or fu-
    ture. [1985:256]

Chung and Timberlake also say that mood "deals with events
and worlds" while aspect deals with "events and time" (1985:256).
Perhaps the overlap between these two categories in Koyukon is
analogous, then, to an overlapping view of time and space, often
noted in studies of Athabaskan. Pinxton, van Dooren, and Harvey,
for example, include the following as one of the basic conceptual
clusters of Navajo natural philosophy:

    The dynamic nature of the world: in opposition to the common
    Western belief of segmentability of an essentially static world,
    Navajos systematically represent the world and every discrete
    entity as a dynamic or continuously changing entity. A complex
    time-space notion seems more applicable than clearly distinct con-
    cepts of one-dimensional time and three-dimensional space. [1983:
    36]

How differing views of temporal and spatial constituency affect, or
are motivated by, the linguistic expression of those categories will
be an important issue in the developing field of cognitive studies.

References

Anderson, Stephen R.
  1988   Inflection. *In* Theoretical Morphology, edited by Michael
            Hammond and Michael Noonan, 23–24. San Diego: Academic
            Press.
Aronoff, Mark
  1976   Word Formation in Generative Grammar. Linguistic Inquiry
            Monograph no. 1. Cambridge, Mass.: MIT Press.
  1983   A Decade of Morphology and Word Formation. Annual Review
            of Anthropology 12:355–75.
Attla, Catherine
  1983   Sitsiy Yugh Noholnik Ts'in': As My Grandfather Told It.
            Edited and translated by Eliza Jones and Melissa Axelrod.
            Fairbanks: Alaskan Native Language Center.
Axelrod, Melissa
  1990   The Semantics of Temporal Categorization. Ph.D. disserta-
            tion. University of Colorado, Boulder. (UMI order number
            9032809.)
Bybee, Joan
  1985   Morphology: A Study of the Relation between Meaning and
            Form. Philadelphia: John Benjamins.
Chung, Sandra, and A. H. Timberlake
  1985   Tense, Aspect, and Mood. *In* Language Typology and Syntactic
            Description: Grammatical Categories and the Lexicon, edited
            by Timothy Shopen, 202–58. Cambridge: Cambridge Univer-
            sity Press.
Clark, Eve V., and Kathie L. Carpenter
  1989   The Notion of Source in Language Acquisition. Language 65:
            1–30.
Coleman, Linda, and Paul Kay
  1981   Prototype Semantics: The English Word 'lie'. Language 57:
            26–44.
Comrie, Bernard
  1976   Aspect. Cambridge: Cambridge University Press.
  1985   Tense. Cambridge: Cambridge University Press.
Croft, William
  1984   Semantic and Pragmatic Correlates to Syntactic Categories.
            In Papers from the Parasession on Lexical Semantics, edited
            by D. Testen et al., 53–70. Chicago: Chicago Linguistic

Society.

Dahl, Östen

1985   Tense and Aspect Systems. New York: Basil Blackwell.

DeLancey, Scott

1982   Aspect, Transitivity and Viewpoint. *In* Tense Aspect: Between
         Semantics and Pragmatics, edited by Paul J. Hopper, 167–83.
         Amsterdam: John Benjamins.

Dowty, David

1979   Word Meaning and Montague Grammar. Dordrecht: D. Reidel.

Fillmore, Charles

1975   An Alternative to Checklist Theories of Meaning. Proceedings
         of the 1st Annual Meeting, pp. 123–31. Berkeley: Berkeley
         Linguistic Society.

Friedrich, Paul

1974   On Aspect Theory and Homeric Aspect. International Journal
         of American Linguistics 40:1–44. Memoir no. 28. Chicago:
         University of Chicago Press.

Givón, Talmy

1982   Tense-Aspect-Modality: The Creole Proto-Type and Beyond. *In*
         Tense Aspect: Between Semantics and Pragmatics, edited by
         Paul J. Hopper, 115–63. Amsterdam: John Benjamins.

Golla, Victor

1970   Hupa Grammar. Ph.D. diss., University of California, Berke-
         ley.

Hale, Kenneth

1956   The Distribution of the Class II Prefixes in Navaho. M.A.
         thesis, Indiana University.

Hall, Robert, Jr.

1964   Introductory Linguistics. Philadelphia: Chilton.

Hardy, Frank

1979   Navajo Aspectual Verb Stem Variation. Ph.D. diss. University
         of New Mexico, Albuquerque.

Hoijer, Harry

1945   The Apachean Verb. Part I: Verb Structure and Pronominal
         Prefixes. International Journal of American Linguistics 1:193–
         204.

1946   The Apachean Verb. Part II: The Prefixes for Mode and Tense.
         International Journal of American Linguistics 11: 123–25.

1948   The Apachean Verb. Part IV: Major Form Classes. Interna-
         tional Journal of American Linguistics 14: 247–59.

1949   The Apachean Verb. Part V: The Theme and Prefix Complex.

International Journal of American Linguistics 15:12–23.

Hopper, Paul J.

1979   Aspect and Foregrounding in Discourse. *In* Syntax and Semantics, vol. 12, Discourse and Syntax, edited by Talmy Givón, 213–41. New York: Academic Press.

1982   Aspect between Discourse and Grammar [introductory essay for the volume]. *In* Tense Aspect: Between Semantics and Pragmatics, edited by Paul J. Hopper, 3–18. Amsterdam: John Benjamins.

Hopper, Paul J., and Sandra Thompson

1984   The Discourse Basis for Lexical Categories in Universal Grammar. Language 60:703–52.

Jacobsen, Wesley

1984   Lexical Aspect in Japanese. *In* Papers from the Parasession on Lexical Semantics, edited by D. Testen et al., 150–61. Chicago: Chicago Linguistic Society.

Jakobson, Roman

1957   Shifters, Verbal Categories, and the Russian Verb. Cambridge, Mass.: Harvard Univeristy Press.

Jetté, Jules, S.J.

1905   Ten'a Dictionary. Ms., Crosby Archive. Gonzaga University, Spokane, Wash.

1906   On the Language of the Ten'a. Ms., Crosby Archive. Gonzaga University, Spokane, Wash.

Jones, Eliza

1979   Aspectual Stem Variation in Koyukon. Proceedings of the 43d Congress of Americanists, Vancouver.

Jones, Eliza, ed.

1979   Chief Henry Yugh Noholnigee: The Stories That Chief Henry Told. Translated by Eliza Jones. Fairbanks: American Native Language Center.

Jones, Eliza, Melissa Axelrod, and Jules Jetté.

Forthcoming Koyukon Athabaskan Dictionary. Fairbanks: Alaska Native Language Center.

Kalmar, Ivan

1982   The Function of Inuktitut Verb Modes in Narrative Texts. *In* Tense Aspect: Between Semantics and Pragmatics, edited by Paul J. Hopper, 45–64. Amsterdam: John Benjamins.

Kari, James

1979   Athaskan Verb Theme Categories: Ahtna. Fairbanks: Alaska Native Language Center.

1990   Ahtna Dictionary. Fairbanks: Alaska Native Language Center.

Krauss, Michael E.

1964   Proto-Athabaskan-Eyak and the Problem of Na-Dene. Part 1: The Phonology. International Journal of American Linguistics 30:118–31.

1969   On the Classifiers in the Athabaskan, Eyak, and Tlingit Verb. Indiana University Publications in Anthropology and Linguistics 23/24: 53.

1980   Alaska Native Languages: Past, Present, and Future. Fairbanks: Alaska Native Language Center.

1982   Native Peoples and Languages of Alaska [map]. Fairbanks: Alaska Native Language Center.

Krauss, Michael E., and Jeff Leer

1981   Athabaskan, Eyak, and Tlingit Sonorants. Fairbanks: Alaska Native Language Center.

Lakoff, George

1987   Women, Fire, and Dangerous Things. Chicago: University of Chicago Press.

Leer, Jeff

1979   Proto-Athabaskan Verb Stem Variation. Part 1: Phonology. Fairbanks: Alaska Native Language Center.

Li, Fang-Kuei

1946   Chipewyan. In Linguistic Structures of Native America, edited by Harry Joijer et al., 398–423. New York: Viking Fund Publications in Anthropology 6.

Lloyd, Albert

1979   Anatomy of the Verb: The Gothic Verb as a Model for a Unified Theory of Aspect, Actional Types, and Verbal Velocity. Amsterdam: John Benjamins.

Midgette, Sally

1987   The Navajo Progressive in Discourse Context: A Study in Temporal Semantics. Ph.D. diss., University of New Mexico, Albuquerque.

Mithun, Marianne

1988   Lexical Categories and the Evolution of Number Marking. In Theoretical Morphology, edited by Michael Hammond and Michael Noonan, 211–34. San Diego: Academic Press.

Morice, Adrian Gabriel

1932   The Carrier Language. Vienna: Anthropos.

Pinxten, Rik, Ingrid van Dooren, and Frank Harvey
  1983   The Anthropology of Space. Philadelphia: University of Penn-
            sylvania Press.
Rice, Keren
  1989   A Grammar of Slave. Berlin: Mouton.
Rosch, Eleanor
  1973   Natural Categories. Cognitive Psychology 4:328–50.
  1977   Human Categorization. In Advances in Cross-Cultural Psy-
            chology, edited by N. Warren, 1–49. New York: Academic
            Press.
  1978   Principles of Categorization. In Cognition and Categorization,
            edited by E. Rosch and B. Lloyd, 27–48. Hillsdale, N.J.:
            Erlbaum.
Sapir, Edward
  1936   Internal Evidence Suggestive of the Northern Origin of
            Navaho. American Anthropologist 38:224–35.
Sapir, Edward, and Harry Hoijer
  1967   The Phonology and Morphology of the Navaho Language. Uni-
            versity of California Publications in Linguistics, no. 50.
Schriffrin, Deborah
  1981   Tense Variation in Narrative. Language 57:45–62.
Silva-Corvalán, Carmen
  1985   Tense and Aspect in Oral Spanish Narrative. Language
            59:760–80.
Smith, Carlota S.
  1983   A Theory of Aspectual Choice. Language. 59:479–501.
  1989a   Characteristics of Situation Types in English. Ms.
  1989b   Comments on Situation Types in Navajo. Ms.
  1989c   Temporal Aspect. Ms.
  1991   The Parameter of Aspect. Studies in Linguistics and
            Philosophy, v. 43. Dordrecht: Kluwer Academic Publ.
Tai, James
  1984   Verbs and Times in Chinese: Vendler's Four Categories. In
            Lexical Semantics, pp. 289–296. Chicago: Chicago Linguistic
            Society.
Talmy, Leonard
  1985   Lexicalization Patterns: Semantic Structure in Lexical Forms.
            In Language Typology and Syntactic Description: Gramma-
            tical Categories and the Lexicon, edited by Timothy Shopen,
            57–149. Cambridge: Cambridge University Press.

Thompson, Chad

1977   Koyukon Verb Prefixes. M.A. thesis, University of Alaska,
        Fairbanks.

Thompson, Chad, Melissa Axelrod, and Eliza Jones

1983   Han Zaadlitlee Koyukon Language Curriculum Scope and
        Sequence. Nenana: Yukon-Koyukuk School District.

Vendler, Zeno

1967   Linguistics in Philosophy. Ithaca: Cornell University Press.

Wallace, Stephen

1982   Figure and Ground: The Interrelationships of Linguistic Cate-
        gories. In Tense Aspect: Between Semantics and Pragmatics,
        edited by Paul J. Hopper, 201–23. Amsterdam: John Ben-
        jamins.

Waugh, Linda, and Monique Monville-Burston

1986   Aspect and Discourse Function: The French Simple Past in
        Newspaper Usage. Language 62:846–77.

Young, Robert

1983   Navajo Verb Themes. Ms.

Young, Robert, and William Morgan

1980   The Navajo Language: A Grammar and Colloquial Dictionary.
        Albuquerque: University of New Mexico Press.

1987   The Navajo Language: A Grammar and Colloquial Dictionary.
        Rev. ed. Albuquerque: University of New Mexico Press.

1992   Analytic Lexicon of Navajo. Albuquerque: University of New
        Mexico Press.

Index

Categories, verb theme
Vowel lengthening: in aspectually
modified verb stems, 13, 48,
50, 54, 56, 60, 73, 113, 115; in
superaspectually modified
verb stems, 91, 94, 97, 99-100
Vowel reduction: in aspectually
modified verb stems, of motion
verbs, 13, 54, 56, 59, 113, 115;
of activity verbs, 66, 70, 75,
77, 115; in superaspectually
modified verb stems, 97,
99-100

Wallace, S., 158
Waugh, L., 158
Williams, S., 8

Young, R., 30, 35, 37, 98, 147
Yukon, Central (Koyukon dialect),
10

Zones, of prefix positions, 14-16

Other volumes of Studies in the
Anthropology of North American
Indians include:

*From the Sands to the Mountain:
Change and Persistence in a
Southern Paiute Community*
By Pamela A. Bunte and Robert J.
Franklin

A Grammar of Comanche
By Jean Ormsbee Charney

The Canadian Sioux
By James H. Howard

Koasati Grammar
By Geoffrey D. Kimball

*The Medicine Men: Oglala Sioux
Ceremony and Healing*
By Thomas H. Lewis

*Wolverine Myths and Visions: Dene
Traditions from Northern Alberta*
Edited by Patrick Moore and
Angela Wheelock

Ceremonies of the Pawnee
By James R. Murie
Edited by Douglas R. Parks

*Archaeology and Ethnohistory of
the Omaha Indians: The Big
Village Site*
By John M. O'Shea and John
Ludwickson

*Traditional Narratives of the
Arikara Indians* (4 vol.)
By Douglas R. Parks

A Grammar of Kiowa
By Laurel J. Watkins

25-
C